D0339823

THE

Conscious Wedding

HANDBOOK

THE

Conscious Wedding

HANDBOOK

HOW TO CREATE AUTHENTIC CEREMONIES
THAT EXPRESS YOUR LOVE

LILA SOPHIA TRESEMER & DAVID TRESEMER

NO LONGER PROPERTY OF
ANYTHINK LIBRARIES/
RANGEVIEW LIBRARY DISTRICT

sounds true
BOULDER, COLORADO

Sounds True
Boulder, CO 80306

Copyright © 2015 David Tresemer and Lila Sophia Tresemer

Sounds True is a trademark of Sounds True, Inc.

All rights reserved. No part of this book may be used or reproduced in any manner without written permission from the authors and publisher.

Published 2015

Cover design by Rachael Murray
Book design by Beth Skelley

Printed in the United States of America

Library of Congress Cataloging-in-Publication Data
  Tresemer, Lila Sophia.
  The conscious wedding handbook : how to create authentic ceremonies that express your love /
  Lila and David Tresemer.
     pages cm
  ISBN 978-1-62203-488-8
  1. Weddings—Planning. 2. Marriage. 3. Couples. 4. Interpersonal relations.
  I. Tresemer, David Ward. II. Title.
  HQ745.T74 2015
  392.5—dc23
                              2015000679

Ebook ISBN: 978-1-62203-553-3

10 9 8 7 6 5 4 3 2 1

*This book is dedicated to all who are willing
to cross the threshold into a conscious partnership,
and to realize the potential to cocreate
your relationship as a spiritual path.*

Contents

Preface

We have imagined a sixty-second television ad for weddings that would go something like this:

Voice of a wise elder: "You're planning a wedding. How is it going?"
Bride's voice: "Oh, we've been so busy. We've got the dress . . ."

Images show quick scenes of trying on dresses, with mother and friends looking on, finding the right one, everyone nodding approval, smiling, squealing, a significant look from the mother. An empty box appears:

☐ The Dress

> *Then is checked:*
☑ The Dress

> Bride's voice: "And the place—we've got a great place . . ."
> *Images of the many choices of venue, then:*
☑ The Venue

> Bride's voice: "And the flowers . . ."
> *Images of the many choices of flowers, then:*
☑ The Flowers

> Bride's voice: "And we've found a good wine selection."
> *Images of tasting wines, choosing the right ones:*
☑ The Wine

Bride's voice: "We've chosen the invitations on a beautiful paper . . ."
Image of sitting with the designer of invitations, with many choices on the table, then:
☑ The Invitations

Bride's voice: "And we're finally finished with the list of who's invited!"
Image of list with some names underlined, and some names crossed out:
☑ Who's Invited

Bride's voice: "And we have some really cool things too!"
Images of limousine, boutonnieres, bungee jumping:
☑ Cool Things to Do

Voice of wise elder: "Good work. Is there anything missing?"
Bride (thinking about it): "No, I don't think so . . ."
Image of the list, as she's pondering all that she's accomplished:
☑ The Dress
☑ The Venue
☑ The Flowers
☑ The Wine
☑ The Invitations
☑ Who's Invited
☑ Cool Things to Do

Voice of wise elder: "Perhaps you've forgotten something???"
A new item arises at the bottom, box unchecked:
☐ Meaning

Bride's voice, confused, vulnerable: "I thought meaning would take care of itself?"

We have imagined doing this as a commercial, but there is no way we could pay for such an ad. For all the other items on the list, money exchanges hands; you hire people to make them happen. Not so with meaning! You've got to figure that one out for yourself.

A Conscious Wedding:
Gateway to a Conscious Marriage

Every year, over two million couples get married in the United States alone. Statistics on 182 countries compiled by the United Nations (Fertility and Family Planning Section) show that, from Albania to Zimbabwe, in wealthy countries and in poor, in times of conflict and times of peace, many millions of people marry!

How many realize the fullness of this opportunity? Weddings often turn into a flurry of activities and to-do lists, while the potential to cocreate a ceremony that could be magical and foundational to the rest of the couple's lives is overlooked. It's as though the Beloved sits in the middle of the living room, neglected and ignored, because the energy is going toward dresses, food, and wine. Instead of focusing on building the core connection with the Beloved, the wedding industry has hijacked many of the resources and much of the attention involved in creating a deep and meaningful wedding ceremony.

Statistics from 2013 reveal that the costs of weddings have escalated since the financial crisis of 2008, with the average wedding in the U.S. costing $29,858. The dress itself averaged $1,281. Averages can be deceiving, and we know weddings can range between hundreds of thousands of dollars to near zero (a pot-luck wedding we attended, where friends brought food and music, the couple wore recycled clothing, and the celebrant was an old friend). That the wedding industry drives many of the choices is obvious. Explore any wedding magazine to see what is promoted as "absolutely necessary" to fulfill the dream you have for your special day. Then calculate the costs involved! With these prompts, a bride is far more likely to stress over her wedding gown than to give deep consideration to the vows she is making to her partner, which are intended to form the foundation of their life together.

Accurate wedding and divorce statistics are challenging to pin down. Divorce rates are high; the threat to long-term, sacred, and fulfilling relationships is real. However, there is a way to build a firm foundation for personal growth, deep soulful support, and true delight in partnership. All of that can be woven symbolically into the vision of the ceremony. Your wedding can be one of the most significant and meaningful celebrations on which you will possibly ever collaborate!

When recognized as such, a marriage and a deeply committed relationship provide an astonishing opportunity for growth. They open a portal toward understanding Love—how to create Love and how to receive Love. We capitalize "Love" (and "Beloved") in this book because we recognize the astonishing power of this wonder, this cohesive and cocreative energy of the universe itself. The vision of the relationship you choose to craft can be enhanced by the highly valuable project of cocreating a wedding. It is an opportunity, a "mythic" one, to build a ceremony that captures the depth, the magic, and the passion of your Love. And, it doesn't need to cost a fortune! When the soul is present in the ceremony, the cost of creating the "look" in the staging of the ceremony becomes secondary—not unimportant, simply secondary.

The portal to a conscious marriage is a conscious wedding. Both require a conscious relationship, which in turn requires skills. These skills need to precede the design of a ceremony. In this book we will focus in Part One on some of the tools we have found useful. Many of those tools will then work their way into the design of the actual ceremony in Part Two. Our research and counseling with couples has indicated that the wedding provides an opportunity to script what's most important to the couple. In your life there are mythic moments, which we might call rites of passage, threshold crossings, or points of initiation: meeting the challenges of puberty safely and wisely, the first time you make love, the death of someone close to you, marriages, divorces . . . All are meaningful transition times in life. Our culture has lost many of the rituals for marking threshold crossings. A wedding is one of the few remaining rites. We can use that opportunity to create a ceremony with meaning.

Defining "Ritual" and "Ceremony"

It's important to clarify what we mean when we use the words "ritual" and "ceremony"; in many contexts they are interchangeable, but they have distinctions. We use them together in this text, often as "the ceremony or ritual you are creating." We prefer to deepen the word "ritual" to regain some of its original meaning, related to "rites" and to "spiritual" ("spirit-ritual"). Ritual is often defined as the repeated practices of a religious order; psychologically, it can include the daily rituals of eating the same breakfast each morning or repeating an affirmation every time you look in the mirror; spiritually, ritual means a repeated action that engages both seen and unseen energies.

Ceremony can include many different rituals, and it is its own thing. When you do something ceremonially, you don't necessarily repeat something you've done before. Rather, you invest it with meaning. You notice the subtleties of your senses: what you see, taste, hear, and feel. Color becomes not only a sensory impression but an emotional tone. You notice the nuances of gestures, and often you slow them down so that you can feel them more deeply. In short, you become present to the moment in all of its diversity. You do this because you sense that these experiences have consequences for the depth of your being, and at times consequences for others and the world. A true ceremony matters for the whole world.

This book speaks about reclaiming the depth of spiritual practice and expressing it through a wedding ceremony as well as through rituals you develop in your relationship. When a relationship develops greater intentional depth, it often involves more ritual—the performing of repeated spiritual rites with each other, most of which we take for granted. Many of us don't have the same allegiance to religious rituals that accompanied many cultures in the past, and yet we do have the right to create rituals and give them meaning. Repeating rituals is what gives them power; repetition is one of the foundations of magic.

For example, we, David and Lila, have a ritual practice in the mornings. It has grown out of many decades of studies, practices, and meditations. It is now uniquely our own. Because we repeat a version of it daily, it has become our morning ritual. It has assisted us in developing our will forces in the relationship; it gives us a container to strengthen the spiritual work we are doing together; and it gathers strength because of the repetition, just like building a muscle by repeating the pump of the weights.

Our Story

We (David and Lila) met after each of us had been married twice before. We were in our mid-forties. We had each reached a point of recognizing that living as a single person would be fine. We had both independently acknowledged that we would not create another marriage unless it was founded on the solid ground of Sacred Union and true partnership. Our coming together has depended on understanding the value of relationship as a spiritual practice. It fits our cosmology and our sense of universal principles, and we have made it the most important element in our life. Because we sense that all life generates from the balance and integration of opposites, we know that our ability in relationship to create harmony, passion, ritual, joy, and emotional support is fundamental to creating anything at all.

Our decision to work together is part of this spiritual practice. We have written theater plays together. We created a community around our property in Boulder, the StarHouse, which relies on spiritual practices and rituals in the course of the seasonal year: solstices, equinoxes, full and new moons. We also spend part of each year in Tasmania, Australia, where we have created an Arts and Wilderness Retreat Center dedicated to connecting with the wild in nature (MountainSeas.com.au).

We each have our own areas of individual expression and creativity, as well as our areas of expertise in the relationship. We have learned to effectively negotiate around the mundane (Lila usually cooks, David usually cleans up—and sometimes we shift roles), as well as the financial, emotional, and spiritual areas of our lives. Our emphasis is on cocreating a fun, functional, and inspiring life together, not on being right or spending a great deal of time in processing our relationship.

An Overview of the Value of Relationship

Relationships are easily the most challenging, promising, compelling, and misunderstood part of our lives.

People are drawn to relate to one another, especially in a one-to-one primary relationship, even in the most extraordinary circumstances. A friend of ours has the job of assimilating refugees from war-torn African countries. She reports from her initial interviews that, even after her clients have lost everything, lived in horrible conditions on the edge of starvation, and survived a difficult journey by boat from the site of conflict, they tell her, "On the boat I met this guy, and he was really cute. What do you think?" Through thick and thin, in sickness and in health, we are drawn to relationship.

Some people who have died and then recovered report that one of the questions of the final exam after a life is, "How have you learned to love more?" Whether you believe in near-death experiences or not, these reports open an inquiry about the purpose of a life. Because relationship is the way we grow Love at our deepest foundations, we offer this book to create more consciousness in the crafting of relationship, and therefore of Love.

Excellence in any art or craft requires practice. The exercises here will offer you and your partner that opportunity. Whether you are planning a wedding or a simple dedication ceremony, you will find useful tools. You can see these tools in action in the companion DVD, *Couple's Illumination: Creating a Conscious Partnership* (along with its predecessor, *Brain Illumination*). We focus in this book on the design of a ceremony or ritual, and dedicate our work to the pursuit of deeper clarity and expression of Love.

The word "relationship" has in it a genius. The prefix "re-" means bringing back, or coming back to. The next part, "lat," comes from *latus,* meaning something you bear or carry. The next part, the suffix "-tion," confers on the word a thingness, as in a state or condition. You keep coming back to this thing, whatever it is, that you are bearing. The "-ship" part comes from the Proto-Indo-European *skap,* meaning to create or ordain. You create or ordain or recognize a thing that exists within every relationship, and you keep coming back to it. The word itself collects reminders about what relationships are and what their possibilities can be. It also lends itself to the metaphor of a "relation-ship," a vessel (ship) whose structure and form is intentionally designed to carry you both from where you are now to where you wish to be, as you craft the form of your relating, your creating, together.

In this book, we emphasize the one primary relationship/partnership in your life. However, nearly everything we say here can be applied to the many relationships in the numerous areas of your life. We are interested in increasing your level of consciousness: "con . . ." meaning with, "-scious" meaning to know, and "-ness" meaning a state—thus a state of knowing with oneself or another. Becoming more conscious means increasing your awareness of that of which you have previously been unaware. When you are conscious, you can make use of more possibilities and not come to regret opportunities missed.

We also want to help you find and create the magic in that great occasion of the conscious wedding, whether it's your first wedding, your second, your third or more, a rededication of an existing marriage, or a commitment ceremony to a relationship that does not involve legal or religious documents. "Wedding" comes from older words involving a pledge, a covenant, a promise. We will guide you to better understand what a pledge means to your being, and to that of an apparent other.

Some people may say, "Let's have great music, good wine, all of our friends, beautiful clothing—the rest of the ceremony will take care of itself." In our experience, "the rest" won't take care of itself. You have to take care of it. We have found that the wedding's success and its memorability rely on the foundation of your knowledge of yourself and your partner. The exercises in this book can help you increase this knowledge. Then your wedding becomes an honoring of the beauty of your union, which can bring healing to yourselves, your family, your community, and, honestly, to every living thing.

Who Is This Book For?

- For those planning marriage to which the gateway is a wedding

- For those who want to create a conscious ceremony that represents their uniqueness as individuals and as a couple, and who have not found the full potential of the wedding they envision in the choices available through their religious or cultural contexts

- For those who sense their partnership has changed and would like to mark their recommitment with a ceremony

- For couples who have been through a difficult time and wish to deepen and redefine their partnership

- For those who would like to bring their relationship agreement to an end (chapter 17 deals with "Divortex" as the basis of divorce)

- All of the above, for couples of both heterosexual and same-sex relationships, though we will use the traditional "him/her" pronouns. Just make the adjustments as you need so that the book works for you!

How To Use This Book

There are other workbooks on relationships. What makes this workbook different are the ways in which it can help you to experience your relationship and your wedding as sacred. The short-term rewards of relationship may seem important, but the long-term—and the very long-term—rewards are even more important. In service of this sacredness, we offer the notion that ceremony or ritual can add vitality and depth to relationship.

Toward that end, we invite you to engage actively in this process with each other. Each chapter gives you an opportunity to apply the information in an exercise. It can be highly valuable to do the work together, and bring some of your discoveries into the creation of your wedding, maybe in crafting your vows, or writing a poem together that you will read aloud. This book will help you build a lasting "ship" for the creative passage of the time you spend together.

Our culture has largely lost touch with the power of ritual and ceremony as an enactment of transformation, its stimulation and confirmation. We will help you plan an event that becomes a reflection of the values and vision of your relationship. A ceremony is like the seed of the tree you are choosing to grow—it has all the information in it to get the tree growing in the best way.

Whether you are planning a wedding or wishing to deepen your relationship without a formal ceremony, this workbook will be helpful to you. Committed couples of every sort—indeed, partners in every relationship, no matter what their gender or age—can make the tools and processes in this book into the vessel that will carry that partnering, the relationship, into new territory. Dedicating time to crafting that ship together will support its strength and integrity. Making agreements now about how you will choose to maintain the ship will help ensure a vessel more likely to weather storms, even to be strengthened by them.

The process we present can—and likely will—bring up difficult places in the relationship that many couples avoid addressing. Our philosophy is that these challenges should be celebrated, as they present an opportunity for expansion. Some have spoken of "relationship as guru," meaning that the process of relationship is a teacher of your development. Very few experiences will bring us face to face with limitation, denial, exhilaration, and ecstasy as clearly and perfectly!

If you're already married but find that both you and your partner have changed through the years, you may wish to create a rededication, the focus of Part Three. Much of Parts One and Two will also be useful to you. Or you may simply wish to enliven your present relationship by doing some of the exercises in this book with your partner, to get things going again. That in itself will be rewarding.

We highly recommend that you each buy a personal journal for this work. Use these journals throughout the recommended exercises. What you discover by tracking your own experiences can serve as a basis for your ceremonial design. We recommend that you make a commitment to spend time together on some or all of these exercises, especially if you are planning a formal wedding or ceremony, because you will be cocreating this event. We will respect your individual belief systems, so don't worry that we may try to coerce you toward any specific design. This workbook will allow you to make choices with full respect for your religious affiliation and what is sacred to you. We simply share tools to help you create a design that will be the most fulfilling given your goals, dreams, and visions.

We've designed the book in three parts. Part One, "Creating a Conscious Partnership," includes tools and perspectives for the crafting of your vessel. The exercises here will assist in making the whole adventure more real for you.

At the end of Part One (chapter 9), we suggest that you work actively together on questions about the foundations of your relationship—whether you are planning a formal commitment or not. Along with these questions, we suggest some exercises that you can use to work on your physical, emotional, mental, and spiritual capacities, sensitizing yourselves to the possibilities of conscious relationship.

Part Two, "Creating a Conscious Wedding," addresses the logistics of ceremony and preparation. We emphasize the structure of a ceremony that makes space for a magical transformative event that we call the Sacred Moment. Part Two also addresses the details of a wedding and how to put them in perspective. There exist many guides for wedding etiquette—which side whose parents sit on, who pays for what, whom you're supposed to choose as bridesmaids—and you may need one of those guides as well. This book is dedicated to the often unseen, yet palpably felt, essence of ceremony and communion. We emphasize the creation of meaningful vows and how to sustain your relationship past the wedding. Ideally, these vows, which express the living word of your Love, are woven into your "ship maintenance." We repeat our vows on a regular basis, because it keeps the focus of our attention on positive creation. You can't hire out these essential elements to a specialist or expert. Only you can create them.

We also recognize that because relationships are forms, by their nature, those forms will change. Part Three, "Endings and New Beginnings," addresses the ceremonies of divorce, renewal, and rededication. A healthy couple can bear to look ahead at the possibility of change, and in doing so may be freed from certain fears. Indeed, we recommend the divorce chapter ("Divortex") for everyone in relationship in order to clear out the past for a new relationship. In addition, more and more couples are finding that after ten, twenty, thirty years or more, the relationship needs to be dedicated anew. Over the course of a life, family structures change, children leave the nest, careers shift, goals change, and visions modify. Again, the power of simple ritual and ceremony can acknowledge and actualize these changes, making them more conscious and therefore more enduring for the evolving future of you and your relationships.

We call this a workbook because it takes work, and leads to transformation. Without someone to relate to, you could easily stay the same. Relationship provides a compelling opportunity to transform.

We believe that the intelligence and spirit that go into creating a successful wedding ceremony reflect the foundation of the whole relationship, which deserves to be well thought out, watered, and nourished. We emphasize conscious weddings in Part Two because they are a sacred opportunity to become more aware, more awake, more present to the spiritual realities that will arrive at a well-designed ceremony.

Mount Maslow

Our culture holds a subtle prejudice against the sacred, which we ought to investigate. In 1943 Abraham Maslow, a psychologist at Brandeis University, wrote that humans operate according to a "hierarchy of needs"—basics first, then relationship, and finally spiritual needs. Maslow's hierarchy of needs was picked up immediately in the professional and mainstream media. It was depicted widely as a pyramid, which eventually became known as Mount Maslow.

At the bottom of Mount Maslow lie the lowest-common-denominator items, essential foundations for living. You spend most of your time and energy on these basics. Only when you're warm and fed can you rise to relationship or, eventually, at the top of the mountain, to "meaning."

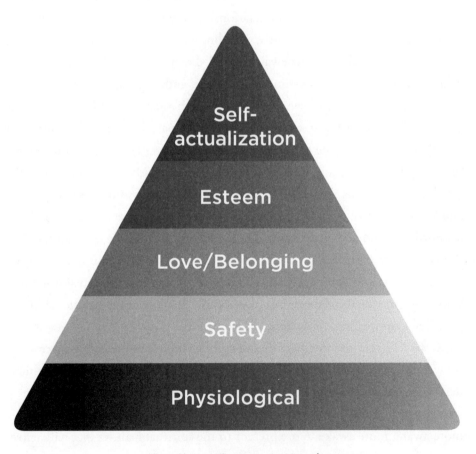

Mount Maslow: The hierarchy of needs

Some recent presentations have taken the analogy further and likened Mount Maslow to an ascent, as of Mount Everest, where you need tanks of oxygen to make it to the top. Using this metaphor, they conclude that many relationships don't have enough oxygen to rise to "meaning." If you don't have enough oxygen, you stay at base camp, low down on Mount Maslow, tending to life's basic needs.

Many feel relieved by this analogy, off the hook. Let meaning take care of itself if there is time, which there isn't.

But hold on! Research does not support a strict differentiation between these needs, saving the needs near the peak only for those with enough oxygen—enough time and energy—to enter those realms. All of the needs operate all of the time. As Viktor Frankl found in his experiences in a World War II concentration camp, even in the most extreme circumstances, meaning is as important, or more so, than basic physical needs. From these experiences, Frankl wrote *Man's Search for Meaning,* in which he presented the psychotherapeutic approach of logotherapy (from the Greek *logos,* meaning pattern, order, or meaning). If you have a "why" to live, then you will find a "how"; the "why" is not a peak that you struggle to attain, but rather a star from which you suspend the rest of your life.

Why is this excursion into the history of psychology so important? Because wedding planners and the vendors of wedding gear press the model of Mount Maslow: if you get the right dress and the right flowers, etc., at the base of the mountain, then the summit perhaps has a chance for a brief encounter; without these essential things at the bottom, forget it. Our approach: meaning is present in everything you do, including in your choices of dress, flowers, etc.—which are, from our point of view, secondary to your conscious presence in a palpable matrix of meaning.

When Relationship Is Strong, Illusions Disappear

Relationships, ideally, are all about lifting the veils of illusion to rediscover truth. Our culture has many notions of relationship that can create illusions between you. You put on the rose-colored glasses and your partner sure does look rosy! Some think that working on relationship means finding ways to maintain that illusion. The country singer who complains, "A girl trying to find herself a perfect man is like trying to find Atlantis," in a tattered wedding gown and a bouquet of flowers falling apart, nurtures illusions in multiple directions.

We haven't seen any couples who can successfully fool themselves for very long. If you connect to your soul and to the soul of the other, the veils will lift and something extraordinary happens. You come into relationship with a living, breathing, life-filled inspiration of soul! The question is how to accomplish that. How do you lift the veils and become authentic with each other, deliberately and by choice? The communication tools in chapter 7 are one good place to begin, and you can go straight there if your partner resisted getting this workbook. This resistance may stem from a fear that some rose-colored bubble of relationship may be popped. We suggest that the reality is far more dazzling and wonderful than the illusion, so pop the bubbles and enjoy more fully!

Would you like to have a relationship that settles forever in the chronicles of your heart as something beautiful, something right, and something good? Something that has gone from individual experience to partnership to communion? Are you interested in taking your relationship further, in creating a celebration that is a statement of your unique Love and an expression of your unique selves? Some consultants may tell you, "We'll design you a ceremony that you will remember." That's important, of course. There are many weddings that are not memorable and some that everyone would prefer to forget. Something worth remembering is a good start. But what is it remembered for? Is it remembered because of the great cake, the wine that never stopped flowing, the flowers that adorned every person and piece of furniture, or the beautiful dress?

We would suggest that something more than fond memory is possible. You can easily have fine food and all-drinks-for-free at other times and places. We suggest that you have a unique doorway to the brilliant lightning flash of a magical moment when everyone is electrified by Love.

This book's intention is to help you cocreate a Sacred Moment, a magical experience for all involved that will cast your wedding into the "unforgettable" category. It becomes an event that continues as a living memory into the future, providing fresh warmth and fresh Love. The Sacred Moment is when a transforming magic occurs, and your witnesses can feel and applaud the union of the Two into the communion of the ONE.

A British man who with a buddy rowed for fifty days to cross the Atlantic Ocean said in an interview, "I had no training in long-distance rowing. I'm not an athlete. My day job is at a TV station. I don't like being cold or wet, certainly not both. And I prefer my midmorning tea. Therefore I thought it was a proper challenge." Somehow we have the notion that it's sporting to be unprepared, a true test of grit.

In most relationships the two people arrive completely unprepared. Perhaps it's "a proper challenge," and perhaps it's a setup for some very difficult experiences. The British man who rowed across the ocean admitted that he prepared for his next adventure, spending months in training. He admitted that he had been lucky with the crossing of the Atlantic.

What is the crossing of the Atlantic in this book? A relation-ship built on Love transports two independent individuals into a partner-ship, a team of Two that can accomplish a great deal. One person plus One person makes Two. Together they can cross an Atlantic Ocean impossibly wide for an individual. Together they can then experience the ONE: communion, a deep sense of well-being, peace, and power. How can this happen? We aim to guide you through the process. It's challenging enough when you're prepared. The rewards are immense and well worth training for.

Relationship encompasses the mystery of what we are, the quality of our awareness, and how we integrate all the different parts of our experience, including the ones that take us suddenly into scary places and the ones that take us suddenly into joy. To create a successful marriage, you have to begin to form ideas about who you are. The intention of the tools offered in this book is that your partner will help you in the continuing saga of discovering the miracle that is you.

exercise

Journal

Buy a journal for each of you to keep notes and to record your discoveries with the exercises. The act of buying the journal can be an important step toward working together!

PART ONE

Creating a Conscious Partnership

So, You're Committing to Relationship

The gateway to a fulfilling marriage is the wedding; the foundation for both wedding and marriage is a healthy relationship. Yet nothing brings up greater challenges than stepping into a deeper conscious commitment with another human being. Preparation for this commitment throughout childhood by churches, temples, schools, or government is often absent or ineffective. Whom do you emulate? Nearly everyone with whom we work on planning a wedding says, "There aren't any models out there. We mostly see what we *don't* want to create." After many trials and heartaches, we become too disillusioned to trust in Love. Many people become bitter or just settle for an appearance. If you were lucky, you may have had some basic training, such as a sex education course or instruction in how to communicate effectively. Physical bodies and emotions need to be understood in order to operate properly, and seldom are these things taught. Most of us learn as we go, reinventing the wheel through heartache, projection, misunderstanding, and poor communication . . . until, eventually, we learn from many mistakes and much pain how to care for our bodies and how to meaningfully engage our lives with those of others.

It doesn't have to happen this way. Accept that you have equipment—your body, emotions, mind, and spirit—for which you were not given a manual or training course. Then start the process of finding those who can teach you how to manage and develop those systems.

exercise

Preliminary Questions

To walk down the aisle prior to walking down the aisle, we recommend highly that you answer honestly the following questions, either individually or as a couple. Go through them yourself, share the questions with your partner, and then share your responses.

- You're interested in a conscious wedding. Are you planning a wedding ceremony? Do you have a date for that event?

- Or are you exploring, seeing if your relationship is strong enough to go those next steps?

- Are you willing to work through the issues brought up by this book?

- Are you willing to try the exercises offered throughout?

- Do you feel comfortable enough with each other to dive into this work with a good sense of humor and a willingness to learn from the process? If you don't feel that comfort, have you identified someone with whom you can work to help you achieve those abilities?

- Can you make an agreement with each other that if things get stirred up, you will work together?

Making Love

We dedicate a huge amount of our time and resources to creating life partnership. Beginning in our teenage years and continuing through our maturity, we ask one another, "Who are you seeing now?" or "Who are you sleeping with?"—which means much more than sleep. For that matter, it means much more than sex, too. Some of your most vulnerable hours—the ones when you are naked or clothed only in your pajamas, caressing, acting silly, sharing the day, unconscious and defenseless, dreaming and recollecting those dreams—are in bed. You spend more vulnerable time with your partner than with any other person.

Whom are you making Love with? Pause on that question: *making* means you're creating something. *Love.* You are creating the most precious substance on earth! This is a most important vocation, in that word's original sense as a calling to action. We are speaking here of Lovemaking, beyond sex but including sex, as well as intimacy, sensuality, and awareness. In true Lovemaking, everyone should thank you for your contributions, as everyone benefits! Love fuels the energy grid or the morphogenetic field of the whole earth. All life can be fed by conscious Love. When people speak about you becoming "a productive member of society," they ought not mean only that you volunteer your time in this or that place. Being a productive member of society ought to include the notion that you make conscious Love—if not in large quantity, then certainly in high quality.

One–Two–ONE

One–Two–ONE—a system which we've worked on over the years and presented many times—is designed to help you understand the dynamics of relationships. We will explain it more fully in chapter 5. Here's an introduction.

There are three modes of experience when in relationship:

> One: I experience myself as an individual, a mature and independent human being. I = I.

> Two: I experience my partner as an individual. "I am I and you are you." Energy and conversation move back and forth: One speaks to One. I + I = II.

> ONE: I experience the feeling of "we" as unity, in vibrant communion. The One (individual) matures through Two (the couple) to ONE (the unity). I + I = I.

All healthy relationships have the capacity for each partner to move from One to Two to ONE and back again.

Twoness, Threeness, and Commitment

What makes a relationship—or a ceremony celebrating that relationship—successful? Both require focused intention and hard work. We don't have a just-read-these-words-aloud-and-you'll-be-fine approach; prewritten scripts miss the opportunity of a vibrant wedding. To have a successful celebration, you may need to come to know your partner better. You may need to come to know yourself better! A "conscious" wedding and One–Two–ONE: these comprise a journey you have begun together.

Commitment means pledging together, moving forward together. It takes an action of will for the Two, each One saying, strongly, "I'm in!" The relationship itself is a third entity in addition to the Two of you and your partner. The "third," your "us-ness," depends on two strong individuals who are consciously choosing the way of partnership. Your commitment to another really means committing to that third, the relationship itself. What you do and feel and think serves that third, which is the unique mixture of you and your partner. You serve it with your attention—your commitment—and it serves you. As you honor this third, it can take on a numinous, sacred quality. It opens the door to bringing that quality into your lives on a regular basis.

You may not see the third, because every time you look at your partner, you're looking through that third part. You can see the third feature when you look at the relationships of others. This is well worth doing. As you get better at observing others' Two with the third of relationship in between, you will learn a bit more about how you look to others. That will help you become more conscious of how your wedding appears to others.

Some of our suggestions may seem like opening a can of worms. When previously hidden feelings and issues rise up, we affirm and suggest you open up the can of worms and put them in the pile of kitchen waste. In a short time you'll have good compost, which will grow beautiful flowers. Make your garbage into flowers! When you see a can of worms about to be opened, celebrate, don't hide.

Each chapter in Part One opens up new possibilities, with new cans of worms, and you will see how they lead to beautiful flowers.

One–Two–ONE

Your Story, Your Myth

Let's begin at the beginning. When you know where you've come from, you have a much better idea of where you may be going.

When you become known as a couple, the question comes up, "How did you two meet?" You tell your story. You ask for their story. Everyone experiences a kind of wonder at the twists and turns and near misses in the path to commitment between two people.

This is your origin story, just as there is an origin story for the universe and an origin story for the nation and for the town in which you live. Every tribe, village, and culture on earth has an origin or creation story that it holds sacred, for in it live the themes that enliven the people's daily experiences. Notice right off the kind of passion that people have in asking that question, "How did you two meet?" That's because something has moved them in their story, something mysterious, and they hope to learn something about themselves by listening to your story.

exercise

Origin Story

You've heard the question, "How did you two meet?" And you've answered it. First off, on a blank piece of paper write down a brief version of your answer. Write it down! You'll see why later. Each of you write down your story. Set what you've written aside.

Just after you've written your stories, or maybe a day later (we trust the wisdom that comes from a night's sleep in between steps), take out your pieces of paper and begin to add in details: the qualities of the scene, the colors of the sky or of people's clothing, the actual words that were said. This is still the recollection stage. You're like Sherlock Holmes paying very close attention to every detail. And you're writing it all down.

Note especially the moments in which things could have easily gone another way, where a certain gesture or turn of phrase could have meant that you never saw each other again—but that's not what happened. Something else happened. What was it? Describe it.

Now go over your origin story with each other. You could trade the pages that you've each written, and read each other's words aloud. Or describe the drawings that were made—one of our clients drew a picture of how they met, because two cars just happened to turn from different streets at just the right time. Sharing these notes can be delightful. You may have already settled on how you tell your origin story. Take the time now to expand it and examine its many details.

Origin myths often have alternative renditions, and you may recall different versions. Enjoy the telling and the sharing. The themes stay the same, but the actions can differ. If your version differs from that of your partner, don't try to craft an "official" version. There are likely aspects of both versions that inform your relationship. And don't be surprised if your origin myth changes over time—that happens with every tribe, family, and nation. The function of the story is not so much to settle on the facts, which seem to change anyway, but to express something of the power underlying your relationship.

The Guiding Hand

The power of myth has served whole cultures with notions of how the people came to be in a particular place, what the spirits of that place are like, and how the animals and plants and sky around them came to act the way they do. "That's a myth" can be a terrible put-down. Yet myths have a powerful binding effect, and, as modern psychology has shown (in the work of Carl Jung, Marija Gimbutas, James Hillman, Joseph Campbell, Michael Meade, Otto Rank, and

Bruno Bettelheim, among others), contain much hidden truth. Your life is not only about the "facts"—it's also about your feeling life. To cultivate your relationship, cultivate your myth. And begin to sense what unseen forces might be moving through your lives.

As you listen to and share the story, entertain the possibility of a Guiding Hand. You can call it destiny, fate, coincidence of astronomical improbability, Divine Intelligence, whatever you like. That's one reason that a couple likes to ask another couple about how they met, so that all can experience and reexperience the Guiding Hand working behind the scenes to bring two souls together. There may be moments when she might not have called you back, or when he might not have walked down that particular street. Imagine those moments and consider what might have happened if another path had been followed or an opportunity had been missed. Then feel the Guiding Hand gently moving you in the direction of this particular other human being.

Entertain the possibility that your guardian angels (or your Inner Knower, or your destiny, or your higher self) have to work quite hard, especially at certain key junctures, to help you through the twists and turns of the path to relationship. You can sense these divine influences through remembering in detail the occasions when you met and remet.

This exercise may help you find the Guiding Hand in any ceremony that you design with each other. Play with this notion, even if you think that angels don't exist (or destiny, or a higher self). We find that most couples met under "extra-ordinary" circumstances, with at least one near miss. Imagine what helpers were there to guide you together.

exercise

Guiding Hand

Stand next to your partner, not looking at each other. Turn your head and body away from your partner, yet stay close to him or her. Then feel the presence of a tug or impulse or attraction gently turning your head or moving your arm toward your Beloved. It's that gentle, almost indiscernible nudge that moves your body toward your partner that occurred in the first times you met. You can think of this as a Guiding Hand.

You may feel nothing at all, and wonder what this is all about. Try it again, and see if you can feel how the subtle forces of attraction turn you to interact with your partner. Does this gentle nudge have the shape of a gesture that you could repeat with each other? We mean an actual gesture of body, arm, hand, and face that expresses that attraction. This may be a body memory of what happened when you first met. By reenacting that movement, you can feel the Guiding Hand at work.

Every story of two people finding each other has at least one of these moments, and maybe several. Your body may remember better than your brain. These things are stored in your body memory, and that's where you can find a rich resource for connecting again to that Guiding Hand. At first you may only imagine the turning of your body. Later you may actually feel the Guiding Hand.

The Guiding Hand does not always connect immediately. We, Lila and David, met originally in a training workshop, and felt an attraction to each other. One of us was married, and the Guiding Hand pointed us in opposite directions for the next two years. Seriously! When one entered the room, the other felt compelled to leave. Only when we were both able to turn toward the relationship were we able to follow the Guiding Hand.

Repeated Questions

The Repeated Question exercise can be helpful in understanding deeper streams of the origin myth of your relationship. It features a technique we learned from the Diamond Heart approach of A. H. Almaas. One person asks a question and listens for three to five minutes while the other responds. When you are the questioner, determine that you will not interrupt your partner or react to his or her words. This agreement will keep the space safe enough for exploration.

The depth of learning that becomes available with this approach is astonishing. You find yourself saying things that had not occurred to you before. Sometimes whole areas of your relationship open up seemingly from nowhere. Your creativity, and your partner's creativity, will impress you! The process may feel challenging at first, but by committing to stay with it you open up areas of

Love—and disagreement—that call for your attention. This is the closest thing to voyaging out in your relation-ship into uncharted waters, which can be an exhilarating adventure.

exercise

Repeated Question 1

Decide which of you will act as Coach to begin with, and which as Respondent. (You'll switch roles after the first three to five minutes and repeat the process for the same length of time.) Then introduce the repeated question as follows:

Coach: "Tell me, what brings us together?"
The Respondent says what occurs to him or her, such as:
Respondent: "I believe it is fate."
The Coach thanks the Respondent and repeats the question exactly.
Coach: "Thank you. Tell me, what brings us together?"
Respondent: "Maybe it was angels, and still is."
Coach: "Thank you. Tell me, what brings us together?"
Respondent: "Pass."
Coach: "Thank you. Tell me, what brings us together?"

The Respondent can say "Pass" when nothing arises in that moment, and the Coach thanks him or her, then goes on. The Coach accepts the challenge of remaining neutral, even when addressed directly by the Respondent, and always thanks the Respondent for whatever she or he has said, in recognition of the real work involved. "Thank you," every time. The neutrality of the Coach sets a tone of safety for the Respondent to permit responses to arise.

Simply notice all of the material that arises. Here you are taking a reading, as in temperature or heart rate. Any material that is gathered remains confidential between the two of you. Let anything arise as an answer, even words that might seem negative at first. For example, a Respondent might say, "I don't know what brought us together," or other words that might evoke an emotional response. As Coach, you stay neutral, though you can mark these comments to discuss them later.

But for now, you say, "Thank you," and move on. This exercise can be used for all sorts of questions: "Tell me, what's your favorite dessert?" We're using it here to help you flesh out the foundation of your relationship, your origin myth.

A Mythic Crossroads

Ceremony and myth are related, and there may be deeper territory to access regarding the mythic undertones of your coming together. There may be key patterns or information that came through in the early hours and weeks of your courtship.

Here is an origin story that includes a Mythic Crossroads:

story

LILA   A Mythic Crossroads

When I first became aware that David was "available," after the two years when the Guiding Hand had separated us, I heard a strong voice that said, "This is your partner." I was uncertain how to acknowledge this voice in waking life.

One night I dreamed: "I am standing behind three large projection screens in a theater. David has his arm around me, and we are gazing out through a gap at a thousand people who are giving us a standing ovation for a theater piece we have just coproduced. I am aware that we are partners as well as cocreators in the dream." It was on awakening from this dream that I decided to telephone David, whom I barely knew. I left a phone message saying, "Hi, I don't know if you remember me, but I just had a very interesting dream about you, and if you want to hear it, give me a call." Then I sat down anxiously and wondered, "What did I just do?" David did call back, and once we came together for tea, we never separated again.

We collaborated on several theater productions together over the years. When we had been together for five years, we did one that involved three screens. At one moment, as we stood behind the three screens, David said, "Do you remember that first dream you had about us?" We both ended up in tears, as we had fulfilled a prophecy and met a Mythic Crossroads. 🌸

This takes us to the next exercise.

Mythic Crossroads

STEP 1: Recount your origin story in mythic proportions. You're expanding from "how did you first meet" to a larger story, the finding of enduring relationship, and you're seeing it as the unfolding of a myth, of which the Guiding Hand is a part. As a myth, what were the key crossroads, where a choice was made that affected everything thereafter? What influences may have been involved that brought you together? What purpose in your relation-ship might have been revealed through a dream or an intuition? Play with it. Write it as if you were telling a fairy tale to a young child. This is a larger story taking you up to the place where the mythic tale often ends: "And they lived happily ever after." Meaning for adults in the real world: "They came together in an enduring relationship; they ended a chapter of their lives, ready to start another." Share your story with your partner.

STEP 2: Read mythic tales (and fairy tales) that involve relationships, such as "The Queen Bee" or "Psyche and Eros." Note how the characters have to develop skills in order that they may discover a mythic crossroads, then find each other.

Just as Lila completed writing her origin story, we took a walk on the beach. We spend a good portion of the year on beautiful Flinders Island in Australia. We find it to be an enchanted place, with a powerful mountain and glorious air, water, and energy. As we walked, we talked about Mythic Crossroads and how they are gifts to a relationship. Just then, we glanced up from the beach, looking toward the mountain, and beheld a perfect, full-spectrum rainbow, arcing over our home across the valley. It reflected the dance between elements of air, sun, and water particles; it was the smile of the Fire of the Sun, blessing the moisture over the mountain. It truly offered us a new Mythic Crossroads where we could say "yes" to the perfection of the synchronous celebration in color.

These moments of interaction between ourselves and the whole world are available more often than we know. Everyone has them, and we believe that they happen more often when you cultivate intention and awareness. The natural world will often offer a reflection when we open our perception toward it as a messenger of the dreamtime, or of mythic reality.

Though you may have settled on the details of your "how you met" story—your origin story—every aspect of that story is still available for further exploration. Let it become an origin myth in the best sense, a source of continuing inspiration to your relationship.

Re-viewing the mythic for clues from the beginning of a relationship can give you the opportunity to identify the challenges that bring you together. We choose to see these as knots of energy that require a correction, rather than as "troubles" or problems to be solved. Knots are quite common as little points of intensity in the early stages of relationship. It helps to name them (playfully, if possible!) to see how they may have shown up early on. We will review them more fully in chapter 4.

We will work with the power of myth and the power of the symbolic in many places.

Why Relationship?

chapter 3

In the last chapter, we asked what brought you together in the mythic story of your meeting and becoming intimate. And we asked, in a preliminary sort of way, what is the Guiding Hand synchronizing your movements, and where is it leading you? Now we're going to get very focused in our questions.

Why be in a committed relationship? In fact, what is relationship for? (And then, why get married? We'll leave the marriage question for Part Two, and concentrate on conscious relationship here, which is, after all, the foundation for marriage.)

Sometimes we have expectations of each other that originate from our parents, or from popular magazines, or from what our culture defines as "being human." We are told that people are drawn into relationship for biochemical and procreative reasons. And then they start dating or living together. It's "normal." But why? What is this hide-and-seek play between masculine and feminine that rules so much of our world, our commerce, our consumerism, our neuroses, our finances, and general life striving? Why do they say, "Love makes the world go round?" Why do novelists, screenwriters, playwrights, and songwriters rehash the same territory, concluding with the happy ending boy-gets-girl or any of the other possibilities of one-gets-the-other?

Part of relationship can be seen as social necessity—someone to talk to and to help with the household chores, what society deems is the right thing to do. Part of relationship meets physical needs—sex, safe partners for intimacy, someone to snuggle with, someone to make a home with. Some part is fantasy—the Barbie and Ken fairy tales that end in "happily ever after."

29

"Happily ever after" continues to be repeated—especially at weddings—over and over again. It views the Ship of Relation as a beautiful vessel on an ever calm sea, sun shining, dolphins jumping.

We have asked many people why they seek out relationship, and we have received dozens of different answers. It's just the thing we're guided to do; or, the sex is good; or, our parents expect it; or, we prefer being with a partner to being alone; or, the baby-making years are upon us. Then a puzzled look takes over the person's face.

In the end, when they really look at it, people conclude that they have absolutely no idea why they are propelled into a relationship! Biologists say, "A male and a female are necessary for sexual reproduction," whether we are humans or apes or reptiles or flowers. In some cases, we may be aware that we have a connection to the other person, and we just go for it because it feels "destined." We hear people say, "We are fated to be together." There may be "karmic" reasons you are drawn to the other person, which is a way of saying you have something very specific to work out with her or him, and diving into a long-term relationship is the fastest way to jump in very deep.

This odd collection of organizing principles is not sufficient to support a vital relationship.

story

LILA   Choice

I have been married three times. I consider that the first two marriages were also successful, because I learned so much about myself, about intimacy, and about communication skills. The methods of this learning were sometimes tumultuous and painful. I found that as I matured, I developed a clearer sense of the grand design—not one that was destined, but one that I *chose*—a design of the relationship that I truly, fully aware and awake, chose to create. It is from these years of study, practice, and actualization of the relationship we now have that David and I came to write this material. We feel there has been a missing piece in the relationship design department of Project Humanity, because humans have had to make up most of it! How you conceive that relationship design will be apparent in the relationship that you choose to create.

Back again to the opening question: Why relationship?

Turn the page for an unexpected answer.

Relationship is not for happiness.

Of course, happiness will occur; indeed, a kind of bliss is possible in relationship that is unavailable any other way. But it's not the "happily ever after" that still catches people—catches both in its promise and in its betrayal. Most people say that they feel happiness is possible. However, when pressed, many can think of only one or two relationships that they've observed where the promise manifested as true. Some people survey their acquaintances and find no instances.

When the bubble pops, the lovers feel betrayed, and their Ship of Relation joins the other wrecks in the relation-ship graveyard.

Everyone who sees this picture nods in recognition. They immediately remember relation-ship-wrecks going back years. They number or name the wrecks of ex-partners. Why are those wrecks still there? Why don't they rust and rot into the basic elements that can then be used elsewhere? Because you have your energy bound up in those wrecks. They can't function, but your energy stuck in them prevents them from naturally decomposing. The exercises in this book will help in the natural process of returning all that energy into its basic elements, ready to be used again.

So, if the reason for relationship is not happiness, what is relationship for? We suggest that:

Relationship is a living process through which each person becomes a better human being.

A committed, conscious, living relationship will cause you and your partner to develop, to mature, to grow, to blossom. The process may include experiences that are painful. Your partner becomes partly your live-in therapist, who will learn about your secrets and your irksome habits and will—either gently or with exasperation—cause you to look at yourself, and perhaps—yes, we should say it—*cause you to change!* You will *change!* We didn't say you *may* change—we said you *will* change!

Brain research has revealed that the complex connection matrix between your neurons continues to transform until the moment of death. What you put into your brain, by your choices of what you see, what you think, and what you feel, leads to changes in how the dendrites of your neurons hook up with one another. If you dwell in worry and fear, your dendrites hook up to pay attention to that. If you dwell in Love, your dendrites hook up to pay attention to that. The technical term "neuroplasticity" suggests that you mold your own nervous system, as a sculptor molds clay. Whether it's a sculpture of stress or one of beauty is your choice. That's why this book is so important, and why we don't accept people's excuses for choosing difficulty or grumpiness, such as, "Well, that's just the way I am." Everything can be changed. Relationship can assist you in that process.

exercise

"How Has Relationship Helped Me Become a Better Human Being?"

You can work this question using the repeated question technique, or you can simply ponder the following sequence. We suggest that you take notes. You have held these feelings unconsciously for a long time; we recommend that you make them conscious.

1. Recall an important teacher in your life, someone from whom you know you received some teaching or blessing, for whom you feel a deep gratitude. Now answer the question, "How did I change from knowing this person?" It may be that you left knowing more—but that always comes with a load of feelings. Admiration? Imitation? Warm, wistful memories?

2. Bring to mind others with whom you felt growth and a soaring happiness.

3. Recall a relationship from which you gained much though the person and the situation were challenging. You may have hoped that the other would not be so difficult, but you must ask if you would have learned as much had the person been nice.

4. Bring to mind others with whom you felt growth amid difficult and even tragic circumstances.

5. Now you're ready to recall past peer relationships, ex-partners, ex-lovers, ex-boyfriends, ex-girlfriends. This step comes after the previous two because peer relationships are often a mix of warm and cold, soaring and crashing, sunlight cruises with the dolphins and relation-ship-wrecks that persist.

It's very helpful to assess the different ways in which you have grown from relationships in your life, and to recognize that happiness is not a prerequisite nor a guarantee. It's terrific when it happens, but a bigger bliss comes from becoming a better human being.

Now answer the question, "Do I believe that challenges in my life present a gift to me? Can I see these difficult relationships as helping me gain strength, insight, and character?"

And now ponder the question, "How can I help my partner to grow? Do I want to protect him or her from every bad thing? Or do I offer support to him or her in growing from encounters that span the full range that the world has to offer?"

The process of your partner acting as catalyst for your self-discovery can sometimes be joyous. You become a better human being through the front door, so to speak.

Sometimes, though, this process is frustrating. In the mirror offered by your partner, you see that you have worked up little eccentricities and private routines. How do you find out about these? He tells you; she tells you. You may find that you have odd habits that you have conveniently hidden from yourself. You may find that some of these habits are nasty, or thoughtless, or cruel. You may not like to have these mirrored back to you. But mirrored back they will be, either explicitly or through your partner's reactions, and you have the opportunity to improve through seeing yourself more clearly.

You have the potential for becoming a more loving person. Perhaps that sounds too easy or too schmaltzy. Let's put it another way: You have the potential, with the help of your partner, for learning what true Love is, a Love that will change the way you think and feel about everything in the world, making everything more potent and delicious, a Love that fires you in each morning's dawn to engage with the world and everyone in it, a Love that acquaints you with angels. This is latent in everyone. It can become your experience, and relationship helps you in this process.

Those who have been in relationship for a long time know that human beings aren't given at birth the tools to make a relationship work. They are given an impetus—sexual attraction or the mystery of Love—that draws them together. But most people don't know what to do after that. You have to learn the skills to make the relationship endure, grow, and teach you what it can about yourself. This takes extraordinary vulnerability. It takes openness to bubble-busting. It takes intention, choice, and work.

story

DAVID   Some Science Metaphors

Certain metaphors from modern science have helped me understand my own experience more deeply. In physics, "work" is force multiplied by change of location (translocation, or distance). "Force" is your directed will or intention to move something. You can apply force by pushing against a wall. If the wall moves—that is, changes location—then it has been transformed and "work" has been accomplished. If the wall doesn't move, then no work has been accomplished. The phrase "it takes work" refers to more than the exertion of force. It means that movement happens. If you don't move—that is, if you are stubborn and set in your ways—then no work is accomplished in your relationship. For things to "work out," you both have to use directed will (force) and you both have to move. With this in mind, I understand that I have to move, even when I think I'm right in my position.

In an alchemical process, two ingredients are put together in a closed vessel. Heat is applied, often a very low heat over a long period of time. The substances change, merge, separate. Each becomes purified, transforming into something completely different. The process goes through a dark stage (*nigredo*), then a white stage (*calcinatio*), and other stages as well, ending in the great "marriage of opposites" (*coniunctio oppositorum*), creating a miraculous, radiant new substance. Each of us must gather the right ingredients; each of us must generate the right level of heat and other conditions that cause transformation. For example, if you are marrying for the first time, there may be an assumption that you will have children, within the alchemical vessel of the womb. Seriously reflect on the question of whether to have children. Be deliberate in choosing, and if you do decide to have children, realize that your responsibility is to purify as much as possible the ingredients that make this child. It's commonly known that you should stop smoking and drinking; the ingredients that go into the alchemical vessel include your thoughts. Are you ready for that fire of self-observation? Going through the stages of an alchemical process has potent meaning for me in every encounter with my Beloved.

We have wondered why human beings pair, rather than bond in threes or fours or larger groups. Evolutionists might say that we do this because deep down we're only interested in mating and making babies. That explanation doesn't account for the vast majority of our lives, and the meaning of relationship at a soul level. Evolutionary theory does not explain consciousness, and after all this is a book on conscious weddings. Let's look at it this way. If you have two people, each has to pay attention to my-One, to your-One, and to the Two. Thus, you have three things to manage. If you expand to three people, all of the actors in the drama plus all of the possible relationships (three Ones, three Twos, and one Three) adds up to seven things to manage. For four people, it's fifteen things (four Ones, six Twos, four Threes, and one Four). For five, it's thirty-one. The answer to the question of why we choose pairs is perhaps simply, "More people quickly increases complications." Add some complexity to each individual—different streams of head, heart, and hand—and it all becomes even more complicated. As we are drawn to relationship through body, heart, and soul, two-people is the least we can do and still be relating.

Saying Yes to Choosing

In a healthy partnership comes a stunning gift—bearing witness to the life of another. From the most mundane to the most glorious moments, a life that has a witness through the eyes of the Beloved is a life that can be enjoyed with a different perspective and depth. I am witnessed in my ecstasy and in my suffering; I am witnessing my Beloved in the same. I learn how not to judge. I learn how to allow and to appreciate that life *is,* how life happens, and that my partner and I choose to traverse its winding road together. We choose, daily, our relationship as a vehicle for that journey. It's a conscious choice, and by making it in full consciousness, we light each other up. It's actually a miracle, because it's so simple! When we're asked what is the key to a successful relationship, our response is brief: Choose it. Moment to moment. And when you notice you are "not-choosing" or denying the relationship, then simply shift. If you really value the relationship, then choose it, repeatedly. You can look at your partner and say to yourself, "Yes!" You need to be comfortable with saying it both out loud and quietly to yourself.

exercise

Yes!

Prelude: Look at your partner and say to yourself, "Yes!" Do it again, and again, and again. You can do this silently, or you can look at each other straight on and exchange these affirmations, alternately softly and loudly.

Now look your partner in the eye and say, "I choose relationship—with you!" Your partner silently affirms the "Yes," then says, "I choose relationship—with you!" back to you. You then silently affirm, "Yes!" Feel what happens when you affirm choice.

When two people do this on their own, without our benign supervision, they report embarrassment after the first few exchanges. Persist over that hump. Accept that it's an artificial setup, and enjoy what happens after a minute into this exercise.

Simple, yes—and fundamental. Each of those moments of choice becomes a bead of affirmation on the necklace of loving. Ultimately, you can affirm with your partner, "I am choosing Love." It's not always a personal love; sometimes it moves mysteriously into the reflection of Divine Love itself, pouring through the Beloved. Sometimes it's the joy of knowing Love is in the world, and that in your small way you are able to focus it through your personal story, through the players in your life, in a way that transforms suffering into joy. The choice any two people make to be "related" carries with it the opportunity to go beyond partnership and into states of communion—communion with the Divine, as we experience it. Relationship can be an engine of growth that allows us to unfold the possibility of true Sacred Union, which is the path of Love. In some core essential way, moving from duality to union needs to be understood at an individual level first. A sense of wholeness in the Self—that part of you that stands tall and wise and is not distracted by the dramas of the little self—allows the dance with the apparent "other." From there, a Beloved can be found within the partner, maybe not all the time, but often enough that you are transported from the mundane to the sublime. The vehicle of relationship can be chosen to be the vehicle of awareness of this greater Self.

Whatever you desire from this relationship—Love, communion, maturity, ecstasy, truth—choose it! To whatever degree you are capable in the moment of your commitment to each other, choose to walk this path of relationship to its fullest. When you do this, even if the time comes when you part ways, you can part consciously, choosing that also. Rather than falling into reaction, blame, and sabotage, you will both know if it's time to part. (More on this in Part Three.)

Here is an exercise that may help you understand what you are choosing, and the feeling of choice.

exercise

Repeated Question 2

Decide which of you will act as Coach, and which as Respondent. Use the same rules as before. It looks generally like this:

> Coach: "Tell me what you choose in our relationship."
> *The Respondent says what occurs to him or her, such as:*
> Respondent: "I choose ecstasy."

The Coach thanks the Respondent and repeats the question exactly:
Coach: "Thank you. Tell me what you choose in our relationship."

Do this for two or three minutes each.

In the end, when your life comes to its conclusion, you can't take with you the things in your life, nor the books you've read or written, nothing of your fame or fortune. Spiritual traditions remind us that you take with you the quality of your relationships. Whether you are aiming toward marriage or not, it's worth improving your skills at relationship. The next chapters will help you strengthen that foundation. Keep always in mind that relationship is a living process that makes us into better human beings.

Shadows, Thorns, and Knots

chapter 4

In a healthy relationship dedicated to mutual growth, stuff comes up. Sometimes you say things you regret—words you can barely believe came out of your mouth. You feel stormy emotions swirling about inside. You don't tell the whole truth and you sometimes tell lies. You can feel your own behavior tearing you away from your partner, and you are horrified by yourself. Those parts exist in every human being, deep down, in a shadow realm, unconscious.

How do you craft a "conscious wedding," or a "conscious" anything, when there is that realm of the unknown? You begin by learning as much as you can. The term "shadow" is used in some schools of psychology to symbolize aspects of yourself that have been held deep down in your personal unconscious—stemming from mistakes or misdeeds or traumas that you don't want to remember. Added to this are reports of ghosts and things that go bump in the night. You don't know about them; psychologists can't tell you what they are; no one knows about them. Yet it's premature to reject their existence, as we have all had experiences that have confirmed that "something is happening."

We like to give these hidden, unknown, and shadowy bits some sort of form. One kind we call thorns, as in something you stepped on that went in deeply, snapped off, and now has worked its way to the surface. A thorn is simple, acute, and painful as a sharp jab. It's a broken-off piece of something from the past.

Another kind of shadow we call knots. These are more complicated, chronic, painful as an ache, a twisting together or a tangle of many threads of energy and history. We view knots as more serious than thorns. A thorn you can extract, painful as that might be; a knot has to be unraveled and straightened out before its ache can be eased.

Thorns and knots often arise unexpectedly. You say something silly or hurtful. Oops, too late, the damage has been done. Apologies can help soften the territory. Feeling guilty doesn't help. Understanding the phenomenon in yourself and in your partner does help.

Sometimes the thorns and knots are the rusty parts of your older relationship-wrecks, patterns left behind by your former partners. Sometimes they come from parents or those powerful in your childhood. Sometimes they come from your partner. Here is an example from David: "Lila asked why I had not included her in a list of those whom I thanked at the end of a talk. I turned red. It was true. Even though I am very careful to include everyone in my acknowledgments, I had forgotten her. Later I learned that Lila had been left out in this way repeatedly through her childhood. I had effectively continued that knot from her early life." Note how important it was that Lila mentioned the knot, rather than simply suffering through a repetition of the pattern.

Sometimes these thorns and knots don't belong to you. They can be world issues that have found a handy place to land: your heart. You might feel sorrow for the suffering of people elsewhere in the world and in your frustration shout at your partner. Empathy with the suffering of others is the mark of a compassionate human being, though you have to be able to set this aside when the two of you are exploring issues specific to your relationship.

Your partner's acceptance and support of this very human process are essential. The best attitude to hold is, "Hmm. How interesting! Here is something arising in me or in my partner, and it's difficult, and it is tearing us apart, but our Love is stronger than that. I wonder what will happen next." Real interest, warm yet disengaged, describes this mode of observation. You're awake to the process, even though you don't know what's happening. You mix in some laughter because, when you look at the little thorn, painful but small, you wonder how serious it really is. (This laughter is not derisive, but finds humor in the way that human beings are so easily capsized by tempests in teapots.)

Sometimes, just after you and your partner have experienced a fabulous communion—the ONE part of One–Two–ONE—a thorn or knot arrives as a sabotaging agent that forces you apart. We have found one thing in common about many of these apparent disruptions: they carry a gift within them. To paraphrase Richard Bach, we seek (or create) the problems because we need their gifts. Examine the notion that the difficulties, tensions, thorns, and sabotage have a gift for you, a gift of insight and consequent deeper Love.

The barbed thorn or the gnarly knot wants to grab you again, but it can't if you simply observe it and apply a healing ointment to the wound. However, it may be that the pattern seems bigger than you can handle together. You may need professional help. You will still need your partner's support, more than ever, as professional help can accelerate the thorn's surfacing. This is healing, and on the other side of it you will be wiser, more capable of Love. Some of our exercises, too, may bring thorns or knots to the surface. Greet them, as you will be more mature after dealing with them, and your vision less blurred by fantasies of 100 percent happiness now and evermore. Remember: relationship is the means of growing a better human being.

We're serious about the place of a professional counselor in helping you get over the larger bumps. A counselor can help you find answers to these questions:

"What shadows, knots, and thorns am I not revealing to my partner?"

"How do I tell him or her about my fears?"

"Do I yearn for someone with whom I can share every aspect of my life?"

"Is there something I distrust about my partner?"

Trust is the most fundamental of all emotions, one that we develop or don't develop in early infancy. It is the most satisfying aspect of a close relationship—one could say, a necessary prerequisite. It is, also, not easy to develop. Patience is very helpful. No matter how many relation-ship-wrecks there are in your past, you can develop a culture of trust in your relationship.

Knots

Thorns are sharp foreign objects that you learn to draw out. Other shadow parts of your biographies and personalities hide by turning in upon themselves, becoming knots, which are more complicated. When a thread is straight, you can see where it comes from and where it leads. When it is knotted, the threads disappear into loops and whorls. You lose the thread and lose the plot. You can feel an energetic knot in your own physiology, as in the expression, "My stomach is in knots." Everything seems bound in upon itself, stuck and unmoving. Similarly, in relationships, a knot will arise between two people who create a unique pattern of energy that repeats. Every time the pattern arises, everything contracts.

Sometimes habits reinforced by a predictable reaction create knots. The man slices onions in such a way that his partner's eyes well up with tears and she makes a show of wetting a towel to put over her nose and eyes. Repetition causes the energetic knot to grow more convoluted, a black hole of contraction that continues to tighten out of sight, sucking your radiant energy into it. Even old relationships hold energy like knots—those are the relationship-wrecks below the surface, still binding your precious energy. And some knots come from the culture: formulas about how you should think and act, prescriptions, assumptions, rules, and regulations. These are some of the most difficult, though with your partner's help, you can at least accomplish the first step of naming them.

One researcher has identified four kinds of knots in relationship: contempt, criticism, defensiveness, and stonewalling. If you encounter any of these with your partner, you are dealing with a tight knot that will require patience. The tools in this book are strong enough to untie these knots. If not, then there are terrific counselors available to help.

Here's a knot for which you might not be prepared: trust. You trust your partner to be honest, caring, listening. But trust does not mean that your partner will never trigger your deepest vulnerabilities in a way that makes you uncomfortable. Your partner may do this intentionally, or the simple fact of living closely with another may bring out your most hidden secrets. Remember how, in the previous chapter, we spoke of the purpose of relationship as growing? Comfort, familiarity, always being nice: these are not growing. The issue of trust means trusting your partner to feel care for you when your knots begin to unravel. Trust does not mean a guarantee that you will never be disturbed.

You can learn to play with these places in a relationship, and perhaps make them lighter simply by being less attached to the content.

Mythic Knots

In chapter 2, we spoke about the story you tell about your origin, which can be on a mythic scale. In your origin story, you may well find the presence of something unsettling, what a mythographer might call the thirteenth fairy. In the story of Sleeping Beauty, twelve fairies came to bless the babe, and then a thirteenth showed up, angry that she hadn't been invited, and cursed the child and everyone present. The curse turned out to be helpful. Without it, the twelve blessings would have been too sweet. The thirteenth fairy brought in the power of time. Against that force, the characters in the story have to struggle, learn, and grow. Thus, what may appear as a difficulty—what we call a knot—may foreshadow something that will be untied later on, through the growing fostered by the relationship.

A couple came to us to get married. They had met when another couple had invited two men and two women to join them for an outing. Our female client had gotten in the backseat of the car first; the other woman was getting in when she realized that she had forgotten something, so she got back out again; our male client then got into the cramped backseat and managed to step on the female client's foot. This was their first meeting. His apology led to a conversation during their cramped ride to the picnic . . . which led to them sitting with us many months later to design their wedding. The second woman's sudden recollection of something forgotten is an example of a Mythic Crossroads. The hurt foot is an example of a knot. It was necessary to create the conversation, and gave an opportunity for the man to show just how caring he could be. It was a knot that was readily untied that same day—mostly untied, since they continued to tell the story and to hold it as a knot that needed more untying.

Knots

Take a twenty-foot length of half-inch rope or cord, gather it together in a heap, then let it fall on the floor into a tangle of knots. (Or ask another person to tangle the rope, or put some random knots into it. David makes the knotted tangles in our workshops.)

Name the tangle as some well-known issue in your relationship. For example: "This tangle is what it feels like in my stomach when you choose to spend a weekend with your friends rather than with me." You can label the tangle with something specific, or just get the feeling of untying knots together. Approach the tangle with your partner and begin the process of teasing apart the knot and undoing the loops. Observe how the rope bends and twists. Work together as four hands and feel the confusion clear. Observe how your four hands cooperate to untie the knots and straighten out the rope or cord. Does one of you think that she or he can do it better? Does one of you become agitated? The untangling trains you in patience and cooperation. Your mind works more slowly than your hands, and you will be amazed at how efficiently your hands work together to untangle your mythic knot.

Share with each other what you observed and felt.

Identify the Knots in Your Origin Story

Sit facing each other, and look back at the origin myth you shared earlier. Locate the bumps, the blips, the mistakes, the faux pas, the knots that were there from the very beginning. "What went wrong that we nonetheless got past?" Can you identify a knot that lingers in your current relationship? Does it challenge you? Make it bigger—it's part of your relationship myth! Become the filmmaker or director of your own play. What are the elements of the unfolding plot, and how did they originally reveal themselves? Become playful with the knots in your biography—name them and tease them apart.

Secrets that you tell no one become knots in your psyche. They bind energy. As you hold on to them, they bind more energy. In effect, you blackmail yourself over a secret, demanding hush money in the form of energy to hold it all in. You may find it liberating to share your secrets with your Beloved, and they will no longer hold power over you.

exercise

"What Would You Do If . . .?"

Another way to approach knots goes like this:

Person A says to Person B, "What would you do if I told you that there was something that I couldn't tell you?" In other words, "What would you do if I revealed one of my deepest knots?" In this exercise, you don't reveal the knot; you simply ask the question as stated.

What would Person B say? The biggest mistake here is that B assumes that A knows that B would be accepting, interested, warm, supportive, and patient—in other words, a caring and concerned partner. But B should not assume that A knows that. This exercise permits B to say and be all of those things: not by assumption, but by behavior.

All right, Person B, now respond to Person A.

Of course, do the opposite as well. B says to A, "What would you do if . . .?"

exercise

"What Do I Say, and When?"

How many movies have you seen in which one partner meant to say something to the other but waited, and then tragedy befell them both? Everyone has something that they hide; it seems that this is part of the human drama. Telling all may not be a solution. What you have to tell changes too. People mature and are able to say—and to hear—more than before. This exercise asks you to write down a few items that you feel you're holding that you can't yet speak. You already know that these confessions are heavy to carry. That's where a professional counselor may come in. You may reach a point where your partner can be told.

For now, simply bringing an issue to awareness can have great power for you. As you write them, you may evaluate what it would be like to share this story with your partner. Just entertain the possibility! On the other hand, if you have any concern about writing down something that you are not ready to reveal, you may choose to write it and then burn it. The very act of burning something can begin to release some of the energetic patterns you have.

story

Chocolate

"I had a little habit of hiding chocolate in a closet and sneaking a little piece here and there. I watched to see that no one was looking. I was very sensitive to any noise that might indicate that [my partner] was nearby. My precautions become more elaborate. It took so long to finally tell her. But after I told her, it seemed less serious. Now I have my little chocolates not whenever I can sneak them, but right after meals, in full view of everyone. My chocolate consumption has gone down, and I enjoy them more than ever."

This story could be told about any addictive process. It is much easier to address an addiction pattern when both you and your partner know how it is eating up the attention of you both.

exercise

Repeated Question 3

This is a very potent exercise, and one that you might decide to use after you've done others. It makes a fitting end to this chapter on shadows.

Choose which of you will act as Coach and which as Respondent. Use the same rules as before. It looks generally like this:

Coach: "Tell me, what would separate us?"

The Respondent says what occurs to him or her, such as:

    Respondent: "The way you slice onions."

Remember, the Coach does not react, or try to fix anything, or respond in any way but with warm interest. The Coach does not smirk and say, "Onions? You can't be serious!" If that happens, then it is best to agree, "Whew—this exercise isn't for now." Or perhaps you think, "Onions? That is minor!" Respect these apparently small examples, as they can lead to big discoveries.

    Coach: "Thank you. Tell me, what would separate us?"

    Respondent: "If you had an affair."

You see, this is an exercise that gets everything out into the open.

Whatever comes up, take note, and don't interrupt. The issues may seem trivial or profound. Keep going for three minutes, then switch roles. The three minutes will lift up many important realizations into the light of day.

Write down what you've learned. You may have to use some of the exercises in chapter 7, such as Heart Talk, to understand what happened.

This process will likely bring up knots and thorns, which you can ponder and discuss. Several of the tools we give you in later chapters will be helpful for challenging issues. Watch out for times when one person says that a particular issue is a problem and the other one says it isn't. Take the example above of slicing onions in a manner that bothers your partner. If you dismiss this concern as trivial, you may be making a mistake. You're seeing the situation from your individuality—your One. Going to Two requires that you listen.

Through these exercises, you've collected some very good material. We will suggest ways of working with what you've learned in the next few chapters.

Building the Core of a Conscious Partnership

Sometimes in a life, we are blessed to find a tool that works simply, elegantly, and profoundly. The Concentric Circles is one such tool. Lila devised this pattern and has used it in workshops all over the world, for individuals, couples, and groups.

The underlying principle of the Concentric Circles is based on a statement by Albert Einstein: "No problem can be solved from the same level of consciousness that created it." Therein lies the key to just about everything! It's all about using our challenges in order to grow. Richard Bach wrote, "You are never given a problem without a gift for you in its hands; we seek the problems because we need the gifts."

Concentric Circles creates an opportunity to name a problem and then to enjoy the discovery of the gift of insight that the perceived problem offers. Seen as a representation of the field of consciousness, Concentric Circles can help you locate where you are in the contraction of the problem, and then see your way to the expansion inherent in any given issue. For couples, it is an opportunity to listen with interest as you understand aspects of your partner and certain behaviors that either of you may not have understood before.

When we work with a couple, we create the pattern of Concentric Circles on the floor so that the couple can stand in the center (a circle three feet in diameter is good). They stand in the "Story," the part with the drama and the details—the misunderstandings, the reactions, the recriminations. After modeling the process for them, we ask them to step over the boundary marker of the inner "Story" circle to the next circles out, "Psychological Understanding" and then "Mythic, Symbolic, Expanded View." Moving one's body from circle to circle makes the process, and one's life, more playful and engaging. The pattern can also be worked on paper, or in the imagination, and we've found it has greater impact when the body moves. An example will illustrate the model.

The couple started by naming their issue: "We have always argued over where to go for vacations. Now, we want to plan our honeymoon, and we have very different ideas. Sarah wants to go to Paris, or some other place of high culture. Anthony wants to go into nature and wilderness." They stood facing each other in the center circle. They spoke about their desire to pursue the trip they individually wanted. They were passionate and articulate. It was easy to hear that both wanted to convince the other that their own point of view had greater merit.

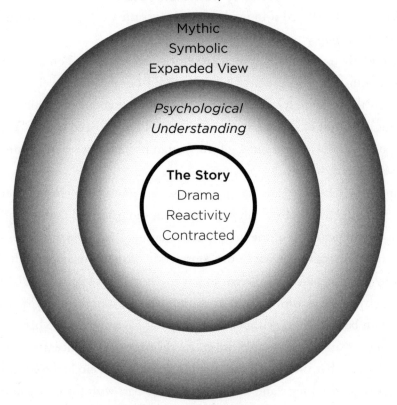

Concentric Circle transformational model

When they had heard and felt the whole story from two points of view, they each took a step out into the "Psychological Understanding" circle. The simple act of expanding from the more constricted inner circle in itself creates a sense of more space. From the second circle, they spoke about their family vacations. Anthony's family never went camping or into the wilderness; their vacations were to tourist locations, which he avidly disliked. Sarah's family had not had the financial capability to travel, and she craved more connection to the pinnacles of culture, through museums, fine cuisine, and history.

They each listened to the other's story, and heard it differently from how they'd ever heard it before. There was a quality to their listening that was deep and appreciative. Then each stepped out one more circle into the "Mythic." From this place, deeper insights arose. Sarah recognized that she finally had some resources in her life, and that she could spend them in elegance; she wanted to mark their marriage as dedicated to culture and learning. Her imaginings of romance, fine wine, and great art experienced together showed that her sense of the mythic took her to the most refined creations of human culture. Anthony found in the mythic his vision of the life forces of nature herself; wild nature was for him the source of power and creation. Both discovered that they valued creativity and life force. Both valued romance in fields of creativity. For one, those were nature's fields; for the other, they were fields of artistic endeavor. Anthony made the first bridge, bringing a wild poetry to his vision of them "glamping" (that's glamorous or high-end camping) in nature. They didn't have to rough it.

In the end, they designed a truly fine honeymoon which had elements of both. Once they understood that they both wished for a romantic experience of the Beloved that honored nature, culture, wildness, good food, and creativity, they designed something far better than either had envisioned previously. Days later, they shared that they had made arrangements to go to Barcelona to experience the Gaudí sculptures and the art museums; afterward, they would head south into Andalucia and go glamping.

Working with the Concentric Circles pattern, it is easier to identify that the process of cocreating relationship is both energetic and structural. It moves in and out, from contraction to expansion. The human adventure is not intended to be lived entirely in the expansive mythic. We learn from the drama in the contracted "Story" circle, even if it is, as Richard Bach wrote, "seeking the problem because we need the gifts." We circulate from the grand view of the Mythic through the understanding of the Psychological to the details of the Story, and back again, in and out—with ease.

This is a flexible model; it can be experienced by physically creating a pattern in sand or dirt or with rope on the ground. It can be drawn on paper and talked about, or it can be felt in the imagination. We recommend initially working with this form physically, that is, creating a space where you can stand in the center circle and feel that it is more contracted. Then walk out to the outer circle, and feel its expansiveness. Engaging the physical body helps us to feel into a problem or issue, perceiving it with a different part of the brain.

You begin on the inside, where the story feels dense: full of details, full of emotions such as blame, full of explanations for why things happened this way and why someone else is in the wrong and you are the victim. In the center, you live out the dramas, the passions, the slamming of doors, the writing of hurt letters, as well as the great sex scenes.

It can take years (or possibly only a very short time!) to realize that you've had enough struggle with your various dramas, and to choose to move out into less dense zones. In the psychological circle, you can observe the motivations for your own behavior and the behavior of your partner. You might see that you have had a pattern since you were very young, perhaps one that you learned in response to your parents, which caused you to act or feel in a certain way. In the psychological circle, you gather the facts and the impressions of the past. From this research, you can make a better assessment of what is going on in yourself and in the other.

Then you can step out even further, into the mythic or symbolic level, where you can see the greater dynamics at play. This often has the feel of truth beyond personal drama and even beyond the personal life. You find yourself acting a certain way because of great streams of evolution, or feeling touched by transpersonal forces. Here you may meet Venus or Mars, Inanna or Gilgamesh, and discover how they have influenced the events that you experienced in the center as so dense and personal. In the mythic circle, you can feel and perceive the influence of the Guiding Hand (see chapter 2).

Take a moment to reflect on what the Guiding Hand has brought to you through these Concentric Circles. Can you trace the influence it has had on developing and furthering the details of your story? The Guiding Hand is an excellent reflection of the mythic in our lives. And we have found that it isn't "just a myth," but absolutely real.

You can move out even further, beyond the mythic, beyond the last circumference, into the state of Awareness or Unity or Oneness—the spiritual realm—where all the activity in the center is held as the tremor and agitation of existence. In this rarefied place, you have pure equanimity, and nothing seems important enough to get upset about.

Imagine that you are a multidimensional being who occupies all these circles simultaneously. Any situation can be viewed from any place in the circles, and ideally, you move deliberately in and out of each ring. When you get stuck in any one of them, you create a challenge or a puzzle for yourself, or for your relationships.

Picture yourself in the center circle, where you are in some kind of drama or story regarding your relationship. You assert, "My story is the truth!" If you stay here, without being able to move to one of the expanded circles, then you create a feeling of being victimized in some way. You become caught in a role, often that of the righteous person who has been wronged. Life experience and sometimes the simple passage of time can help you gain perspective. You begin to expand beyond the center and gain some psychological understanding of how the situation arose and how it repeats a familiar pattern. You then understand why people respond in the way they do, sustaining the old pattern. This begins to create more space around the stuck feeling you had in the center. Then you can move further out, embracing the pattern from the perspective of its mythic roots.

Concentric Circles helps you keep a healthy perspective when dramas arise. The ideal is to move freely in and around the circles, keeping some sense of awareness of them all simultaneously. Don't aspire to dwell in the mythic or spiritual realm all the time! Feeling ever expansive, cohabiting with the mythic gods and goddesses, can leave you ungrounded after a while. Besides, the story at the center is engaging. Yet feeling stuck or victimized by the story is not fun, nor does it feel like freedom.

Concentric Circles

Sit with your partner and name an issue that comes up in your center "story" circle on a fairly regular basis. It might be a repeated pattern of some kind. Start with something simple in order to develop this tool.

Here is a mundane example that was a pattern for us. Lila tended to set lids back onto bottles of liquid, rather than screwing them back on. Sometimes, if David grabbed a bottle of juice, the lid would fall off and the liquid would slosh out. Similarly, Lila often left doors open and, from David's point of view, let insects into the house. He screwed the lids on tightly and slammed the doors.

Once you have chosen your issue, draw a circle and name the story in the center. Go over its details with your partner: who said what, the circumstances, the things present, the scents, the colors. It may help to write down key words in that first circle.

In our example, "lids," "spills," "insects," "slammed doors."

Just looking at the details already begins to put you into the next circle of observation, the psychological. When you're "in the story," you have little capacity to observe yourself.

Draw that next circle, and name some of the psychological patterns of which you are aware. How do you see each pattern when you are able to understand it and give it a little more space? Can each of you take responsibility for how you create your part in it, and how you each react?

In our example, Lila spoke about openness and the sense of boundaryless existence; David spoke about his desire for order, his need to keep things in their place because of a concern that otherwise everything would fall apart. David could share how this was rooted in his experience of his parents' home, which had chaotic aspects that David, as the eldest child, tried over and over again to fix. Lila, who wanted to throw off all constraints, to nurture that which is wild and free, had longed as a girl to break out of a constraining household. The issue of the loose lids expressed a great longing in one person, and a great fear in the other. These are psychological insights.

Now go more expansive, and name the mythic or symbolic. The issue might show up as a mythic story with which you are both familiar, or you might name principles, like forgiveness or compassion, that you believe the story is attempting to teach you.

See if you can create a shift in the way you see and experience the habit pattern of this old story simply by looking at it from different perspectives.

Find out what principles or features or beings or gods or goddesses embrace your point of view, or with whom you identify.

At the mythic level, Lila felt that, once the lids of life were loosened, she was flying, free even of gravity. She values freedom above all else, and freedom from nearly all form is pure joy for her. At the mythic level, David felt that he was bringing primeval chaos into form, guiding clouds of radiant hydrogen gas in the cosmos into the shape of a planet, and then into a beautiful garden. Lila's freedom tended to the destruction of old and limiting forms, to the function of Shiva. David's admiration of the preciousness of forms and protection of form led him to feel akin to the gods who create form out of primal substance; he felt akin to Brahma. We felt the complementarity of the functions of Shiva and Brahma. At the outer levels of the mythic, we shared a deep Love for the divine play of life on earth, though each identified with a different cosmic role.

When you can move your awareness out beyond the myth, to the most expanded place past the last circumference, there is no story. There is no myth. There is only the unconditional Love and sense of communion with all that is. Each story we get stuck in can be seen as a perfect design to assist us in moving toward the immense vistas and freshness of this communion.

When Lila and David began to see loose lids on jars and open doors as manifestations of form and formlessness, boundaries and freedom, creation and destruction, to make way for new creation, the whole dynamic changed. David didn't need to feel threatened by the chaos of a loose lid on a bottle of apple juice. Lila didn't need to express her freedom by leaving doors open. The story in the everyday world became unimportant. Behavior began to change without prompting. Lila fastens lids and doors more often and David has ceased to react. We do joke about it, because we see the mythic humor in it.

How do you move from one circle to another? By making a choice, and by being able to perceive what each circle is reflecting. Write about each circle, talk about them with your partner. By moving freely, being fluid and appreciative of all the aspects of the Concentric Circles, it will become clear that as you work with them, you can go back to the contracted story with new information, appreciation, and spaciousness—thus the story starts to transform.

The "core" of a conscious partnership can be seen from very different points of view, and no point of view is more important than the others. If you get too spiritual (further out in the Concentric Circles), you can lose touch with the stories and concerns of the world. Learn to move in and out of all of these realms.

In this book we go back and forth easily from life stories to psychological understanding. We press into the mythic and sometimes beyond. People seem to have the least experience with the mythic zone. We suggest you practice more in this realm. Sometimes you find yourself giving voice to great insights, or speaking with a gallant air, or making a flourishing gesture or a seductive one. These are mythic elements, and perhaps mythic beings peeking through, via your words and gestures. Cultivate your relationship with the mythic.

exercise

Walking the Circles

Practice using this pattern in your body. Create the circles on the floor or ground. You can find rope or string to accomplish this, or even stones to mark the form of three circles. It's easy on a beach, where you can draw them in the sand. Walk by yourself into each realm, and recall the focus of each. Start with a simple issue in your relationship that may be just a bit challenging. Don't start with your biggest issue; learn the pattern first. The most important coaching we can offer at this point is to encourage the spirit of play. Don't take it all too seriously, no matter what issue you're working with.

Now that you've practiced with a simpler issue, you may want to take on something more challenging. After you've created the pattern on the ground, decide what topic you will explore, and agree to listen to each other and enjoy the process! It takes some maturity to walk through the pattern without getting reactive. Do your best, and learn from the experience.

Name the situation, and listen to each other as you speak about it in the center of the circle. This is meant to be dramatic, and storytelling at its most engaging! Do your best to listen and hear your partner from a different point of view from the one you've had in the past. Each of you can speak two or three times, trading off as you flesh out the situation.

When you feel you've heard it, step out to the next ring, and share any psychological insights that have come in relation to the topic.

The last step involves moving to the mythic realm, and reflecting on the big picture. The following exercise may help you discover insights from this place.

exercise

Working with the Mythic

The mythic realm can be intimidating to some. It's often used to mean a statement is incorrect: "Aw, that's a myth!" In contrast, we use it to mean something more true than the apparent reality. We regard the mythic or symbolic as the expanded essence of the story, and of the identity that is behind it. The mythic can be expressed as a character you know from cultural mythologies, or it can be a quality or vibration. Take, for example, Kwan Yin: in Asia the goddess of mercy and compassion. The qualities—mercy, compassion, goodness—may be more comfortable for you to work with than the actual character of Kwan Yin. Make a note of your favorite mythic characters or qualities, and invite your partner to offer insights that he or she can see more clearly than you can yourself.

Practice taking on a mythic figure. Imagine that this being (or quality) works through you. You might adopt Athena, goddess of wisdom, and ask her to help you find a particular quote that you've been seeking from a nineteenth-century poet. It could be Aphrodite, the juicy goddess of Love, who, expressing through you, buys lingerie and scented oils. It could be Hephaestus, the brawny blacksmith who can fashion anything from wood, stone, and metal, and who, expressing through you, repairs the bed and the bathroom sink, and makes useful and artistic things for the household. Any role you take on can bring out an aspect of yourself. Observe who and what you are drawn to. You may even notice, when you choose a particularly great outfit, that in that action you are invoking a mythic identity.

After you've practiced with preset roles, permit the mythic to arise naturally in you. What principle or what character arises when you open to the mythic realm? What would happen here if you each took on the voice of the Guiding Hand, and told the story of your meeting and coming together from the perspective of the mythic? (We become very excited by this step because we have seen a blossoming in many couples when we get to this part.)

Perhaps you ask why we do this. Your wedding—and your relationship that precedes the wedding, and your marriage that follows on from it—invokes by its nature the mythic. You can see all the aspects of the wedding, from dress to flowers to vows, etc., in terms of the Concentric Circles: each and every feature! Then they will combine synergistically to give you something far more powerful than what you may have expected.

Embarrassing Stories

Sharing embarrassing moments in your relationship with friends and family is a good way to notice when there's still stuck energy around the "story" level. When you tell a story about your partner, or when you hear your partner tell a story about you, notice how it feels. Are you reactive in some way? Is the telling of the story creating more intimacy between you or is it accentuating separation?

We notice this happening at dinner parties, where one partner needles the other with some continued pattern. "Lids" is our example. David told the "lids" story many times in public before we understood it in the context of the Concentric Circles. Telling stories about your partner is like letting off steam from a container which is about to burst, but the teller isn't fully aware and awake. In the pressure cooker of your relationship, when the top starts rattling, it releases steam to keep the whole thing from exploding. It can be a semi-useful tactic, but more valuable would be to wake up in the pattern and understand how to complete the unfinished story, and go on to one that's more constructive.

This pattern of reinforcing the old embarrassing story by retelling has been called "negative pleasure," or what we would call thorns, because you each enjoy the fact of stimulation, even though the stimulation comes in the form of shaming, accusation, and defense. The niggling never resolves anything because the relationship bumps along in a reactive way. Often the partner who has been shamed in public by the telling of an old story initiates another story that shames the one who started telling stories in the first place. Pay attention if you find yourselves doing this, and then notice what really holds that story in place. Move outside the center circle into the psychological and then into the mythic realm. It's likely to lead you to a delighted "Aha!" There are constructive ways to feel stimulated by each other. You don't need to settle for the ones that hurt.

exercise

Embarrassing Stories

Do you have recurring stories that you tell about your partner? Here's a good clue: you notice your partner squirm or try to defend himself or herself. This should raise a red flag and the question, "What am I doing to my partner and why?"

Perhaps you don't notice your partner's struggles. You might ask a friend to tell you when and if you do this, as often a couple seeks the stimulation (the "negative pleasure") of the shame story and doesn't perceive the repeated destruction that the story wreaks upon the relationship. Name your stories—"The Lids Story" or "The Time You Locked the Keys in the Car" or "The Time You Dropped Aunt Tillie's Antique Vase" or "The Time You Sent Out that Facebook Picture"—and take them one by one through the exercise of the Concentric Circles. Take your time with each story, as we have found that stories hide a wealth of your origin myth as well as a wealth from the mythic realm under something seemingly mundane. Once unlocked, these discoveries become resources rather than thorns.

Once you've observed the energy dynamics of your favorite shame story, you may not be telling it anymore. Find another, more constructive way to present yourselves to others.

The Concentric Circles exercise helps you build a conscious relationship, a relationship that is sacred. So, what is sacred?

Defining the Sacred

You are not alone, the two of you. There is the relationship that you are actively creating between you—an energy field in between, all around, and permeating you, a field that has a growing power, a field that has its own intelligence, a field whose main nutrition is Love. You can nurture your creation with your honesty and the Love you generate with each other.

You may see this third entity as a quality, or as the balance of yin and yang, or as a sacred being. You both discover and cocreate the awareness of that third presence, and there may be differences in how you define, experience, and describe it.

When understood as sacred, the third entity can nurture and enhance each of you continually, immeasurably. You can also see it as two notes—the note of you and the note of your partner—combining into a chord, a field of sound or electromagnetic energy. It requires vibrating fields from both of you to make the particular chord of your relationship. The music metaphor can on occasion become more than a metaphor: some report being able to hear that subtle music created by your notes and the notes of the other making chords, the notes and chords changing with every glance and touch.

Religious traditions and cultures define "sacred" variously. Some of these definitions can point you in a helpful direction as you build this sacred space between the two of you. If you do not share religious, cultural, or spiritual beliefs, then you may need to discover how your core values and definitions of the sacred can be held in trust by each other. You come to feel the sacred as you move through the Concentric Circles, out from the story into a place where you embrace a reality larger than the story, a reality that orders the details in meaning.

When you get the three-ness going—the two Ones and the field of your relationship—you will find that a functioning couple becomes an instrument of expanded awareness. Your combined power can more effectively sense answers to questions about the world. You become a team, capable of greater understanding, greater compassion, and bigger deeds. You become aware of a vastly grander view of creation and your place in it.

Helpers, Presences, Angels

We have different perceptions about how "beings" show up in the world. David experiences angelic and intelligent presences. Lila attunes more to qualities, and tends not to experience them as "outside," but more as a resonance that ultimately is part of the Whole. We are aligned in the important essence of this inquiry, but we express it differently. Hence, in this book David will speak about angels, while Lila will speak of qualities, values, and archetypes. We heartily invite you to insert words that work better for you. If angels and "spiritual beings" don't resonate with you, find a way to describe the sacred that does. We will encourage you to create the experience of this "presence," however you define it, in your ceremony.

Some will scoff at the notion of the sacred, and name it in terms of illusion, claiming that the only true reality is in the base of Mount Maslow: what you can see and touch, what will feed you and keep you warm. To complete the picture, some attending your wedding may go way off in the other direction, believing that the world is full of angels who have a personal interest in them. We take a middle view, one that is based in personal experience—your experience—though it requires that you have an open mind.

We all have some connection to unseen forces. You may be a deep lover of nature, and sense unseen spirits in the trees. You may feel a quiet presence in a temple, church, or mosque. You don't have to become an esotericist to appreciate deep quiet, or a feeling inside, or the sense of power in a place. We each have a place, literal or figurative, where the sacred resides. Name that; find it in a word or phrase. It may be the spirit of Adventure (this can become the goddess energy of Artemis or a Knight of the Round Table); or the energy of Enthusiasm (from *en theos,* "in god"). It may be the fact of Beauty—and don't be put off by that awful adage, "Beauty is in the eye of the beholder," suggesting that there is no objective Beauty. An objective Beauty does exist. It is full of life and purity and passion—and we recommend that you invite it to your wedding.

Even the scoffers and skeptics, the materialists and those living at the bottom of Mount Maslow, are occasionally swayed by their own feelings, or by awe at the beauty of nature, or by the warmth of a greeting. You may not change the committed philosophy of your materialist friends and relatives, but stay with your job: to cultivate first your own openness of mind and heart, and to design a wedding that makes space for unexpected positivity.

story

DAVID   Angels

You may not believe in angels, and certainly there is a lot of fluff in print about angels and what they are supposed to look like, and so forth. That puts off some people who can't see them that way. However, everyone most likely feels or perceives the presence of something extraordinary in moments that we call "special" or "blessed." I have met people who are skeptical of anything that is not observable fact, verified by the senses, witnessed by several qualified people, and replicable on demand—modern scientists, in short. Yet these same people will glow with warmth and speak in hushed tones of "extraordinary" experiences they've had and cannot explain. The skeptic might call them "inexplicable occurrences of very low probability," even "anomalies," which means that, in those instances, they don't even try to explain what they've seen or heard. I say that angels are at work, and I have sensed the tremor in the air and the quickening in my heart.

In moments of confidential sharing, scientists have told me, "A newborn child is a wonder." "The whole world is a puzzle." "The cosmos is unexplained." That's the kind of openness that can bring the power of mystery into a relationship and into a wedding ceremony.

In a well-designed wedding I believe that angels show up, lending their light and perfume to the celebration. You can call upon spiritual agencies and invite them to assist you. The section "In Whose Name," later in this chapter, guides you in this.

story

LILA   Qualities

I have always sensed the quality of vibration as dense or as expansive. When David talks about angels, he is very expansive. I feel that quality around him, bearing witness to the fact that he is sharing a perception that is sacred to him. The experience of that is a treasure for me. I may not share his perception, but I appreciate what he feels like.

My personal revelation of the sacred is mostly embedded in the natural world. I feel mountains are beings (as the South Americans name them, the *apus*). I listen to the weather as though it were the medium of conversation with a huge intelligence that I call Sophia, or the Great Mother. The elements are aspects of her wisdom and presence. ✿

The Sacred Elements

You can bring the sacred into your lives in ways that are nonreligious and nonthreatening. Work with the basic elements of earth, water, air, and fire. Everyone will readily agree that these elements exist. Sharing your experiences of these fundamental elements of our world can excite your mutual appreciation of beauty, which in turn leads to a loving time together. We also suggest including the elements in any ceremony, as they can work as an organizing principle around which different aspects of a ceremony can be created.

Befriend earth, the element of substance, soil, crystal, structure, and form. In these times of high technology, fast movement, extensive travel, and rapid communication, we all can benefit from simple grounding techniques, that is, a connection with the ground of earth beneath our every step. Many practices, from yoga to qigong to tai chi to eurythmy, include stances that are intended to ground the body, slow the breath, and bring us to deep center in our bones, the earthiest part of our bodies. Stones and bones share a connection to the earth element.

The simplest of these exercises is to stand in balance on the earth and feel as if you are sending your roots into the earth. Slow down the breath, and feel the connection through the ground. This is an actual sensation, not only an imagination. Simple awareness like this is also appropriate when dealing with the nervousness that can arise in a ceremony or ritual. Here's a suggestion: learn how to stand. You'll be standing for a while at your wedding ceremony, and it will be helpful if you are comfortable with your bones before that event.

exercise

Befriend Earth

STEP 1: Each of you, find one thing in your environment that is heavy and represents earth energy to you (and that you can pick up!), such as a stone, piece of wood, or metal object. Holding your object, stand facing your partner, and allow a sense of roots to grow into the earth. Stay with it until you actually feel more grounded and slowed down. Feel the weight of the object pulling you into the earth, into gravity. Appreciate that feeling of being grounded.

Then sit and face each other and complete the sentence, "I feel most grounded when . . ." or "I feel most solid when . . ." You can do these as repeated questions, or simply complete the one sentence and move on.

STEP 2: Feel your partner's hard places: the cranium, the sternum, places like elbows and knees where the bones stick out. Notice what's the same and what's different about the quality of your individual structures. Name some of those qualities that you sense in your partner's bones and form. Rejoice that your partner's earthy structure is animated by vitality and life force!

Get to know the structure and shape of your Beloved as would a sculptor, caressing the whole and the parts. A sculptor feels the shapes of the model and then feels the clay, wood, or stone that is being worked, back and forth from the living to its imitation. Ponder making a sculpture of your Beloved, and how intimately you would have to know her or his body. The bony structure of your Beloved provides the framework within which her or his essence finds expression. Crystals express the ordered geometries that underlie all earth forms. The rings on your fingers are probably made from gems and metals, the earth realm's finest productions, showing in their structure the orderliness of crystal. The ring exchange in a ceremony is one place that these earth energies can be honored.

Befriend water, the element of flow, rhythm, and moisture. Our bodies are about two-thirds water (with our brains at four-fifths).

exercise

Befriend Water

STEP 1: Fill a glass with water, and decide what quality you wish to imbue into the water. It might be joy, or healing, or love. Both of you place your hands on the glass and imagine all the water molecules receiving the impression of the quality and somehow changing their interior composition to reflect that they now carry that quality. Do this for at least one full minute before you sip it, one person at a time, holding the water in your mouth before swallowing it. Make it real! Create the experience of the quality you have chosen, and feel it as it slides down your throat and is quickly assimilated into your blood and into your entire body. Medicines work swiftly when imbibed, and so can qualities. (Dr. Masaru Emoto has studied imprints into water in the way presented here; though controversial, his findings have recently been verified.)

STEP 2: Find two glasses, preferably ones that are special or beautiful in some way. Have a small pitcher of water ready. Sit facing each other, and align yourselves with your choice to be together. You might do this with the previous "Yes" exercise, and really choose to be together.

Pour water into both glasses, and each hold a glass between your hands. Decide who will speak first to offer a blessing for the relationship or for your partner. When the blessing is done, pour the water from that glass back into the pitcher.

Now the other person speaks a blessing. Bless your water by feeling energy move out through your hands and into the glass.

Pour the second glass back into the pitcher. Now imagine that the two prayers intermingle in the pitcher, and the water molecules happily align with these prayers. Pour the water into the glasses again, and slowly drink, expressing what you feel, or what you imagine might be happening as these prayers move through your body, cells, and blood.

The imagining here is that water is impressionable. It does respond to energy and intention. Changes in molecular structure have been found when water is prayed over or blessed.

Because our physical bodies are mostly water, we naturally flow, undulate, gyrate, vibrate, and pulse. Explore your Beloved's mostly watery flesh, fed by the very watery blood. If tears are ever shed, be they of grief or joy, realize that these are special distillations of the water element within us. Don't brush them away with a tissue, but set them someplace special, onto your skin, onto the skin of your Beloved, or into the water that you drink. Enjoy water together: springs, streams, waterfalls, the ocean's waves. Move together fluidly. Enjoy this discovery of your Beloved's watery expression.

Now to the element of air, which we often forget about, as we look right through it. It disappears by its presence everywhere, yet we can honor it for its gifts to us.

exercise

Befriend Air

STEP 1: Breathe! Air carries *prana,* or life force, into us with our every breath. Sit facing each other and intentionally synchronize your breath, letting it out together, pausing, and inhaling. Pay attention to each other, and don't speak! Just be aware, and inhale and exhale together. Do this for at least five breaths together.

Now alternate your breaths with your Beloved, faces close, sharing breath. As you inhale, your partner exhales. Have your faces close together, but not touching; simply feel the breath and breathe in each other's essence. Begin to see that a lover's exhalations are full of Love energy. You breathe in prana, and you can fill the air with Love as you breathe it out. In every tradition you can find the notion of life-giving breath. Exhalations need not only be waste; for healers, the exhalation holds something very positive that they gift to others. Because of your love for each other, you can do this too, with each other.

STEP 2: Chant together or speak together. Take an in-breath together, and find the same tone or a harmony with the sound "Ahhh." Play with your voices, carried between you and your Beloved through the air. Explore how your voices blend. Sing together, and don't say that you can't sing. David and Lila have joined choirs open to all that demonstrate that everyone can find beautiful tones. Indeed, all speaking has a singing component. So enjoy whatever sound you make together, as this is the discovery of your Beloved's airy expression.

STEP 3: Laugh! Air carries prana into us with our every breath. Intentionally laugh. It's great medicine!

STEP 4: Watch birds together as messengers of heaven, and clouds as domiciles of angels. Trace the trails of birds in the sky, and try to see the afterimages of where they have flown.

STEP 5: Design a banner with colors and words that have meaning to the two of you, then construct this banner and wave it in the air. Thus you use the air to witness your banner.

Befriend fire, the element of warmth, creation, and destruction. Fire glows in your belly, flaring up into passions of emotion or sexuality. Explore your relation to fire by contemplating the stars and galaxies in the heavens, all points of intense heat.

exercise

Befriend Fire

STEP 1: Create an intentional fire together. Either build a big fire or share the little fire of a candle. Before striking the match that will ignite your flame, speak an intention and dedication. To what do you dedicate this heat, this miracle of flame? What lives in flame that stays with that flame? Why is it important that the Olympic torch never goes out? What kind of flame might you light together that will stay lit for a long time?

The nature of fire is to consume and transform. It burns, it warms, it cooks, it comforts, and it can destroy. To honor the power of fire is to acknowledge that it is inherent in us all as a creative force. Speak to each other about what you choose to create with your fire together.

STEP 2: Dance together until you are both hot.

STEP 3: Watch for the flash of fire in the eyes of your Beloved. Enjoy this discovery of your Beloved's fiery expression.

Thus you can befriend the elements, finding supports and ritual opportunities for your relationship. A wonderful poem and song goes like this:

> Earth my body
> Water my blood
> Air my breath
> And fire my spirit.

Releasing

You eat to nourish your body. In digestion, you break down what you've eaten into its basic constituents. From these basics, your body builds something useful to you. What you couldn't digest, your body efficiently eliminates. Excretion has gotten a bad reputation, but it is essential to your health—the health of your body, and the health of your emotions and thoughts, too. We all need to let some things go.

Fundamentally, "releasing" is an acknowledgment that energy that has been locked into a pattern must transform. Did you know that you exchange every cell in your body for a new one every seven years (the pancreas every month)? Habits of movement and of thought can last much longer. Whenever we change a habit or a pattern, we let go of the previous way that energy moved through us, freeing up that energy to move in another way.

In chapter 3, we discussed relation-ship-wrecks that persist. Even with patterns smaller than entire relationships, such as grudges and shocks and little traumas, we tend to hold on for too long. One reason is because we don't understand elimination. When you eliminate an indigestible part of something you ate, you don't also eliminate the memory of having eaten it. You simply remove its power. The aim with emotions is the same. There are two aspects to an emotional memory: 1) The fact of it, the faint impression of its outlines, the details of what happened, and 2) its power to excite you positively or negatively every time you trigger that memory. You may not wish to get rid of the first aspect, because you can continue to learn from your life experiences. The second aspect is the most wonderful for positive recollections, and the most bothersome for negative ones.

When you change, you release aspects of yourself that were difficult, things that you didn't like. You also must release some of the things that you did like. To the extent that your old pleasures slow your growing, then they must go too. We'll get to that after the more familiar releases of things you don't like.

In releasing, you say, in effect, "Yes, I had that experience. I survived it! Here I am to tell the tale! I don't need it anymore. Thanks for the experience, and now it's time to move on."

exercise

Releasing

Releasing the difficult, with some clear thinking:

- Perhaps you tell people a story of woe, something terrible that happened to you. You have told it dozens of times. Now tell it to a mentor, therapist, trusted friend, or partner, while listening closely to the story. Ask what benefit it's giving you. Often there is an unspoken plea: "Please have pity on me! Please make me a bowl of warm soup! Please acknowledge how much I've suffered, and don't ask me to do anything else! Please stroke my hair and whisper soothing sounds!" It's helpful to determine if these requests are behind your story of woe, because there are much more efficient ways of getting those needs met.

- When you identify stories of woe, acknowledge that those stories occurred; acknowledge that you may have been treated unfairly; say thanks for the tough lessons; and set them aside. It is as simple as picking up a stone and moving it to a new place, further out from the center of you. The stories remain part of your history and may even go into the novel you're writing, but for your future they can only hold you back.

- Decide where you're going in life, what kind of person you would like to become. Here is a sound-bite that has some help in it: "Fake it till you make it." It doesn't mean to exaggerate the artificiality of an artificial smile; it does mean to put some art into your smile, some intention. Neurological studies show that a refocus of your attention on a way of being will, in a short time, reconnect the neurons of your brain to attend to that new way of being. If you decide to notice the wonders in every experience, it does in fact become easier and easier to do so.

- The Concentric Circles exercise works potently for any issue that you would like to bring to it. Perhaps you have a series of stories proving that you can't trust romance. That's at the story or drama level. Because loss of trust is such a deep issue, you may need someone's help to find your way to the psychological and then to the mythic levels of these experiences. That helper could be your partner, as doing deep work with each other can enhance your loving commitment to relationship. If shame arises, well, that becomes the topic that you take through the Concentric Circles.

Releasing with the help of the elements (working with the previous section):

- Write whatever is ready to be released on a piece of paper and tie it to a small piece of wood. Build a little bonfire, and ask that the pattern be transformed as it burns. This involves both the earth element in the wood and the element of fire. You can do this process as a couple or individually.

- Ritual bathing can provide a vehicle for release as well. If you add salt to the bathwater, such as Epsom salts or sea salt, that brings in the earth element, to soak up the old patterns and lead them down the drain to be transformed by natural earth processes.

- In the element of air, speak the troubling patterns, and then breathe them out. Consciously breathe fresh air into every corner of your lungs—do you know that the surface area of your lungs equals that of a tennis court?—and clean out all traces of the old. You may find that certain sounds and words hold portions of the pattern. Let it all be breathed out. Articulate in words your new freedom.

- The earth can receive things we are letting go, when we bury them. An object (such as a crystal, or a piece of jewelry, or a piece of paper) can come to represent something or someone. If it isn't burnable, consider a ritual of burying it.

Releasing the good times:

- You may realize that some of your comforts, habits, pleasures, favorite foods, and routines are holding you back from growing. For couples especially, when you are living separately, completely comfortable and familiar with the routines of your separate lives, you may decide to release the independence, permitting yourselves to join together to explore relationship more deeply. What seemingly positive things are ready to be released?

When you use these techniques, you will notice that your relation-ship-wrecks dissolve into the sea, giving you more energy to build a new relation-ship.

In Whose Name?

The Christian Gospel said it best: "Wherever two or more are gathered in my name, the I Am is in their midst" (Matthew 18:20). "Two or more"—that covers the relationship of two, and the "more" of your community of friends and neighbors, or, at a wedding, your witnesses. "In my name" is a transla-tion of words that can also mean "in my breath" or "in my vibration"—in other words, not just a word but a feeling, too. The "I Am" is one way to see and hold the divine awake consciousness in which we all partake. The part of us that can say "I," as in "I feel," "I perceive," "I know," "I exist," is very pre-cious. The usual "I" is sometimes petty, sometimes grand, but you can give voice to a greater "I" that expresses its joy of existence in and through you. The part that says "I Am" is awake, just as you hope to be in marriage, and at your wedding.

We have found this to be one of the most important questions for a couple desiring to marry: "In whose name do you marry?" Those of you who are not planning a wedding can ask yourselves, "In whose name are we conversing? In whose name are we living together? In whose name did we meet?" These questions are important for all levels of commitment in a relationship.

Many people who have rejected traditional religion find it difficult to work with this idea. They may think of themselves as individuals, separate from any mystery of life or creation, and they like it that way. But we all are capable of awakening to the freshness of the air we breathe, the deliciousness of the water we drink, the nutrition of the food we eat, the beauty of the things we see . . . The wonder goes on and on. All of creation comes alive in the awareness of sacred qualities, presence, and grace. These are the "names" in which we relate to each other, and it is very helpful to state those names.

Even those who understand a relationship merely as an economic unit, a convenience, a mechanical efficiency, will on occasion appreciate the distinct language of the heart. Those occasions may be more plentiful in some relationships, and less in others, but they are always there. That shows movement toward the sacred, and is done in a name other than that of efficiency. What is that name?

Can you identify a principle that has power for you? It could be a traditional figure such as an angel of mercy, Jesus, Mary, Buddha, Father, Mother, or Great Spirit. It could be Beauty, Love, Cocreation, or Truth. Choose not just a nice principle, but a real principle, something you would stand up for. If someone said, "Beauty doesn't exist," would you stand up and assert your connection with Beauty? "Yes, Beauty exists—I know Beauty!" If someone said, "Love doesn't exist," would you stand up and assert your connection with Love? "I affirm Love! I am a champion of Love!" Are there other principles that are important to you? You see how we're working toward the mythic realm of the Concentric Circles? And finding a name for the Guiding Hand?

The virtues were once understood as independently existing helpers who had attributes—sometimes as archetypes, sometimes as gods and goddesses. Sensual Love had her near-nakedness; Grace had her fluid, upright posture and delicate fingers. The Greeks and Romans named their divinities with words that we use—Grace, Harmony, Patience, Love—relating to them as living beings that could visit you and permeate you. The nine Muses personified nine qualities of art and beauty that could be contacted through invocation and conversation.

Whether you see Grace, Beauty, Harmony, Patience, and Love as principles, independently living beings, or resonant frequencies that permeate creation, these qualities definitely exist. You know someone who has Courage, and someone who does not. Can the latter person be awakened to the being of Courage—the presence of Courage or the vibration of Courage—in such a way that he or she can find this Courage in himself or herself when the situation calls for it?

Or, if you feel moved to do so, name a divinity that you feel as a living force. Perhaps it is Sophia, the Wisdom of the Divine Feminine? The Divine Mother? Christ Jesus? Some people choose Light. Some choose Consciousness. You can also consider Great Spirit, Shiva-Shakti, Father-Mother God, the Divine Feminine and the Divine Masculine, Radha-Krishna, Love, Life, and Brightness! Or other names of the Divine Spirit or qualities of life that move you. As celebrants, we like to know what quality or essence we are invoking in the sacred space of a wedding; the same goes for any relationship at any stage of commitment. The "name," the vibration, the quality of breath, can be invoked before the witnesses at your ceremony or can remain private if you wish. Whichever you choose, "in whose name" is extremely important for the two of you.

Discussing this question can create a lovely sharing between you and your partner. Think of whose attention you would like to have, what power you would like to come and bless your union! You're sending that power a letter, and the more specific you can be in the address that you're sending it to, the more likely that being (or principle or angel) will arrive.

exercise

Repeated Question 4

Decide which of you will act as Coach, and which as Respondent. Use the same rules as before. It looks generally like this:

Coach: "What principle or being has power for you?"

The Respondent says what occurs to him or her, such as:

Respondent: "The power of beauty."

The Coach thanks the Respondent. If the Respondent says, "Pass," the Coach also says, "Thank you." Then the Coach asks the question again:

Coach: "Thank you. What principle or being has power for you?"

Keep at it for three minutes, then switch the roles of Coach and Respondent. You will be surprised at what emerges. Talk with each other about what came up. Wait a month, then try it again.

Another variation is the repeated question, "What principle or being do you love?"

You've just named many names that are important to you. We recommend that you find the one or two that really sing to you, for you, and in you as a couple. A list of a dozen divinities and virtues is not practical. Focus on one or two. Of the many essences that have been mentioned, choose a very positive one that will support a loving relationship between you. This principle or spiritual presence overlights your entire relationship, and also your wedding. It will show up during the ceremony, especially at the Sacred Moment. You may end up including it in your vows or having the celebrant invoke this quality, so that all who are there can feel it and align with it as part of the ceremony.

In some traditions, these names are repeated over and over again. In the Hindu tradition, this is called *japa,* repeated names of Divinity: "Om namah Shivaya. Om namah Shivaya. Om namah Shivaya . . ." Or, "Love, Love, Love . . ." You can speak the name quickly or slowly, or vary the rate of speaking. If it really means something to you, and you say the word each time with meaning, repeating these words can have a powerful impact on you. They can draw you closer to the living energy of the quality of being. Sometimes you have to reinvest meaning into words that have been overused. "Heart" and "Love" and many others have been wrecked by wrong use, and you simply have to resurrect them with the way you say them.

Repetition of the Name

We know of several traditions wherein one chants the names of qualities and beings who personify those qualities. One story: A friend traveled to the Middle East where he was invited to a Sufi chanting meeting. The men came together in a room and began to chant the names of the Divine, first with confidence, then very fast, then very slow, then loud, then softer and softer until there was only a whisper, then no apparent sound at all as they continued the chant inside, then after a time started up again vocally. After five hours, the chant ended, everyone happy to have bathed in the vibration of Divinity for the entire time. Our friend said that his heart-understanding of the invoked Divinity and all its qualities progressed through stages of increasing intimacy. He felt that he couldn't have come to what he experienced in the last hour without the previous hours of chanting.

There are no limits to how familiar you can become with the name that blesses and guides your relationship. Remember, "name" can mean vibration, meaning you can sing or make tones to invoke what's important to you.

exercise

Toning the Name

Take any word or phrase that you hold sacred and stretch it out. Exaggerate the consonants and savor the vowels. For example, "Love" begins with a long, luscious, and liquid "l" sound. You follow with the vowel, a combination of "ah" and "uh." You can go back and forth between the two vowel sounds, and back and forth between the consonant and the vowel. Finish with a wavy, vibrating "v," often dropped, well worth the tingling vibration on your lips. Try it loudly and softly.

Try other words that are important to you. Find your way to a more intimate experience of each important word through the sounds of that word.

Now you know what to do if you're stuck in a long line at the grocery store: repeat the names of the virtues that you admire, as well as the name of your Beloved, over and over again, with feeling. A simple practice like this can take a potentially irritating situation and transform it into one of Divinity, for yourself as well as for those around you.

The Mentor

A relationship can benefit from a grounding element in the form of a third party, a mentor. In the case of a wedding, the third person can assist you in the creation and manifestation of your ceremony. In the case of a relationship, this person reminds you of the names that nourish your relationship and the sacredness of your union. Depending on where you live and whether you are working in a religious tradition or not, this person may be a minister, rabbi, counselor, celebrant, coach, great-uncle, consultant, dear friend. . . . No matter what the costume, guise, or label, this person functions as your Mentor.

We suggest that you identify and agree upon a third person whom you admire, a responsible person whose advice you might choose to follow. If stress ever overwhelms you beyond the capacity of the tools in this book, go to this person for counsel. Many couples are shocked, when we ask them to name such a person, to find that they cannot do so. The traditional role of the minister or priest or rabbi who once filled this slot has eroded in many places, and may no longer be imbued with the respect you'll wish to afford your Mentor. Make it a project to identify such a person, even if you see him or her very little. Mentors need not be personal friends whom you see regularly. You simply need to know that they are there if needed for counsel in trying times.

A mentor can also help you understand the Concentric Circles from the beginning of this chapter—in other words, when you are "in the story," when you are in your psychological and emotional reactions, when you are in the mythic, and when you are beyond it all, in pure spirit.

A Mentor Couple

We were recently asked by a young couple we married if we would adopt their relationship. At a meeting over lunch, the new wife stated that they each had active parents in their lives, and both sets of parents were very supportive. However, if there were any signs of strife, the parents tended to side with their child.

We were asked if we would, therefore, be the parents and mentors of their relationship, and offer guidance and insights toward the good of that third entity. It was completely endearing; and it reminded us that there are few seasoned couples around who can model conscious marriage. But they do exist, and it's worth finding one from which you can learn!

If it isn't possible to find such a couple, mentors can be found in the mythic realm. You might even discover them when doing a Concentric Circles process. There are Divine Couples in every tradition, and their stories abound: Shiva and Shakti; Christos and Sophia; Yeshua and Magdalene; Inanna and Dumuzi; Isis and Osiris; and countless indigenous examples as well. Explore some stories and see if there is a pattern in a mythology that can assist you.

exercise

Mentor

Together gather names of those whom you consider older and wiser. Discuss the qualifications of each of these people—and, most importantly, the feelings that you have about each. In whose name do you feel that they live their lives? Don't rush through this. If you discover that there is no one in your life who is wiser than your peers, then name the ideal qualities of such a person, and together invite such a person into your lives, and into your relationship. Then note who shows up in your life in the next days or weeks.

Transitions: One–Two–ONE

In this book, we seek to establish the foundations for a conscious wedding. We find that the simple formula One–Two–ONE helps you establish that foundation, and helps you remember it when the distractions of the ceremony cause you to forget.

As humans, we begin with a sense of self, perhaps an egocentric and immature version of identity. We mature to a sense of a free individual: the One. Two individuals can have a healthy relationship: a Two, a partnership. From this partnership, we can evolve into communion with all creation: the grand ONE. However, the course of development seldom moves straight ahead, and obstacles abound. In this chapter we will look at some of those obstacles.

One (Individuality)

> **One:** I experience myself as an individual, a mature and independent human being. I = I.
> **Hazards:** narcissism; there is only me; I versus It; dominator and victim.

Early in adult life, each of us thinks, "I know who I am!" We take on an identity: "I'm an artist," or "I'm a doctor." The world seems like a collection of objects to be manipulated into serving personal needs. Objects include people; like other objects, they are "It" in relation to my "I." How do we mature beyond the ego definition of "I am the one!—the one and only one"? How do we go beyond entitlement, demands, and manipulation?

A mature adult has a sense of "I" that is sustainable and self-directed, that knows the Self, is aware of impulses and has them under control, asserts the right of freedom for all individuals, does what he or she says that he or she will do, does not impinge on others, and has a feeling of self-sufficiency. This is the One at its best, and the development of that One is necessary before entering into a mature relationship (the Two).

Riane Eisler, author of *The Chalice and the Blade, The Partnership Way, Sacred Pleasure,* and other excellent books, has called the immature development of the One the dominator. It is loudly reflected in our world, where college degrees, awards, achievements, and financial net worth have become the most prevalent measures of personal value and wealth. You acquire those assets by any means possible, by taking control and dominating your surroundings. This implies that there must be a victim whom the dominator dominates.

Most of us have some dominator voice alive in our psyche. Those voices that direct our behavior give us monologues that range from controlling to abusive, and that cover topics from sexuality to finances and power. Whatever the topic, the dominator is unable to admit any other person's point of view. Have you ever observed a conversation where the two people talk to each other but aren't listening to each other? They carry on two monologues, each pointed in the direction of the other, but never connecting. Each is trying to dominate the world, because each feels that he or she owns the world. It's easy to see this pattern in charge of many aspects of relationship, in marriages, business, and politics.

An intimate relationship that functions primarily in the dominator/victim mode will be challenged if an attempt is made to turn it into a partnership. A successful effort requires deep desire, intention, and willingness on the part of both people. While partners perceive each other as individuals, freely choosing to come together, both dominator and victim are stuck.

Riane Eisler's books explain the cultural significance of making the transition from dominator (the negative side of One) to partner (the positive side of Two). We can only imagine what the world might look like if people everywhere considered that they were partners with the earth and the environment. Or, as Riane has suggested, if a culture spent as much money on child care as it spent on its military, it would begin to grow a balanced partnership society.

In personal relationship, the dominator voice may sound like, "I am in charge of the finances here, and I make all the important decisions." Or, "I'm looking out for number one!" The victim's position might be verbalized as, "You are in charge of finances, and I'll give you all the money and be indebted to you for your generosity." Or, "Yes, you are number one." In a conversation about sex, the dominator would be demanding, threatening, and controlling.

The dominator/victim pattern is alive in many ways in our culture. It includes addictions to substances and gratifications; it includes violence; it includes suppression of the creativity that is everyone's birthright. Let's be clear: we are not that far away from a time when a man owned his woman as a possession. And there are some who still think, "It's all about ME!," consigning all others to the status of object—to "It." Human consciousness is changing, and this attitude can no longer hold. Individualism is rising, which means your One is feeling the power—and so is everyone else's One!

To go to Two, you have to become a mature One first. The individual must realize his or her innate positive potential and grow in strength. Though a victim may be tempted to throw off the previous dominator and become a new dominator, the "I" must find its own strengths and move past imitation of power to real power. A mature One has no interest in revenge. It has the capacity to graduate from "I and It" to "I and Thou," thus moving toward true partnership.

exercise

Identifying a Dominator/Victim Dynamic

Consider all aspects of your life outside of your relationship. Find an example of a dominator/victim pattern, maybe at work, in society at large, or with a parent. At first, you might make this observation about two other people—not yourself. Speak to your partner about the dynamics of this pattern, how the energy moves, how the dominator holds power, and how the victim acquiesces. For now, just become aware of it. Describe in detail how it feels when you are in that situation. Simply listen to each other. This is not a time to offer advice on how to fix things! First observe the pattern.

Save this idea for the nonviolent communication (NVC) tool in the next chapter, and then come back to it. You can use the NVC tool to develop a more mature One from some old dominator/victim patterns.

Two (Partnership)

Two: I experience my partner as an individual. "I am I and you are you." Energy and conversation move back and forth: One speaks to One. I + I = II.

Hazards: insularity as a couple; collusion; "We versus It."

Deep-rooted, sustainable partnership is cocreated by strong individuals who choose to express themselves beyond their independent selfhood. Moving from One into a conscious expression of the Two excites a dance of duality between masculine and feminine, yin and yang, light and dark, myself and yourself. Partnership means "power with" rather than "power over." The two self-empowered individuals stand side by side, moving into the world together, sharing as they go. Each individual has unique skills, which then are dedicated to strengthening the couple. If one is better able to manage finances, you both accept the expertise of that one. The role can be fulfilled without it being a "power over" the other.

exercise

One Eye, Two Eyes

How do you explain partnership to someone who has known only domination or victimhood? Cover one of your eyes with a hand, and keep it there for a minute. (Ask your partner to join you in this.) You see light playing in colors and on forms, and you can describe the capacity of seeing. Take the time to describe what you see; get used to one-eye sight. Now consider the possibility of having a second eye to see with. Will you see double the color or double the intensity of light? Let your hand go, and open your second eye. What you get with two eyes is depth, something quite difficult to explain to someone with only one eye. Two is not a bigger version of One, but opens your experience in completely new ways.

Riane Eisler speaks of partnership in sexuality as involving mutual respect and freedom of choice. It has as its goal the mutual pleasure of both people, and values feminine strengths and masculine strengths equally. We must learn to distinguish sexual anatomical parts from masculine (yang) and feminine (yin) *qualities*. We all have some of each quality; sometimes a female will have strong masculine qualities, and vice versa. We must acknowledge gender differences and learn to reconcile them with the customs of the world today. In partnership, differences are seen more as resources to be shared than as reasons to distance yourself from the other. We call this essential complementarity. You aren't two portions of the same; rather, you exchange resources.

In Lila's work with women internationally, particularly in Israel/Palestine, she has come to experience the feminine power that in certain cultures is often disregarded or demeaned. The oppressiveness of the exaggerated masculine energy (as dominator) makes it more difficult to reconnect with the power that is innate in feminine wisdom. Some of these feminine qualities—available to both men and women—are intuition, nurturing, relationship, tending the matrix and interconnections of life, care of the soul, and earth-based awareness. When these qualities are understood and embraced, many people understand better how to become equal, complementary partners. This is one of the ways in which the mature One complements the other mature One to make a vibrant Two.

exercise

Identifying Aspects of Partnership

Focus primarily on your relationship. Each of you make your own list, in two columns, of the qualities you embody that you might consider to be masculine or feminine. Look at each other's list, and notice how they compare. Can you see where they might complement one another? Can you see where they might feed a conflict if they were not clearly understood?

Return to the dominator/victim exercise, and see if there are ways you can envision that relationship becoming more of a partnership. It may not seem possible if the other person is your boss or a deceased parent. Yet sometimes taking a different role in your imagination can be enough to renegotiate a dominator/victim pattern within yourself.

You can take this discussion to the Concentric Circles by standing in different rings and identifying what these characteristics look like in the story circle, the psychological circle, and the mythic circle.

Partnerships of all sorts (intimate, parental, business, and friendship) can benefit from a resource assessment. How well you work together in partnership often has to do with how aware you are of the complementary nature of the other. Many conflicts can be avoided when there are agreements in place that address the diversity of talents.

A simple example of role reversal might occur if the man loves cooking and the woman is not as interested. It doesn't matter that this is culturally a new configuration; many people have the understanding that the traditional role of woman in the kitchen can be renegotiated. Different arrangements are made for the balancing out of domestic duties and home-making needs.

We have spoken about the challenge of developing into a true individual, the One. When you get through those trials, you breathe a sigh of relief, for now you are capable of having a true relationship. To go further, you have to overcome the hazards of the Two. The couple can become insulated, oblivious of anyone else. "I lost my friend to a marriage" is said frequently by those outside of that marriage. The couple can become the unit that treats the rest of the world as an "It," to be manipulated for personal gain. The partners merge their illusions about the world into a collusion. You overcome collusion only by broadening your experiences and meeting many different kinds of people and situations.

Illusions and collusions prevent you from truly seeing your partner. The general culture throws them at you mercilessly through every possible medium, in thousands of images and soundbites every day. The more you shed these illusions, the better you can access the joys of communion.

Over the span of a life, you move from One to Two, then back to One again. You realize what you've learned, strengthen your One, then move to Two again. To do this many times is natural: it's called practice. Some of the old relationships may hang on in memory, as relation-ship-wrecks. The exercises in this book will help you to dismantle those old wrecks and reclaim the energy you left behind in past relationships. Practice helps you grow as a better One, equipping you to become a healthy Two on the way to ONE.

ONE (Communion)

> ONE: I experience the feeling of "we" as unity, in vibrant communion, expanding to the Unity of all existence. The One (individual) matures through Two to ONE (united couple). I + I = I.
> Hazards: spaciness; ditziness; "All Is One" with a beatific smile; dissolving into dreaming.

The word "communion" has come to be associated predominantly with Christianity, a sacrament of bread and wine. Yet communion actually means unity of all, spiritual union or empathy, an experience in which everyone can partake.

One–Two–ONE resolves in the fullness of merging in one unified awareness. The word communion can be understood as "coming into union." In our experience, moments of communion will originate from partnership, not from the dominator/victim paradigm. The blossoming of communion in a partnership can occur during a brief glance, or can be sustained for hours in conscious lovemaking, or everything in between. The practice of bringing communion into your partnership can be delightful, and we will suggest some exercises to open the possibility. Riane Eisler's fine work on dominators (negative One) and partners (positive Two) becomes a springboard into bliss (ONE).

These are potential moments of ecstasy, where boundaries dissolve and one experiences the fullness of all creation. Many people have had moments of ecstatic merging in sexuality (more on this in chapter 8). Sex that leads to Love has the full power of creation inherent in it!

We have come to accept an illusion that the space between One and One is empty. Not true! Air is thick, filled with currents. Energy fields emanate from every One to every other One. Though we don't see this activity (though some can), the space is not empty but quite full.

Communion from a cosmological point of view is reflected in a simple story. The seeker sits before the master, and the master says, "The only difference between you and me is that you believe the universe is outside of you, while I know that the universe is inside of me." The master knows and lives in the ONEness of communion, the unified field. Physics speaks of fields, as in electromagnetic fields, a realm of pulsing wave effects that emanate from a source. Fields in physics have no boundaries, but dissipate in proportion to the square of the distance from the source. The source point of the unified field is everywhere all the time. You can enter this zone through communion.

The ritual of getting down on one or both knees to ask your partner to marry comes from awe in the face of the power of the ONE.

Communion also relates to communication. Essential, Love-filled communication originates and deepens union. Any successful communication pulls you out of domination. Techniques of mediation and conflict resolution can aid successful communication. And more intentional, focused communication can open the pathway of grace toward transforming partnership into communion. It is our experience that all aspects of One–Two–ONE coexist in a well-balanced human being and in relationship. It may not be practical to be in a state of communion all the time, and there are moments when a dominator emerges, such as to pull back a child who has stepped into oncoming traffic, with commanding and overpowering strength.

The unifying principle through it all is the awareness of one's attention, and being appropriate to the situation at hand.

In communion, the partners engage, merge as ONE, and become intertwined with heaven above and earth below.

exercise

Communion 1

Where in your personal life have you had a moment of communion? It may have been on a mountaintop (physical or metaphorical), or in some other spiritual context. Share with each other what that experience felt like.

Now speak about what communion between the two of you might look like. Have you had moments that you can share? If they occurred sexually, then describe what they felt like. Begin to imagine what communion might look like if you simply sat together. Gaze at each other. Simply breathe together, and allow your boundaries to dissolve. If you feel sexual energy rise, perhaps choose to breathe with it and continue to gaze at each other.

In an earlier exercise, you discovered how the dominator comes into relationships with others. Now examine how the dominator can come into your relationship. Is there any way you can imagine transforming that specific situation into one of communion? (You might find some large tight knots, so begin this inquiry with small things.)

Some hazards exist in communion, too. People can appear to become stuck there. They waft through life as if on a cloud, smiling sweetly. Whenever a difficulty arises, they sing out, "All is One," and drift past. Or they succumb to mass movements, are swept up in a crowd, and sometimes lose themselves in mob hysteria.

Why not let these people be if they're happy? Because life is a riddle that requires all three modes of activity: the individual One, the partner Two, and the communing ONE. Spiritual development is not meant to hike you up into the heights and leave you there, dizzily spinning, crippled at the other levels. You learn to come and go in any of these levels at will. That flexibility makes for a very healthy individual, a very healthy relationship, and a very healthy community. The ditzy space cadet finds his or her way into the mundane, to cycle back again when appropriate.

Concentric Circles and One–Two–ONE

You may have noticed that two of the models we work with interconnect nicely. The story level of the Concentric Circles is all about my life, my experiences, and often my sense of victimization by others. The psychological level permits me to witness my own creations and fantasies. I have a strong enough "I" to

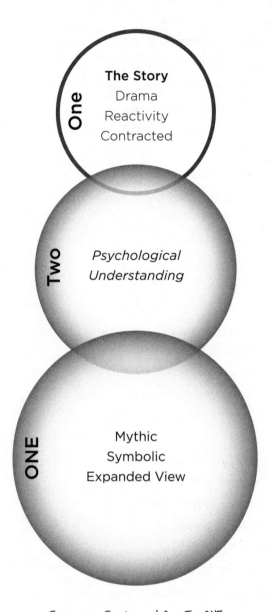

The Story
Drama
Reactivity
Contracted

One

Psychological
Understanding

Two

Mythic
Symbolic
Expanded View

ONE

Concentric Circles and One-Two-ONE

see another's point of view. I am ready for relationship (Two). The mythic and symbolic level of the Concentric Circles begins to move into the same territory as ONE, though ONE also goes beyond to the outermost circle, to all-pervading and boundless Awareness. (You can integrate this further with Mount Maslow, as described in the introduction.)

Again, we must develop familiarity with all the levels, and cultivate our ability to move freely from one zone to another at will.

Tools for Conscious Partnership

To develop a conscious relationship, you have to learn some skills and build some capacities with each other, the primary skill being communication. "Communion" has such a lovely aura of intimacy with all of creation; "communication" is related to that. You may have heard the metaphor that men are from Mars and women are from Venus. The idea goes like this: men are constitutionally aggressive, action-oriented, gruff, warlike, curt, mechanical, practical, and uncommunicative; women are constitutionally pacific, soft, talkative, concerned about appearance, relational, loving, and overly communicative. This view contains some truth, but it does not necessarily determine destiny. Noncommunication and miscommunication are familiar to all men and women, but we don't have to accept the stereotypes. A wise couple understands tendencies and compensates for them by making conscious choices, and by having a reliable tool kit available for times when the right tool will make light work. (We love that pun.)

You may already have learned techniques that assist your communication. If so, write them down in your journal and agree to use them. The important point here is to agree on using a tool when it is necessary, and to practice during times when conflict is not present so that when conflict visits, you have established a pattern. We use these tools regularly and with heartfelt gratitude. Don't try to learn a fix-it tool when tensions are high. It often backfires.

When a problem arises, many people try to avoid it by hoping that time will pass and the problem will simply go away. The tools offered here address the problem directly, seeing the problem as an opportunity to deepen relationship rather than something to be ignored and denied.

Practice creates the "field"—the grid or energy pattern that supports growth and wisdom—that we described in the section on defining the sacred in chapter 5. Rupert Sheldrake has called it a "morphogenetic field," meaning a form-generating field. This energy field contains our mastery and connects us to Oneness. These ways of engaging the field can help reinforce your mastery as a couple.

Building Capacities

To achieve the ability to move freely from One to Two to ONE and back again, as the situation demands and you choose, you must develop capacities in yourself as an individual (One) and in your relationship (Two). Then you will find that experiences of ONE come by grace. Developed capacities means you are less likely to get knocked over by the lightning bolts of relationship—the sudden shocks, positive or crushing, of sexuality or revelation that arise when you get to know your partner and yourself better. You become a bigger capacitor, and can hold a bigger charge of energy. You can tolerate a powerful experience of ONE without blanking out or becoming exhausted. Then lightning becomes lightening.

You build capacity in yourself through attention to the different domains of your being—physical, emotional, mental, sexual, and spiritual. We will ask you about these areas in the questions at the beginning of Part Two, first for building relationship and then for if you are ready to develop further. In between, we give some suggestions for regular practices to improve your capacities in these areas ("Exercises to Ready Yourself for Sacred Relationship," pp. 137–138). Here we give you some tools to make your exploration more effective.

The tools below work at all levels of your being. You may be sitting and chatting, and think that the physical is not involved. In that case, involve the physical! Hold hands, rub your Beloved's feet. Breathe! You exchange breath when you sit together. Make that exchange of breath the physical level of your joy together. Engage your creativity in your intention to increase your capacity as a human being.

Love Languages

In 1995, Gary Chapman wrote *The Five Love Languages,* in which he proposed that there are five very different ways to give and receive Love. Though criticized for being overly simplified, this was a great contribution to human relationships. We will give the five modes that Chapman identified, explain them a little, then conclude with how this is useful to a conscious wedding.

1. **Gifts:** physical items such as flowers or chocolate or the paper on which words (see number 3) are written. Whole industries have grown up around supplying this mode of communication and, we would say, creating the appearance of need. However, receiving or giving things can carry great significance.

2. **Quality time:** making yourself available to be with your partner, the warmth and activity of your simple presence.

3. **Words of affirmation:** general and specific praise, meaning that you see what your partner has said or done, and affirm it. This includes positive affirmation that your partner exists: "I'm so happy that you were born."

4. **Acts of service:** doing things to help your partner, such as washing dishes, picking up a parcel, stacking something that fell down. This means you see what your partner is doing and where the needs are, and you respond with help.

5. **Physical touch:** meaning stroking, caressing, hugging, patting, and otherwise canoodling. Despite the training we receive not to touch each other, science demonstrates clearly that touching is welcomed and very important to health.

The Five Love Languages suggests that you and your partner have favorite modes of communication of Love. We agree. The book, and some who read it, exaggerate favorite modes: "I can only receive Love from you if you use my language!" We don't agree with this. For most people, all of these modes work to some degree. If you have a preferred mode, then you will have to make that clear to your partner. Otherwise, you have to learn all of them.

Special Time

Set aside a time and a place that is just for the two of you. Turn off all electronic devices that might ring or buzz or otherwise disturb you. You don't need to be in a pristine forest; in fact, you need to be able to call for Special Time and make it happen immediately anywhere. One counselor we know told us, "You ought to be able to do the hardest work of relationship in a parking lot!" Even in the parking lot, you can remember how the pristine forest calms you and helps you open up with your partner. You can light a candle. You can turn chairs to face each other, rather than simply flopping onto a nearby couch. You can draw a circle in the sand, or build a circle out of stones, either real or imaginary. Circles symbolize sacred time; they have an inside and an outside. Inside the circle, an opportunity is created to build a magical intention. An extra two minutes to create a sacred circle can make the difference between a tension-filled conversation and one in which each of you can deeply listen to and be heard by the other. If you're in tension, and one of you begins to build a circle, let that intention express itself—because you know this activity is in service of your relationship.

You can agree on the length of this Special Time: fifteen minutes? Half an hour? More? We have found that this is helpful because one person may become restless but wish not to hurt the other's feelings. Just agree on the form, and then you can revel within it. Stay true to your time commitments. If you feel that the time you agreed on isn't enough, then say, "I'd like to stay another ten minutes—would that be all right with you?" If it's not all right with the other, then honor your initial agreement without resentment, and look forward to the next opportunity to create Special Time together.

Special Time sets up the space and allows you to shift your awareness deliberately. It warms you up for another practice we'll introduce shortly, called Heart Talk.

Special Time

Don't make this complicated. This is very simple—and consequently often over-looked in relationship.

Sit with each other quietly. Turn off all distractions, including the lists that you run in your head. This is a very big and important step in service of relation-ship. Simply sit together, quietly. What feelings and thoughts naturally arise between you?

Hold hands. Just that: hold hands. Learn the landscape of your partner's hands. This isn't palmistry, rather palm admiration, and admiration of all the other parts, too. Simply hold hands.

Accept whatever occurs. Lay aside goals for what you're supposed to accomplish or decide. Special Time feels initially like time-out, until you feel how it is, for the relationship, time-in.

You can choose to use Special Time with each other informally, simply relaxing with each other and discussing things that are important. Or you can take a further step and set up a Heart Talk.

Heart Talk

We suggest you find a special item to use as a talking piece for a Heart Talk (a process that we learned from Jack Canfield). It can be anything meaningful to you. People have used a stuffed animal, a seashell, a crystal, even a stick picked up off the ground. There are some simple rules, and they must be agreed to and followed. This is important, because you need to know you can trust each other to hold a sacred space together, even if something very difficult is being spoken about. The key is listening. Listen to each other with every part of your being. Don't just use your ears: listen with your heart; listen with your elbows! Open up and hear each other. Whoever holds the talking piece can talk—or remain silent—while the other listens.

The guidelines are simple, but as with any successful process, you must both agree to follow them:

1. Whoever has the talking piece speaks. The other one does not speak.

2. The person listening is attentive and interested, not planning what to say next. *Do not interrupt,* not even for clarification, as these apparently innocent interruptions often have emotional tone attached. Not interrupting must be honored or the field of trust won't be created. If an interruption does occur (some habits are challenged by change!), simply reaffirm the agreements and start again. As you listen, you may feel tempted to prepare a rebuttal. However, let your prepared comments drift away. You don't have to respond to every single thing that is said. Let yourself listen, rather than prepare, and what comes out of you when it's your turn will be more genuine.

3. Once you're finished speaking, *lay the talking piece down.* Don't hand it to the other person. This allows for silence and relaxation in the communication. The other person will pick it up when he or she is ready to respond. Silence and deep breathing are part of this process, and something we don't often experience in normal conversation.

4. Be as concise as possible in speaking, and don't go on too long or change subjects too quickly. Express one thought. Allow it to sink in. Then lay the talking piece down to give your partner the opportunity to respond. More important than you emptying every nook and cranny in your heart is that you are heard in what you do say. So don't say too much!

5. Don't use this as an opportunity to "dump" energetically or verbally. As much as possible, speak in "I" statements, rather than blaming or accusatory statements. Say, "I feel hurt by the way the communication happened." This opens up things more than saying, "You hurt me in the way you communicated." Speak from your own feelings and experience. If you're the one who feels hurt, that's not the other's fault. These are your feelings, right?

6. Be respectful of each other, no matter how difficult the area of communication might be. Remember, this is your Beloved!

7. As much as possible, take one hundred percent responsibility for creating your experience, reaction, or response to whatever is said in the Heart Talk. This might be a new concept to some. Watch closely and you'll see how challenging it can be!

8. Let the conclusion of the Heart Talk be decided by both parties. Lay down the talking piece and allow the communication to return to easy conversation. Try not to end prematurely, as often breakthroughs happen as a result of perseverance. And don't go on and on until you've touched every possible issue. You have to find the rhythm that is enough. We recommend not exceeding an hour because your heart can't metabolize too much material. Twenty minutes is a good amount of time for a Heart Talk, though that can vary quite a bit, shorter or longer.

In one variation we limit the length of speaking time to thirty seconds (you can limit it even more). Then lay the talking piece down. The other person has thirty seconds, back and forth like that. You begin to find that the flow starts to move between you.

exercise

Heart Talk

Find a talking piece and try this mode of exchange. Simply sit with each other quietly.

Start with something simple: what you thought of a recent shared meal, or something you want to say about your memories of summertime in childhood. Practice with simple topics at first to get the rhythm. Speak a little, set the talking piece down, then listen.

If you are in a calm place together, you can use this tool to bring up some of the troubled places in the relationship. Name a subject that you feel you can both speak about using this tool. Listen to each other's perspectives about a repeating pattern in your relationship. Decide together what the topic will be, and then observe the rules.

Once you have practiced with this process enough, you will have built the trust necessary to use it when situations are hot, reactive, or turbulent. Honor the rules for this tool so you can use it in relationship emergencies!

Highlights—Lowlights

Use this technique every time you are asked for an evaluation from your peers, including from your partner. Too often the pattern looks like this:

> You write or perform or say something, and ask, "Could I get some feedback on what I just did?" Your friend responds, "You need to do this part differently, and that part was really shaky," and the list goes on and on. At the end, deflated by all the critiques, you agree, "Yeah, well, it really was pretty bad all around."
>
> Then you are surprised to hear from your friend, "No, I really liked it."
>
> "What?! You tore it apart!"
>
> "No, I really liked it. Everything I said was fine-tuning. It's a great piece."

When you have something to say to your partner, start with the positive. Even when you have something difficult to share, start with what's working—the highlights. Only in rare emergencies do you need to jump to what isn't working, as in watching your partner begin to pour something into your tea: "Stop! That's salt, not sugar." Maybe there are other times to start with lowlights, though they are very few.

When you begin with highlights, you affirm what's working. Then your critiques can be heard much better. If you begin with and concentrate on what's wrong, the wrongness becomes infectious. The one small smudge in an otherwise clean room takes all of your attention. Start with highlights!

Some have complained to us, "It's more efficient to go right to the problem and fix it. She already knows that I love her." Relationship needs to have the highlights restated again and again. If it's Love, then offer it again and again.

Onto that strong foundation a critique can be given, and the hearer will more likely respond. It's more efficient *not* to go right to the problem.

Even in the exercises of Heart Talk and Nonviolent Communication (on pages 105–107), this emphasis on highlights is very helpful.

A Helpful Hint on Equanimity

Everyone can benefit from a little equanimity, that is, calmness in the face of conflict or drama, accusations, or tragedy. With sufficient equanimity, every situation you look at becomes a fascinating display of the unfolding creation of the world expressing itself to you. A very quick means of accessing equanimity was suggested to David as a young man. An elderly woman advised him how to react when somebody says something outrageous or provoking: Simply nod and say, "That's interesting!" instead of engaging in argument. Listen and ponder, but don't try to educate the speaker, or change the speaker, or vent your irritation. If the behavior is obnoxious, it will pass. Let it go. Simply nod and say, "That's interesting." This was a very helpful piece of advice, which has served David well in many a potential firestorm.

exercise

Equanimity

Try it out. After hearing the daily news or hearing someone rant about having been mistreated by the tax authorities or by an ex-lover, simply nod your head and say, "That's interesting." Listen carefully. Don't numb to the situation. Feel it fully, yet realize that there is a much bigger picture of which this story is a part. Choose to cultivate equanimity. It will be useful in your relationship.

Pure Fun: "Yes, and . . ."

Time for some fun! Our theatrical work together has included not only putting on productions but also using acting exercises to improve communication skills. One of our favorite exercises is "Yes, and . . ." because it gets delicious energy moving and always opens up new possibilities, often unexpected.

exercise

"Yes, and . . ."

Start a fantasy story by speaking a sentence aloud. "We start our vacation in a hot tub." Then your partner takes over to continue to build the fantasy: "Yes, and the hot tub is on the top of Mount Shasta!" Each time you add the next installment, you say, "Yes, and . . ." You affirm what has been said before. You don't say, "No, but . . ." You say, "Yes, and . . ." No matter where the story goes, you say, "Yes, and . . ." as in, "Yes, and a waiter brings us a gallon of rhubarb ice cream"; "Yes, and two elves with little green hats bring the ice cream in little silver bowls with little silver spoons." Take turns adding a sentence or two to the story. You can stand facing each other to do this, so there's room to jump up and down if you get very excited about the creation you're building together.

You'll find yourselves taking astonishing directions. Not only is this fun, but it builds up your fantasy muscle. You can use your greater capacity to devise new possibilities for your relationship.

Create a Relationship Altar

An altar is the place where energy is altered—changed or transformed. It is a sacred space that is created with intention. We recommend a joint altar be created and dedicated to your Sacred Union. Each of you brings to this altar an object that is meaningful to you individually. Take some time with this cocreation. There may be photos of yourselves, or of teachers who have been inspiring to you. There may be the talking piece that you use for your Heart Talks. There may be special gifts from nature that you found either together or alone. Essentially, all the things are there to reflect or invoke sacred memory or qualities that you are choosing to have in your relationship.

A "working" altar provides focus and intention. An altar can share its power if you establish it especially for your ceremony (your wedding or any ceremony of your life) and allow it to work for you before and after the event. Keep it alive, clean, and changing! A dusty altar won't work as well as one that is well tended. Just as the seasons change, so must your altar. This is the home of the third mysterious thing flowing between you: your relationship.

exercise

Relationship Altar

Find a horizontal space, a small table or the top of a dresser, that you declare to be relationship territory. You can begin with one square foot—no one can complain of the altar taking too much space! Put one thing there that has meaning to you. Ask for something from your partner. Share the stories of the items you set upon the altar. Stories will bring the altar more to life and connect meaning to the things you place on it. Then find something that has symbolic meaning for the relationship itself. The next step might be something from the outdoors that indicates the season of the year that you are in. These are beginnings. Don't add anything else for a while; the altar will grow naturally. Tend it at least once a week, renewing water or flowers, and changing the seasonal things if the seasons have changed. If it hasn't been tended for a couple of months, simply clear the space and leave it blank until you have the urge to begin again.

Sacred Geometry

The term "sacred geometry" was coined by Robert Lawlor in the 1970s in his landmark book of that title. It describes the principles of geometry (*geo* from Gaia, the living earth, and *-metry* from system of measure, related to "matter," "mater," and "mother") used in the cathedrals built from the twelfth century onward, and even in some of our present-day architecture. How does this relate to your wedding? In many ways. People like to choose venues for their weddings that have symmetry or that "feel right." People like to stand in circles or triangles or pentagrams. You will notice these things more if you study the principles of sacred geometry a little bit. The drawings in this book, the emphasis on concentric circles, the circle of the ceremony, the circles of the rings: all are complemented by simple understanding of geometry. The "sacred" part means that certain geometries seem to unlock energy that can support your wedding. This is supported by studies of psychology and of energy too.

exercise

Your Sacred Place

You have chosen the site of a relationship altar. Now discover a place that is sacred to your relationship—to you, your partner, and the "third" between you, the relationship itself—a place on Gaia (also the *geo* of "geography"). There are at least a few places on earth where something so supportive and energizing happens to you that you are willing to travel there if the going gets rough between you. Lila and David had three places in mind: one a plane flight away, one an hour's drive, and one very close. We agreed that if we entered a knot that just wouldn't resolve and only got worse, we would travel together—or rendezvous—at one of those places. This is more than a "safe house." It is a last resort. Just having an agreed location, and visiting it occasionally to renew your connection there, has great power to support your relationship through thorns and knots. What are your sacred places?

Shared Affirmation

This process involves crafting strengthening statements about your relationship that you can say together out loud. Why do this together? Because it sets an organizing principle in your energy field. It allows you both to make an intentional choice about what you're all about, whether you're dealing with a specific situation or with a big life situation.

LILA and DAVID   Shared Affirmation

Early in our marriage, we decided to write plays together. You can imagine that such a personal, creative endeavor as writing would bring up uncomfortable issues for a couple! We crafted an intention statement: "We create easily and masterfully together." Before we began a joint writing session, we would empower that intention by speaking it aloud together. When we started to feel any irritation or criticism arise in the creative process, we stopped and repeated the intention statement until the energy shifted. We then were able to speak about the actual issue at hand, rather than being irritable and reactive.

More important than any words on the page was the quality of our experience together. In this way our affirmation allowed us to explore some of the most satisfying and cocreative moments of our relationship, and to create deliberately together. ❁

exercise

Personal Affirmation

If you're not familiar with affirmations, we suggest you practice first with something simple, perhaps, "I am enjoying myself." (We love this one.) Stay in the present tense, as this allows for the present moment of creation, the powerful now, to manifest. Or "I live and love fully in the present." (This has served both of us well over time.) Use one of these, or create a very simple statement.

Keep the feeling of the affirmation dynamic. Speak it with conviction.

Notice the tendency to say it and get it over with. Contrast that to the feeling that you are intentionally creating this statement as you say it. Savor the affirmation as one of your greatest allies.

Repeat it a few times until you feel that creative energy has shifted toward the affirmation.

We strongly recommend that you come up with two or three intentional affirmations for yourself. Then craft two or three shared affirmations that you can say together when you need that extra oomph to get through a challenging moment. These can lift you up and out of your repeating story, and give you the choice to organize around a creative principle rather than around a destructive habit.

It's worth emphasizing again this element of choice. We are all creators, moment to moment, of the experience we're having. We can't always change the circumstances that surround or confront us, but we can always make a choice about how we respond to those circumstances. If asked, "What is the most important thing you've learned in your relationship," our answer would be that we both realize that we consciously, actively, intentionally choose each other as mate and partner. Sacred Union requires creative intention and a willingness to notice when "not-choosing" is going on, and to change it! Working with shared affirmations and intentions is a very strong way to create that change.

"Happily ever after" is a fairy tale we've all grown up with, and it seems to imply that once you get the girl or the guy, the rest just falls into place. Well, no, it doesn't. You need to create the life that follows out of waking decisions and deliberate intention. That includes creating happiness!

Don't slap a happy face on top of something that really needs to be worked through. That's not the point here. There may be affirmations that are challenging to feel as true because there are thorns or knots in the way (in which case, go back to chapter 4). We are suggesting that you can navigate through many kinds of troubled waters with this technique, and keep the Love flowing in the process of deep transformation by stating your intention clearly.

Invest energy in creating and affirming the relationship you desire, and your effort will return bounties to you. Nurture the capacity of words to transmit power. As Rumi writes, "Tender words we spoke to one another are sealed in the secret vaults of heaven. One day like rain, they will fall to earth and grow green all over the world." Those tender words can find their way into your shared affirmations.

Shared Affirmation

Think of one simple situation where you know you need some assistance in relating better. It might be around a project you work on together, or a habit pattern you both have developed that you wish to shift. Define the situation without judging it; just identify it: "When___(x)___ happens, I tend to become____(z)____." Perhaps (z) is "irritable" or "ditzy." You might be able to change the "I" to "we," if you both agree on that.

Create together a Shared Affirmation that will work for you when (x) happens next. Some version of "We create easily and masterfully together" is likely to work! (Example concerning the (x) of jar lids askew and doors left open: "We open to life's surprises." Or, more comprehensively, "We open to life, setting boundaries when necessary.")

Imagine in your own silent space that you have just recreated the triggering situation. Now state your Shared Affirmation until you can feel that you are choosing to create that affirmation instead of choosing to react to the trigger. Notice how you feel. Share your experience with your partner. Agree to remind each other gently of this the next time you find yourselves creating the familiar pattern.

Nonviolent Communication (NVC)

Marshall Rosenberg, whose books and talks we recommend, has presented some simple and compelling steps that promote healthy and positive communication. Here are the four main steps in the process, plus one that we have added:

1. Share your **observations** of a bothersome situation without evaluating or judging the facts in any way. "You left the room while I was speaking" is an observation. The following communication about the same situation has evaluation and judgment in it: "When I was halfway through telling you something really important, you stood up angrily and stomped out of the room just to hurt me." The implication is that your partner knew that you hadn't finished speaking, knew that your communication was

important, became angry, and wished to hurt you, all of which may or may not be true. All you know for sure is that you were speaking and your partner left the room. That's your observation. Simple works best, one step at a time.

2. State your **feelings** about the observation: "I felt my old issues with abandonment were triggered when you left; I was afraid and hurt." One might be tempted to say, "You made me feel abandoned," but this implies that your partner has power over your feelings. Your partner is potent, but you are not your partner's puppet. Your feelings are yours: "I felt abandoned." The feelings are important, and they are yours. As another example, "You made me feel humiliated" is different from saying, "I experienced humiliation." The first statement presses your partner into a defensive posture; the second describes your own feeling dynamics. This is an opportunity to be aware that "no one is doing it to you." Rather, you created an experience that you labeled "humiliation." Stay with "I" statements; they will work much more effectively.

3. Express your **needs** or values that have become more clear after observations and feelings have been named. For example, "I have a need for intimate time together that we create consciously." This is easier to identify with than "I need you to hear me," which doesn't describe the behavior that you need from your partner. The more specific you can be, the better. "I need to feel that we connect each morning before starting the day." "I need to be held." "I need to feel the warmth of your touch." These are needs that your partner can comprehend. It's important not to stop here. At this stage, your needs are too vague for your partner.

4. Make specific **requests** (different from demands!) of your partner. "I ask that you commit to meeting together at our relationship altar once a week for fifteen minutes" is specific and comprehensible. It is different from "We have to create some time together or we'll never make it!" A request defines a specific behavior that you're looking for, and should

not include hidden angers or resentments. Define what you'd like, the simpler and more specific the better, and ask for agreement. If you don't get agreement, you may have to discuss why, and negotiate for what your partner can agree to. "I request that we look into each other's eyes and smile when we both wake up in the morning." Something simple and measurable. You both know when it's happened.

5. We've added a fifth step to the model: **agreement** to the request. If you don't agree on the request, then you have to go back to the fourth step and craft a better request. We have heard a request, "Love me more!", which led to complete confusion. When that was changed to "Hold my hand at the beginning and the end of the day, just after waking and just before going to sleep," there was agreement. By our next appointment, this simple activity had turned exasperation into a deeper intimacy.

The process can feel clunky the first few times you work with it, but it will reward you with great insights into the ways that you have sabotaged your own communication. Soon you will be able to communicate more smoothly with each other.

Can you see that this is a way of working with the Concentric Circles? Non-violent communication provides a system whereby you can extract yourself from the story in the center and move into the next circle, the psychological and analytical.

Watch out for unreasonable requests . . . for example, "I request that you sit with me every day at nine o'clock for twenty minutes." A partner desperate to make peace might assent to that. However, assent would be a mistake, because no one can promise to sustain a particular practice indefinitely and regardless of circumstance. You can assent to once a week for a month, but not beyond. If things go well, the behavior will likely maintain or increase naturally. Likewise, "I request more love" actually states a need, not a specific request that can be clearly and definitely met.

exercise

Nonviolent Communication

Go through each of the above steps carefully, one at a time. Share your **observations** about a situation that has bothered you, and share the facts of the situation. Identify your **feelings** about it. Express your **needs** about how you would like to feel. Make a very specific **request** of your partner about how you would like him or her to behave in the future. Receive the **agreement** to the request, or fashion another request. Go through all the steps. Skipping steps leads to breakdown in communication and hurt feelings that get worse. Practice this now, when you're not in conflict, to get the steps straight. Then you have a tool ready for when you need it.

Mirroring

These exercises have their origins in the theater/dance world. We start with a simple and familiar game, and extend it in ways that can lead to moments of communion. This is one of those exercises that seems really basic; some have said, "Oh, this is so third grade." When you do it as an adult, you realize just how you've changed since third grade.

exercise

Mirror 1

STEP 1: Face your partner, standing several feet apart. Agree that you won't speak until the end of the exercise. Decide who will start as leader. The leader begins to move, ever so slowly, starting with arm and hand movements. The other matches the gesture of the hands, the tilt of the body, the expression of the face. You can coordinate right side with right side, though we prefer to work as actual mirrors, so that when the leader moves a body part on the left, the follower moves the same part on the right. Keep your eyes on each other's eyes, and use your peripheral vision to match your movements to your partner's.

After thirty seconds, change roles. The follower becomes the leader. Explore your range of motion, how far you can go. Feel the energy moving between you as you slowly reflect each other with your movement.

After thirty seconds, the original leader leads again, this time for ten seconds. After ten seconds, switch roles. After that ten seconds, permit movements to arise naturally, slowly, confidently. Follow the movement that you see. The movement itself becomes the leader. Sometimes one leads and the other follows. Sometimes neither of you feels that you are leading, but movement is happening, and you are listening to your partner through movement.

When you feel synchronized, move farther apart, continuing to match movements. If you lose the connection, slow down and simplify. Notice how far apart you can get and still stay connected. Step back further, and continue to mirror across a greater distance. Feel what it's like to be in a connected field of energy, with lots of space between you.

Pause here and talk with each other about what you noticed and how it felt to lead and to mirror.

STEP 2: Expansion. At some point try this across some distance—at either end of a large space, with no distractions, holding energy between you.

Now try it in a crowded room or train station or sports event or, with small gestures, in a long meeting or lecture that you're attending together. You can imagine how much more interesting meetings can be with this technique.

Discuss the differences you experienced.

exercise

Mirror 2

Stand a few feet apart, and begin to move together. This time, pause in a posture that feels "sacred" to you—uplifting, energized, special in some way. Say, "Pause," when you find a posture you like, and you and your partner both stay there for a moment. Then let it go and move slowly again, until you or your partner find the next "sacred" moment. Move slowly, and find three or more positions that create a mutual feeling of uplift.

Now find a "sacred" position that you mirror to each other, and add in one of your shared affirmations while you're in the posture together. Speak aloud the statement together. Repeat it two or three times, until you can actually feel an energy shift by creating this body–speech connection. Hint: We're preparing you for how you might speak your vows with deeper meaning. This is a training ground where no one else is watching.

exercise

Mirror 3

Sit on either side of a room. Become fully aware of each other and, while still sitting casually, attempt to mirror each other in a subtle way. You may not be able to fully embody the same posture, but perhaps you can create a simple hand gesture together in the same way. Simply feel what happens when you do this. Keep eye contact. Now imagine that you're going to move your hand together in an agreed-upon gesture, but don't actually move physically. One of you will say, "Now," and as you allow your imagination or your energy body to make the gesture, notice if you feel anything in the air between you.

You can practice this together in your home, then try it when you're somewhere in public, at a meeting or situation where you are on opposite sides of a room full of people. You may notice that making this kind of connection across a crowded room creates a feeling of electric energy in your whole body.

Exchanging Stones

Before you exchange rings, you might consider another befriending of earth (chapter 5) in service of your relationship. Exchange stones—stones that you've labeled with qualities that you would like to develop in yourself and in your relationship. If you begin looking for stones, they will poke up out of the most interesting places. Find one or a few that you can keep with you, to hold in your hands, to have in your pocket. Write qualities on them that you have or to which you aspire. After you've held them for a couple of months, give one stone to your partner. Tell stories about the quality written on that stone and held within it, ways you feel you are developing in that area, situations where you feel you could have used that quality more. Speak soul to soul. In holding the stone you have given, your partner also holds an important part of your aspirations and your growing edge. This exchange of something physical helps to clarify and acknowledge the quality you see in yourself and in your partner.

Continue with the other stones, back and forth, weaving together your "third self," the relationship.

story

A Stone Exchange

Lana and Derrick wished to strengthen their relationship, to give it solidity, mass, and weight. So they found stones in a river, smooth on one side. Onto these stones they painted the virtues that meant the most to them—not only the words "Honesty," "Beauty," and "Love," but also little swirls and colors that went with each virtue. Each held the stones that he or she had painted for two months, referring to them daily, a simple affirmation of the importance of these virtues. This gave the words and the stones a kind of life. Then they exchanged the stones. Derrick held the stones and virtues that Lana had painted. Lana held the stones and virtues that Derrick had painted. They held the stones of their Beloved for three months. It didn't end with the stones put away in a dresser drawer. After three months, they put the stones on their relationship altar, one stone at a time, changing them every month from that point onward.

exercise

Exchanging Stones

Take the lead from Lana and Derrick, and invoke the principles important to you in the same way that they did.

Pick stones, just a few each, from a place that has meaning for the two of you. Paint labels on them with qualities that you would like to develop in yourself, such as "Equanimity" and "Beauty," and flares of color too. Hold them in your hands and take them with you through your days, occasionally pulling them out to contemplate the qualities written in stone. After a time, give one stone to your partner. Tell a story or stories about the quality that you've written on that stone and that the stone itself now holds. Speak soul to soul.

Ceremony

One of the best tools for relationship is ceremony. Weddings are not the only ceremonies in relationship. Every tool and exercise that we've presented can be approached as a ceremony—just a simple one, nothing complicated. The talking piece from Heart Talk is a simple ceremonial prop. The items on your relationship altar, including perhaps your stones labeled with qualities that you admire, are props. The ceremony directs you in your use of the props to achieve the purpose of directing your mind, your heart, and your body toward one focus—in this case, your relationship.

A ceremony has five stages: purification, invocation, reception/amplification, distribution, and closing. These same steps are used in settings ranging from religious rituals to meetings of a corporate board of directors. If your partner hesitates to become involved in ceremony, simplify it further, or make it more like a meeting of the astronomy club, which uses the same steps, though they are often implied rather than emphasized.

Purification means cleaning yourself before focused time. This may mean a shower and a change of clothes, or just washing your hands. It also means turning off electronic devices and setting up an uncluttered place to sit with each other. Here you separate from distractions of the everyday world.

Invocation means calling on those virtues, powers, angels, or names that assist you in your own development (the One), in your partnership (the Two), and in your communion (the ONE). Invocation can be calm or passionate. It might involve lighting a candle. It ought to involve some action by both of you. You can set the tone by reading a Love poem to each other. Or you can lift up with your affirmations to the realms of those powers that sustain you.

Reception/Amplification requires openness to whatever insight, fresh feeling, or urge to action may come through to you at that time. When you've created the space during purification, and focused your attention during invocation, something will come through after that. Discipline yourself to receive the gift that is given. Once you feel that gift, choose to make it bigger in order to express it more fully.

Distribution means that you extend the bounty of insights and good feelings into the world, to others who have need of this energizing. You can name people or places or situations that you know need attention. When you distribute, you acknowledge that your relationship functions as a portal through which life energy can flow. You thus become messengers and bestowers of blessings. From this deed, energy continues to flow into you and through you.

Closing means that you acknowledge those who have come to the ceremony, the people in the room, the elements, the directions, any principles or divine beings that you called to attend. Here you move from the realm of the mythic back to the mundane.

You can use these stages of ceremony when using any of the tools in this book.

Advanced Relationship Skills

From these last chapters, you have some very powerful tools in your tool belt, tools powerful enough to confront very serious threats to One, Two, and ONE. These threats come in the form of humiliation, cynicism, contempt, profound distrust, betrayal, fear of betrayal, suspicion, anxiety, or crippling fear. All of those are life-denying, like an icy cold wind that comes seemingly from nowhere and freezes the flowers and buds of the optimistic fruit tree of your growing relationship.

We have found that it's delicate to point out destructive energy patterns to a couple. Sometimes they welcome the observation, and sometimes they band together and attack the observer. That means that there is a contracting knot holding a great deal of energy that nourishes a fundamental mythic story through which each feels served in some way. Some people feel comfortable in a dominator–victim dynamic because it feels familiar. The freedom of becoming a separate and powerful One can seem threatening to either dominator or victim. These tools can help you unravel such life-denying dynamics, and lift toward the Two and the ONE.

For example, the words "I can't trust you," as in, "I can't trust you to take care of the baby," should raise a red flag. Trust is a very deep issue, forged initially in the first years of infancy. In such a case, we suggest that you try NVC with a very simple request, for example, "I request that you hold my hand for five seconds right now." This may sound insultingly simple, but it actually works. If trust has been breached, then you start extremely small, making and meeting very simple requests, to begin building trust again.

In just this way, every one of the tools of this chapter can be used for every situation.

Sexuality, Sensuality, Intimacy, and Love (with a Note on Children)

chapter 8

There are many approaches to exploring sexuality, sensuality, intimacy, and Love. How can they best serve your creation of Sacred Union? Your journey into this realm requires at the beginning that you and your partner cocreate an intention to discover the treasures and pitfalls together. You travel into this magical fantastical realm together, and hold hands through the phantasmagoria of it all.

First lesson: There are three kinds of experience around the core of Love.

We envision Love at the core of an exploration of relationships. We distinguish between sensuality, intimacy, and sexuality as three ways to support the expression and sharing of Love. Knowing which aspect or combination is appropriate at which time helps to create a loving relationship. You may have heard of "slow food." Sensuality and intimacy are "slow Love": spacious, caring, long cooking time . . . for a better result.

Sensuality—the excitement and refinement of your senses—can occur with a brush of your hand against your partner's hand, a sensitive massage using fine oils, a choice of an aroma for the air around you, candlelight, or good music. Makers of fine perfumes note that you can't smell an essence unless you rub a drop into your skin—perfumes by their nature are meant to interact with the warmth of the body before they reveal their secrets to your senses. Add a piece of silk to drape over the body

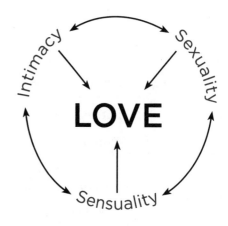

The Three Entryways Into Love

and a peacock feather, and there are possibilities for sensual delight to occupy and educate a couple for a long time! You can choose mood music or wild dance music. You can explore the taste of complicated new flavors. Sharing the sensual experiences of heightened senses becomes a form of Love between you.

Does sensuality need to lead to actual sexual engagement? Not necessarily. In fact, there are good reasons to enjoy simply sensual encounters: for healing, for building trust, and for pure pleasure. Sometimes couples avoid sensual connection because they assume, along with the mainstream of our society, that all sensuality leads to sexuality. On the contrary, it is very important to experience sensuality on its own.

Intimacy does not require physical touch though it is much more profound with touch—simple touch, warm, confident, giving, slow touch. Sitting together and opening your hearts to each other can provide you with a profoundly intimate experience. Sharing some of the deeper, soulful aspects of your past, of your dreams, of your vision for relationship . . . all this can lead to tender intimacy. Reaching across a heart space and gently touching your lover's face can be one of the most intimate expressions of Love. Women often find intimacy easier to access then men. Women friends easily share intimacy among themselves as deep emotional transparency or sincere requests for girl-friend insights. Men may find this more challenging, though we've observed that more and more men are trusting their friendships and building intimacy with one another. Again, intimacy does not necessarily lead to sexuality. It needs to be experienced on its own.

exercise

Intimacy and Sensuality

Write in your journal in response to these questions:

"What is sensuality to you? Describe a time when your senses opened to their most delicate and adventurous. When has sensuality been heightened when you're with your partner?"

"What is intimacy to you? When do you feel the closest and warmest to yourself and your partner?"

Take some risks here, and let creativity flow! Is there some aspect of exploring these territories that you'd like to share with your Beloved?

When you have five good ideas, share some of them in a Heart Talk. Give details, and be specific! At the end of sharing, make a date to explore the ideas you came up with. It's a good idea for one of you to be "in charge" of the exchange, while the other joins in the idea or receives. Then shift roles.

Snuggling, canoodling, and petting can be expressions of the warmth of intimacy, the sensory enhancement of sensuality, and the foreplay of sexuality.

You can experience **sexuality** on its own, without intimacy and sensuality, as a wham-bam-thank-you-ma'am affair. That's possible, even sought out by some. It isn't stable. You need the other two legs of this three-legged stool. Can you engage both intimacy and sensuality to assist your sexuality? The combination of all three elements will lead to the most delightful and meaningful sexual communion, one that has Love at its center. Because sexuality is so hardwired in the brain, it takes commitment to understand the entire picture. It's worth the work to attain deep emotional trust that can transform every person's Love life.

Sexuality includes orgasm, ejaculation, pregnancy, tantric practice. You have to ask yourself, "Where does my behavior lead? Where is it going?" If the only thought in your head concerns the next orgasm—"Let's do it again!"—that is, the repetition of a good time, then nothing develops in you. You just repeat the rise and fall and rise and fall of sexual arousal and completion. If sex takes you to the inner sanctum of Love, then your relationship develops. For that, you will need the allies of sensuality and intimacy.

The spiritual teacher Baba Ram Dass once sat on the ground next to a monk from the all-male monastery on Mount Athos. They looked out over the sea until the monk broke the silence, saying, "The body is bad." Too many people agree with this view: that the whole body, along with sensuality, intimacy, and sex, the three main routes to Love, is bad. You can find such an attitude in every culture and every religion, some fundamentalists holding to an extremely negative prejudice. Those who don't reject sexuality, sensuality, and intimacy nonetheless often feel the subtle influences of Puritanism, obsessive modesty, and shame about the body that shape our cultural institutions.

In our experience, and in our philosophy, the human body has been imagined, energized, and blessed by divine beings. Science has not been able to explain the miracle of life or do justice to the majesty of the body's design. It can study the relation of neurochemicals such as oxytocin and dopamine to feelings of bonding and intimacy, but these chemicals are indicators of experience, not the experience itself. The daily gift of our marvelous physical body radiates beauty in its whole and its every part. The Greeks understood this, and before them the ancient Indian civilization. Statues from both of these cultures portray the body in its naked glory.

Shame about the body insults its makers. Be amazed at your own body, and that of your partner! On the other hand, promiscuity wastes vital life energy, and puts too much weight on the side of sexuality and not enough on sensuality and intimacy. We suggest that you carefully examine your beliefs about the human body in general and your own body. If you hold a belief that demeans the body, then study how you came to those conclusions. We feel that the command over the entrance to the temple of the oracle at Delphi still applies: "O human being, know thyself!" Your method for this knowing comes from observation of your own being and body more than from hearing the ideas of others.

Let's consider a few facts to whet your appetite for pursuing a deeper study of sex together. For instance, many people consider that orgasm and ejaculation are the same. However, each can exist without the other, and it is helpful to look at them separately. Bodybuilders and extreme athletes can have an ejaculation not related to sexual stimulation. Men can learn to have orgasm without ejaculation. Women can experience ejaculation as well as orgasm, and these can occur separately from each other. Men and women can learn to contain their orgasm and/or ejaculation energy, building waves of ecstasy. Drugs are available that manipulate levels of oxytocin and vasopressin, increase blood pressure in the penis, and perform many other tricks. We invite you to explore

Lovemaking without drugs, also without ejaculation, and finally without orgasm (in intimate sensual encounter). Become an expert in the use of your own instrument, your body. When you learn the many possibilities available to you, you then can have the pleasure of choosing which path you take to the palace of Love.

Begin with your body as it is now. Learn to love your body and your partner's body. Start there. No matter what age you and your partner are, you can achieve wisdom, health benefits, and mastery of body and spirit energy when you choose to become aware of the differences between ejaculation, orgasm, and sensual intimate time together.

exercise

Stroking

Stroking and touching tame sexuality acting on its own, to bring in sensuality and intimacy.

STEP 1: Stroke your partner's arm, slowly and thoroughly, over a full minute or for several minutes, not with a primarily sexual goal but simply for the mutual pleasure of touching and being touched. Touching gets oxytocin flowing. Touching has many other very positive psychological effects, such as building trust, ensuring safety, and acceptance. How do you stroke for the sheer sensation of it, and how do you stroke to develop intimacy?

STEP 2: Stroke yourself all over. Become familiar with every part of your body. At the beginning of each day touch every part of your body. It awakens your body into activity and communicates acceptance and trust. If you encounter a no-no part of your body, simply explore that area and wonder why you would feel that way about this most exquisitely designed human body.

STEP 3: Stroke your partner all over. Through sensuality, build intimacy, trust, acceptance, and warmth. These are all pathways to a more balanced sexuality, cooperating to build Love.

Let's go a bit further: have you ever considered that your body can actually experience a heart-based orgasm, in contrast to a genital orgasm? When it happens, the understanding of Lovemaking changes dramatically.

Recall the Concentric Circles. Talk of anatomical parts and how they relate to one another lies in the center, in the story—the facts of the matter in the physical world. Experiment with taking sex through the psychological and mythic levels. At the mythic level the Pillar of Green Jade enters the Secret Garden, the Gallant Knight seeks through the forest for the rejuvenating Grail, the Explorer presses through the jungle to discover a Fountain of Youth. People often giggle when they read these mythic translations of sex, but we find they can be quite wonderful, and pull in a larger experience of your whole being. When someone coos, "Oh, I want you deeply inside," that has to be seen as mostly mythic, also strongly psychological, and, men are surprised to learn, not very practical.

exercise

Sex as Mythic

In sex, feelings are profound, and actions large. Words often fail but can sometimes rise to the occasion through poetry. Enact sex as mythic activity, or as mythic characters. Move more slowly than usual; extend each gesture in time; exaggerate your postures; become a mythic character. Stay with the metaphoric and mythic for more than a minute. That's a first benchmark. Extend that time later as the world of mythos opens to you. You will find that feeling, sensuality, and intimacy increase when you join your companion in the mythic.

The body–brain connection is intimately involved in creating the experience of well-being, intimacy, affection, and health in a primary relationship. Trying some of the different possibilities we've suggested will help you and your partner to cocreate a satisfying, lifelong sexual relationship. And we mean lifelong. Though intimacy becomes more prominent in later years, sensuality and sexuality are not missing among the elderly.

The term "Lovemaking" captivated us early in our relationship. Since we met when we had both entered our forties, we had explored and examined sexuality for many years. We felt a deep sense of responsibility in truly "making Love" in a world that needed more of it. To do so required a new and fresh approach. We both had explored different aspects of yogic and tantric practice regarding sexuality, and we were able to bring that into our relationship. We asked ourselves the question, "Where does this Love energy go?" We observed that it goes somewhere, usually dissipating. We realized that we could direct this delicious Love energy that we had made into specific places.

exercise

The Love Factory

Together, in union, you have a great power to create. Consciously "make"—fabricate, create, manufacture—Love that you can then distribute to the world. Make Love through sensuality, intimacy, sexuality, or any combination of those three. Realize that this sacred act and connection can be of value to the whole of creation. Offer your Love as a prayer to heaven. Offer your Love to the strengthening of your own relationship. Or dedicate the energy to a specific situation of need, such as an individual or community in distress. Simply send the Love that you have made to that person or place. Become more aware of consecrating your Lovemaking, how the experience expands and becomes more sacred. This is another way that communion can be felt, beyond the two of you, toward sharing Love with all life.

To be specific, when you are aroused and becoming more so, speak your intention: "May the Love that we make go to the health of the trees"—or to wherever you would like to gift it.

The increased use of the term "tantra" covers a wide range of ideas and techniques, from clever ways to spice up your sex life, to attention to sensuality and intimacy, to transcendence of the mundane world into bliss. Some techniques can be mastered in a few minutes. Some require daily practice over many months to perfect. Mantak Chia has been writing about Taoist practices for several decades. He offers an excellent perspective on the benefits of gaining awareness and control over ejaculation and orgasm. He promotes a tantric practice to increase health, longevity, and intimacy. His understanding of tantra can be helpful to you, though we suggest you balance it with the views of other authors.

Margot Anand, Brigitte Mars, Marnia Robinson, and others make healthy sexual practices more available to the West, and this material is invaluable for any couple wishing to explore alternatives to goal-oriented, orgasmic sexuality. You can find many books and magazines that demonstrate the mechanics of positions. Look for resources that assist with sensuality and intimacy also. One of our guidelines has been, "Do these techniques increase our sensuality, intimacy, and healthy sexuality, so that we find Love at the center, or do they not?"

Establish as a couple an intention about the sexual realm. When you place intelligent and thoughtful attention on assumptions about sexuality, you can begin moving toward cocreative choice about how that sexuality manifests. Do you choose to have children? (The next section in particular concerns children.) Many people do not acknowledge that sex is connected with children. If a woman does not wish to become pregnant and you have not agreed on a means to prevent this, then you have potential frustrations and misunderstandings. With clear communication and understanding, you can cocreate a satisfying intimate and sensual relationship that will enhance the Love in the core.

With so much information available, this is a time like no other for couples to explore sexuality. Many conditioned assumptions about sex are dissolving, and many paths of exploration are opening. There is no "right way" to express sexuality. You get to create together how you will explore this territory. We highly recommend that you stay *awake* as you explore sexuality. If you don't, you can find an otherwise loving relationship quickly undermined. Because sexuality feels so primal, and has generally been cloaked in so much darkness and judgment (primarily through religious views, fear, and simple ignorance about our bodies), it can feel like a field of land mines to a couple.

In sex, energy can explode. Whether the explosions lead to profound ecstasy or the destruction of a relationship is up to you. We suggest that you explore the many resources available to find support for your agreements in this realm.

Sex expresses the life force of the cosmos. Of all body-based experiences, orgasm comes closest to spiritual ecstasy. You can learn and grow from sex, or misuse it. We have taken up different practices at different stages of our relationship, including periods of celibacy, and do not promote one approach over another. It all depended on our intention at any given stage. A kind of maturity evolves in sexual practice as a living element in relationship. Any time sex starts to feel habitual and disengaging, it's a good time to review. Fidelity is not only some old-fashioned notion. It relates to your depth of commitment. As you create a stronger vessel (the Ship of Relation) of your intimacy, sensuality, and sexuality, you will find the route to communion (the ONE) so valuable that you will not want to poke holes in your vessel. Relationship binds the explosive energy of life force with limitation. When there is no boundary, energy dissipates. When there is the boundary of a container, energy can build. Rhythmic expansion and contraction of that energy creates true freedom.

Our strongest suggestion about sexuality in the context of this book is to encourage you to sit together and speak openly about it. Learn some of the basics of simply breathing together, and apply them regularly and easily. Realize that a successful relationship stays open to change, is willing to explore and be creative, and above all is based on a respectful approach to cocreation and expanded awareness.

exercise

Breathing Together

The next time you are moving toward a sexual encounter and your clothes are shed or partially shed, slow down and sit opposite each other. Hold your hands toward each other, not touching, palms just about an inch apart. Breathe together, matching with each other the rhythm of your in-breath and out-breath. Then switch to complementary breath: one inhales as the other exhales, and vice versa. When you exhale, let the energy of Love build in your heart and travel out from your hand to your partner. When you inhale, let the energy come in from your partner through your hand into your heart, spreading into your whole body. Stay with this breathing pattern until you feel the energy field building within and around you.

At the beginning, do this for only a minute or two. If you can't coordinate your breath, then let one person be the breather, and the other one follows; that is, when the leader inhales, the other exhales. You may have to train each other to observe your breathing patterns. For example, the leader can touch the partner in a certain way to signal that it's time to breathe in, then breathe out. At some point the breath will begin to breathe you, so both are leading and following as one breath. No need to hurry that; for now, find the rhythm of in-breath and out-breath.

Expand the awareness of the energy. When you inhale, let energy come to you from the whole world into the base of your spine, and from the whole heavens through the top of your head, as well as from your partner. These energies travel down your spine to feed your heart, ready for the exhale when you gift this abundance to your partner. When you inhale, you take in from the cosmos, as well as from your partner just opposite you. When you exhale, you give freely and completely to your partner—and to the world as well. This awareness supports the understanding of Lovemaking as the manufacture of a gift to all of life. Your breathing transforms the air that you take in into something wonderful. Many traditions describe holy men and women whose exhalations were sweet and healing.

Children

You have been building from the One of your mature self through the Two of you and your partner to the ONE of communion. What happens when another human being inserts himself or herself into the most intimate center of this crucible? Do you think of One–Three–ONE? David's great-great-grandmother came from a large family that would have been One–Fourteen–ONE.

Children can sometimes feel like distractions to the development of One–Two–ONE. And sometimes children can function as the greatest teachers, offering reminders of the innocence, ingenuity, and passion of life force. Then you feel that their presence is the greatest privilege imaginable and you look forward to every day as the opening of a new adventure.

Nowadays we see so many different constellations in families—the traditional nuclear family of Mommy–Daddy–Johnny–Jane, or single parent living alone with the children, or single parent living with a series of partners or ex-partners, or single people seeking relationship and determined not to have children get in the way.

In this book we emphasize the couple. Even if children are present, the success of the household has to come back to the couple's strength of relationship. We have observed many times how a child may have the power in a family unit, and the parents scurry about trying to meet the child's needs, having little time for each other. This is a time bomb.

Let's look at some basic facts. This will help you refine the One–Two–ONE in relationship. When children are involved, you will need a mentor more than ever.

If you generate children, you are energetically married, even if not legally. The issues about marriage in Part Two are relevant to you, as well as those in Part One. We suggest you consider a ceremony to acknowledge the depth of your relationship, and include a part in that ceremony to welcome and affirm the little ones.

If you enter a relationship in which one partner has children already, you have to find a way to include the little ones in your work with One–Two–ONE. Integrating children into a wedding ceremony becomes a major part of the design of that experience.

The young child has just come from a kind of ONE, communion with the life powers of creation via the mother's womb. The ONE from which babies come does not have consciousness, though it is very alluring. The child in all of us sometimes feels the pull to regress back to that moist warmth. However, the moist warmth is also dark and unconscious. The ONE that we speak about in this book involves expanded consciousness, light-filled awareness of being within the unified field, using the portal of relationship to get there.

The child cannot go with you to the awakened experience of the ONE, not in the same way. The child has not yet accomplished the first step, the creation of the mature individual, the One that is "I." The child may imitate individuality, and act convincingly at times, but then falls back into the egocentric and narcissistic "I," or "little i." "I want! I want! I want!" The "I" is under construction, so to speak, and the parents must lead the little one. Too often we see two-year-olds being asked, "Do you want pasta or spelt bread? Do you want to see Superman or Super-panda?" These are questions you would ask of an individuated adult whose capacities of thinking, feeling, and willing are all functioning. That isn't true of the child. The parents have to act as the thinking and will of the child, otherwise the child will follow only his or her taste buds and eat foods that everyone will regret an hour later when the endocrine and nervous systems react to what's been ingested.

Parents make decisions for small children. Otherwise the whims of children tyrannize the family. When a single mother asks a small child about a new relationship, "I'd like to have Freddie come over tonight for a visit—would that be all right?" the child soon learns that he or she is in control. That's inappropriate for everyone.

Transactional Analysis, a system for understanding human communication systems, names three classes of people: Parents, Adults, and Children. Its simplicity makes it especially useful. Communications between mature individuals are termed Adult–Adult, where One-to-One can lead to the relationship of Two. When there is a child in the system, modern parents often try to create an Adult–Adult dynamic with the child. With a single parent, this often means that the parent is looking for a partner, and trying to get the child to become the other half of the partnership. Confusion joins the household.

Parents sometimes speak as Child–Child. They make baby talk to the baby, and sometimes to the ten-year-old.

Parent–Child is always the better choice between a parent and a child. Parent–Child is not authoritarian. It is very active loving, generating great flows of Love, for a parent realizes that parental Love is necessary nourishment for the child. The Child feeds from the Parent in many ways, and imitates what he or she sees. Receive the imitation respectfully, but don't mistake it for true maturity.

As an Adult, one gives other Adults freedom, and expects respect for one's freedom in return. A Parent gives a Child increasing freedom, starting from zero.

Appropriate

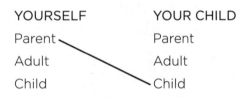

Inappropriate

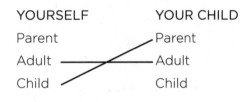

A system for understanding human communication

There are resources for learning how to become a Parent with a Child. *Children: The Challenge* by Rudolf Dreikurs is timelessly useful in this regard, as are Eric Berne's and Thomas Harris's books on Transactional Analysis. The developmental approach of Waldorf Schools makes space for children to be children, rather than prematurely literate pseudo-adults. Much in the Waldorf curriculum can be used at home with children. If the children are happy, then you will have more space to build your relationship with your partner.

Let's say that you've created a healthy relationship with your children. How do they intermix with the One–Two–ONE process? Increasingly they become able to stand on their own feet, to realize the "I" or One of their own individuality. You can then join with them at the next stage, as Two-Plus. They orbit around your partnership, not the same as you, and not ever as substitutes for you. Then you can go to a kind of ONE together, a family communion, a sense of "we" that has a bliss and radiance in it. The foundation for integrating children into your relationship, however, is you and your partner as Adult–Adult.

PART TWO

Creating a Conscious Wedding

The Journey Begins with Questions and Answers

chapter 9

You contemplate crossing a line from healthy relationship to marriage. The portal in between is the wedding. Are you ready? People will ask you that question, and you may feel pressure to answer, "Yes!" However, we have never met anyone or any couple who is ready—as in knowing what awaits them. That's part of the adventure—you are each becoming a better human being, growing each other, and you actually don't know what new experiences might blossom.

You would like the marriage to be a success in its task of growing better human beings. You would like the wedding to be a success as a portal between here and there. You can help by knowing yourself and your partner better.

Who are you? Who is your partner? What are the One, the Two, and the ONE for you? These are big questions that we invite you to explore as you deepen your commitment and begin planning your ceremony together. You see, you can't know about the design of your wedding, nor can you make use of its best opportunities, if you don't know some of the basics about each other. The culture (magazines, movies) glorifies the floating high of a marriage, the rosy glow. When that dissolves, you have to face the challenges of real life in the areas that we will introduce in this chapter. The process of this chapter is an investment in your future.

We suggest that each person in the couple respond to the following questions individually first. Write your answers in your journal. Once you've written your personal response, create a Special Time to sit together and share your responses aloud. We suggest the Heart Talk model for this sharing.

We begin with questions about relationship, how to take your individuality (your Oneness) into partnership (the Two). After that set of questions, we suggest some exercises to help develop your One—your individuality—more strongly and reliably. Then we present questions related to a wedding ceremony and marriage. Begin at the beginning with the process of building trust and communication together. From a strong "I" you can more effectively develop a partnership and a communion. You must cross a threshold to enter the questions about a serious relationship and a conscious wedding.

We have heard the following many times: "I don't know how long I'm going to be with this person. I don't know if I want to get so intimate. I just don't know . . ." We suggest that you use your current relationship as a proving ground for the questions of this chapter. Don't wait for Prince Charming or Princess Alluring before you open up to these issues. Speak to them now. You might find the ice break through this process, awakening intimacy between you in ways that you would never have known without trying.

In answering these questions, if one of you tends to answer with monosyllables—"fine" or "yeah"—then he or she will need some coaxing. We find that is usually (but not always) the man. For such a person, frustration from the partner doesn't help, nor shaming, nor anger; what helps is identification of the undiscovered country, and patient training in how to explore it. The tools in chapters 5 and 7 may help the monosyllabic one open the feeling realm in his or her life.

If one of you writes pages and pages, and the partner hears it and wonders what all these flowery words add up to, then you can ask her or him what the answer might mean in an actual situation.

If you think, "I can't share that!," then ask yourself when the secret will come out, because it most likely will someday. Is that time now?

If this list appears daunting, take on one question at a time. Start at the beginning, and move on to the wedding questions when you've worked through the first section.

These questions might also motivate you to ask married couples how they negotiated these themes and these questions. It seems that people inquire from those with more experience about a new territory in every area other than marriage. Make your marriage an exception, and speak with others.

Questions for a Conscious Partnership

Every relationship has to negotiate agreements about how life works physically, emotionally, mentally, and spiritually. These questions are designed for two people who are intimate with each other and spend a lot of time together. So often these questions are overlooked, and arise later on in the relationship. Focus your attention on them now, and you will come to know each other better.

The Big Why

List the five top reasons why you are choosing relationship.

Take your time. Consider several layers, not just the lofty ones. Be honest! You can change your answers later if you need to.

1. I choose relationship because

a.

b.

c.

d.

e.

Review what you've written, and consider any other aspects that you may have overlooked in the first response. Consider the physical, emotional, intellectual, and spiritual reality of your relationship. How about the financial aspect? Some partners neglect to recognize that relationship (especially marriage) is also a business arrangement, with costs and benefits. That's not the only reason, but it's important to have it on the table.

Now add three more reasons why you are choosing relationship!

f.

g.

h.

You have just described the features of your conscious partnership. You can come back later to add or amend. And, of course, we are in a realm that "words can't express"—but try we must to express the inexpressible!

Get together now with your partner and share your answers to these questions. Notice if any of the responses create stress, excitement, or concern. If you have any reactions, make a note of what they are. Write down the tenor of the discussion, and anything you discover. You will find this invaluable a few years down the road as you measure how you have grown.

What was the tenor of the discussion?

What were my discoveries?

This sharing is an important time to hear one another and exchange your views and perspectives. If there's tension, consider pausing now and going to a Heart Talk (see chapter 7).

Physical Well-Being

What is your intention in regard to your physical well-being? Areas of physical well-being include health, finances, home and property, children, pets, and extended family.

Complete these phrases:

2. For my health and physical well-being, I intend to:

3. For your health and physical well-being, I intend to:

4. My picture of an ideal living situation looks like this: (Be as specific as possible, and—obviously—use more paper to describe this picture. This can include a drawing of your ideal living situation.)

5. Are there children in the ideal picture?

6. Where children (either ones from existing relationships or ones you intend to have) are concerned, I intend to:

7. Are there animals in this picture?

Emotional Well-Being

Now let's consider the emotional well-being of your partnership. The process of relating inevitably brings up areas of intense feeling. Again, respond to these on your own, then come back to the Heart Talk technique with your partner.

Consider the following questions as a place to begin:

8. My emotional strengths are:

9. Your emotional strengths are:

10. My vulnerability seems to show up most when:

11. I experience your vulnerability most when:

12. When it comes to expressing my feelings to you, I promise to:

13. When it comes to experiencing your feelings, I promise to:

Do you see how this can bring up thorns, knots, assumptions, discomforts, and other interesting material? Our view is that you will find out the answers to these questions sooner or later, and we feel that sooner is a better choice.

Intellectual or Mental Well-Being

This area can include material that interests you in terms of your past or current areas of study, mastery, or travel. You might identify things you would like to research together through books that you both read or classes that you might take together. Share your ideals, fantasies, and passions. Find your mutual interests.

Answer these questions first individually, then share your responses.

14. One of the areas of my interest that I am most excited to share with you is:

15. If we could go anywhere in the world together, I would like it to be _____, because:

16. One of the things I've always wanted to study, but haven't had time for is:

Spiritual Well-Being

This is the area of discovery related to the sacred. You may have other words you prefer to use here. Couples we know have found this aspect together through religion, meditation, yoga, being in nature, or caring for life in some way. It can often be that this is one of the most essential aspects of relationship, and the area that can get lost first in our busy lives. This is where the element of true sacred union becomes possible. Complete this statement:

17. I envision spending time each week doing something with you to reinforce the sacred in our life together, including:

Sexuality

This area of relationship touches each of the previous ones but also needs to be considered on its own. Take a moment to contemplate what your dreams are for a sexual partnership. Start by doing this individually. Then speak to each other about this, tenderly! Talk about your hopes and fears, strengths and challenges. Be as honest as possible.

18. My greatest fears about sexuality are:

19. My highest vision of our sexuality is:

20. Here's how I balance intimacy, sensuality, and sexuality:

Your Supports

Realize that there are times when you may need help.

21. These are the friends with whom I feel closest, and the communities to which I belong. (Name the people that you admire in those communities, to whom you could go for advice, physical help, or a listening ear.)

22. These are three mentors in my life—past as well as current ones. (Then talk about them with your partner, and come up with one or two names that feel right to both of you as a mentor in your present life together.)

23. If I experience an unresolved issue or strain in my relationship, would I see a counselor who has been trained in relationship work?

Exercises to Ready Yourself for Sacred Relationship
PHYSICAL

Develop your senses and thus your sensuality. Listen to natural sounds. Contact earth, water, air, and fire. Find a consistent place of connection in nature that you visit repeatedly. Stretch your limbs. Work your body and your heart—walk, climb trees, build stone walls. Dance for flow and dance to awaken your heart.

EMOTIONAL

Read poetry aloud. Listen to songs, then sing them to yourself and to your partner. Write poetry—nurturing metaphor, the language of the soul. Visit communities where life is simple, the people have little, yet their happiness is great. At any moment, ask yourself, "What am I feeling?"

MENTAL

Set aside ten minutes of complete unplugged quiet in each day to clear your mind—simply sitting, without electronics, counting your breaths. Create an altar that you share with your partner; choose what's on it and why. Tell stories, including your origin story. Study some area of knowledge in detail, for example, your own anatomy. Every organ and system of your body serves your relationship in different ways. The study of the intricacies of your organs and systems will lead you to a profound respect for the world.

SPIRITUAL

Open to possibility. Let life arising become a mystery and a miracle. When someone says, "Love is merely the action of chemicals in the right temporal lobe," nod your head, say, "That's interesting," and let come into your mind and body an imagination of something wonderful that you will do for and with your partner. Stay open and observant of your own experience.

Love Languages

Looking at the five Love languages helps you round out your relationship.

24. Gifts: Do I receive gifts from my partner? Would I like to? Do I give gifts?

25. Quality time: Do I have "quality time" with my partner?

26. Words of affirmation: Do I acknowledge what my partner has done? Do I praise my partner for accomplishments, or simply for being? Do I receive words of affirmation?

27. Acts of service: Do I do things for my partner that need to be done? Does this include more than chores? Do I receive this kind of treatment from my partner?

28. Physical touch: (We ask about the physical level in two other sections here. This one has to do with touch.) Am I touched enough? Do I reach out to touch?

29. Non-parallel languages. Do my partner and I agree about the relative importance of the five "Love languages"? Or, if I have different preferences, is my partner aware of that? Has he or she offered to be taught by me in my favorite mode? Have I offered?

Questions for a Conscious Wedding

These questions continue the sequence, recognizing that you are going more deeply into a committed relationship. You will find it very useful to answer these together, or to share your responses after you've had some time to think about them.

Some questions may be challenging. They ask about more than the wedding or ceremony. Some people say, "Let's have a great wedding—the rest will take care of itself." Not true. The marriage's success rests on the foundation of your knowledge of yourself and your partner.

The categories parallel those from the first part, though the questions are different and more intimate. You may wish to pick a number between one and eighty-two, and go to that question to deepen your answer.

Marriage and the Gateway to It: The Wedding

30. Why do I choose marriage or rededication with my partner?

In doing this, you will begin to gather words and information that can serve you in creating your vows to each other. First, you look at the qualities of the overall relationship. Later you will essentialize the information, perhaps for inclusion in the vows you will craft for a wedding ceremony. Those not considering formal marriage should note that vows exist even in committed nonmarital relationships.

You can use these questions to get you started. Do this first on your own, and then share what you've created with your partner; again, we suggest using the Heart Talk technique. You can generate the answers using the Repeated Question technique. (Coach: "Thank you. Why choose marriage or rededication with your partner?")

a.

b.

c.

d.

e.

Physical Well-Being

Recall the traditional Christian wedding vows, which include the phrase "in sickness and in health." If the word "vow" is too strong at this point, you can use words such as "I intend," "I promise," "I would like to," or other verbs of your choosing.

Earlier we went into more detail about physical commitments in your relationship. Here we would like to suggest that you explore one of the more detailed areas of physical support, the value basis of the relationship, which includes but is not exclusively the financial basis of your lives. It can include the maintenance of a household. If you know this issue may be charged for you, take the extra care to create a safe space to allow your answers to arise. Light a candle of intention and do the Heart Talk if that will create more safety. Take care of each other, and do your best to experience the conversation from each other's point of view.

31. Currently, the ways I primarily contribute to my relationship are as follows (list here what you contribute in time, money, and support to the shared well-being of your relationship):

32. The ways my partner contributes are:

33. Our cooperative strengths in this area are:

34. The areas of sensitivity in this area are:

35. What I most want my partner to hear from me about this aspect of our relationship is:

36. My commitment to my partner and to the relationship regarding this aspect is:

Another potentially challenging area of relationship is the extended family. We have found that some ground rules in regard to parents, siblings, and spouses or children from previous marriages are often not clearly addressed in new relationships. In this category we think of their physical needs.

37. The people in our extended family that I am most concerned about are:

38. Our responsibilities to my relatives look like this (name specific relatives here, and specific situations that might arise):

39. Our responsibilities to your relatives look like this (name specific relatives here):

40. About the children, how many rooms do we need in our house? Will this change after some time to a different configuration?

Emotional Well-Being

Deeper inquiries regarding your emotional connection to your partner are explored in this section. Begin with the following questions:

41. I believe we are well suited emotionally because:

42. I feel our greatest emotional strength together is:

43. I feel our potentially most challenging place emotionally is:

44. The key to dealing with me when I'm most upset is: (This is important! Don't assume your partner knows. Don't make it a test of Love to examine whether your partner can help you through your upset in just the right way.)

45. The best way that we can ensure emotional health is:

46. (Consider a deeper dive into emotional patterns of the past by entertaining a challenging question.) "Why haven't my other relationships worked out?" (It helps to be very specific about the story you tell yourself. This is your personal myth. Be honest.) What have I learned about myself from previous relationships that would be helpful for my partner to know right now?

47. Were we to have children who went forth in the world to find their destiny and then came home and asked, "Could I move back in? And I'd like my own room," how would we respond? (Of course, you can change this later, but take a good look at this common situation.)

Parents and Family Dynamics

In a casual relationship, your history with parents and family members may not arise much. As you become more committed, relationship will begin to take you to your edges of development. You will find your family myths there, the many stories that grabbed you as a child and have the power to grab you today.

48. How was I loved by my parents?

49. How was I abandoned by my family?

50. What would push my anxiety buttons from my parents, siblings, or other family members at our wedding? (Can you see how important it would be to alert your celebrant and director to these patterns?)

Intellectual or Mental Well-Being

Now we suggest that you go more deeply into this area of cocreation.

51. A project that I would really like to do with my partner is:

52. A project that I would like to reserve for myself is:

53. Other aspects of intellectual well-being that I want to explore are (these can be alone or with your partner):

54. In the next ten years, an area of accomplishment I would like to achieve is:

55. The best way my partner could support this achievement would be:

56. If I were to affiliate with an ideal mythic character, it would be _____, because:

57. If I were to affiliate my partner with an ideal mythic character, it would be _____, because:

Spiritual Well-Being

Continue to deepen your inquiry with these questions:

58. My dream of Sacred Union with my partner includes:

59. To develop the spiritual essence between us, I would commit to:

60. Other aspects of spiritual well-being that I commit to are:

61. Virtues that are important to me (from chapter 3) are: (Does the list include Grace? Beauty? Courage? Love? Other virtues? Describe one in detail, personified—what this virtue might symbolically wear, what tools or attributes he or she might be carrying, how he or she might move or speak.)

Sexuality

This area of relationship touches each of the previous ones but also needs to be considered on its own. Think about your dreams of a sexual partnership. Start by doing this individually. Then speak to one another about this, tenderly! Talk about your hopes and fears, strengths and challenges. Be as honest as possible.

62. My greatest joy in sexuality has been:

63. My greatest joy in sexuality could be:

64. When I allow myself to envision the most romantic episode possible with my partner, it would look like this:

65. My idea of the perfect wedding night (after the ceremony) would look like this:

Your Supports

66. Three people whom I deeply respect, and whose advice I would trust (ideally living people, but perhaps not!), are:

Money

In a short-term relationship, you can get by without agreements around money. Not so in marriage. Some of these may require a counseling session to get through, which would be a very smart move, as every issue here can be dealt with more easily when you're calm, and not so easily when you're not.

67. How did my parents deal with money? Did one person pay the bills? Did one person make the income? Did they discuss money issues together? Did either parent ever hide money? Did either complain or fret about money?

68. Have I shared a credit report on my creditworthiness with my soon-to-be spouse?

69. Who will pay the bills for running a household? Do I feel that this person holds the purse strings for the relationship? Can I contemplate handing this task back and forth at the beginning of each year? If that's a bad idea, why is it a bad idea?

70. How rich do I want to be one day in the future? If I plan to work hard now and vacation after some cutoff age, am I willing to save what I've earned, and am I willing to support one or both of us working eighty hours a week?

71. Can I make joint decisions about big expenses? What would be the number for big: $500? $5,000? More? Less?

72. What would happen if one of my parents was taken ill and couldn't afford the recommended treatments? Do I have an emergency fund for such situations?

73. Do I have an emergency fund? What is my understanding about what is an "emergency"?

74. Do we have a joint bank account or separate ones? Does it matter to me? Have I spoken to a financial advisor about how to manage finances jointly? If not, why not? (There are some experienced people who can give very good advice.)

The Nonnegotiable Vows

75. (Consider the possibility that you might fall into the percentage of marriages that split up.) What would I like to have in place as an agreement between us? No matter what might befall us as a couple, and no matter what miscommunications might occur, what would I still like to honor with this person in my life? (This is the bottom line of soul-to-soul agreements, which exist no matter what form the relationship might evolve into. These agreements don't change.)

The Wedding Ceremony

76. When I think about our wedding, what one image comes to my mind and heart most strongly? (Be as detailed as possible, either with a specific image or a quality of the ceremony that would have to be present for you to fulfill your intention. You might say, "Well, we must have such and such"—here is the place to state that clearly. Do not assume at this stage that your picture is shared by your partner. You'll soon find out.)

77. What do I think the cost of our ceremony should be?

78. What kind of flowers would I like?

79. What do I see us wearing?

80. What is the word that knits us together most strongly right now? (Name the virtue of this moment.)

Case Studies

Try out these situations and have a good discussion about them. You will have a great deal of fun if you make up your own scenarios, and then exaggerate them with a "Yes, and . . ." exercise.

81. My partner comes home in the afternoon with a large bag and a big smile.

   a. My partner dumps the bag onto the kitchen table—expensive woodworking tools—and announces, "I'm going to make the garage into a workshop!"

   b. My partner empties out cans of paint and paintbrushes. "Now we're going to repaint the living room. I can't stand it any longer!"

   c. The bag contains bottles and tubes of cosmetics: "I've joined a company to sell products. I'm starting at the bottom, but we'll build up our network and soon we'll have salespeople under us and get lots of commissions. The starter kit only cost $700."

These situations have some common features: your partner has made a decision without consulting you, one that involves your space, your time, and perhaps your money. She or he may not think that it involves you, but it will, even if it's to console her or him if things don't work out exactly as hoped or planned. Flesh out each scene, and play with what it might look like. There are many ways such a venture could go, and you can now imagine many of them.

Extra Credit Question

One marriage advisor strongly recommends that early on in the relationship, you each ask the other the question, "How are you mad?"—meaning, "How are you eccentric, quirky, adapted to a world in many ways crazy and unfair?"

You'll save a lot of time if you can share your oddities right up front.

82. "How am I mad?"

Whew!

Once you've written out your answers, take Special Time (see chapter 5) to discuss what you each have discovered. May this process of coming to know each other bring you joy and growth!

Congratulations! Many people don't think about these issues until the issues bite them. Thinking and feeling ahead of a catastrophe will help you grow as a One, better able to achieve the Two of true partnership and thereby enjoy some well-earned moments of ONE. Of course, your answers to these questions will elaborate and change over time. The process of sharing with your partner can create a stronger relationship between you, and set the stage for a much better wedding.

Why Marriage?

chapter 10

Why marry? We can best explore the answer through the Concentric Circles model. The vast number of responses to "Why marry?" can be grouped according to which circle one stands in when answering. We repeatedly make the case that marriage ought to be treated as a verb, both personally and in the collective unconscious of our culture. Whenever you hear the word "marriage," you ought to hear it as an ongoing process, as "marrying." As we shift the beliefs and mythic meaning of marriage, from contracted to expanded, we begin to see that this conscious choice has an influence on a much bigger field of awareness than just our own personal story.

Let's begin in the center circle and look at possible responses from the level of the story, the drama:

"WHY MARRY?" IN THE STORY

I am in love.

We are good companions.

Simply put, sex.

Life will be safer, more secure.

Why Marry?

The Story
The Drama

Story

We want to live happily ever after.

We have great chemistry.

I want to have children with that person.

I don't want to grow old alone.

I'm tired of being single.

Dating and courtship is just too hard.

It's just time to get married.

We believe our love is magical and special.

(Add some of your own.)

In the second circle out, in the psychological and cultural sphere of influence, what comes into play?

"WHY MARRY?" IN THE PSYCHOLOGICAL LEVEL

That's what Mom and Dad did.

My family expects it of me.

It's just the right thing to do.

We need to continue the family name.

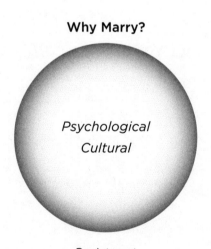

Why Marry?

Psychological Cultural

Psychological

I want to do it differently than my parents and be the family I never had.

I have to keep my religious and cultural heritage alive through a solid family life.

It is compulsory in my religion to marry before having sex.

I want to rebel against my religious and cultural heritage and marry whomever I want.

It's expected for me to be married in order to advance my career.

We have a karmic connection.

Partnerships are the basis for a much more creative and productive life.

Society expects it.

It will make my mother happy.

I've always dreamed of the perfect fairy-tale wedding, and I want it to come true.

We have something to offer the larger community through our example.

(Add some of your own at the psychological/cultural level.)

In the third circle out, we answer from a mythic/symbolic perspective:

"WHY MARRY?" IN THE MYTHIC LEVEL

We want our union to be blessed by God.

We will find the ONE together.

Our vows are sacred; our Sacred Union will heal us.

I am Radha; my partner is Krishna.

We've seen healthy and long-lasting marriages and we know it's possible to be like them.

Love is our true teacher, and will lead us to Life itself.

Everything in creation comes into being through a balanced masculine/feminine communion.

If I can truly see the Beloved in my partner, I also will be truly seen.

We are dedicated to Being and Making Love in the world.

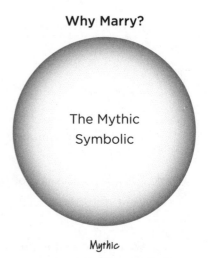

Why Marry?

The Mythic Symbolic

Mythic

In marriage, there is an opportunity for an alchemical blending to occur that is much less likely to happen without the ongoing rituals of marriage, which are prefigured in a wedding ceremony. The blending of the single individual (One) into the strength of partnership (Two) changes both involved, and creates a third, the relationship itself that becomes the pathway to communion with all creation (ONE). Theorists have referred to the "transformation of motivation" which is part of this alchemy. For most people, there will be a transformation in viewpoint, where the single person will now start thinking as part of a unit, and the goals and visions that are part of this particular union will begin to emerge. Passion for sex becomes passion for experiencing the ONE together.

In chapter 3, we asked, "Why relationship?" We examined the reasons that people get together, and now we explore how those who create relationship make the decision to commit to marriage. Some people don't have definite ideas about why they are together in relationship or in marriage. Sometimes couples don't know why they are marrying, which is all the more amazing because of the social/spiritual importance accorded to marriage. We suggest here that the same (and rather confronting) statement applies to marriage as to relationship:

Marriage is not for happiness.

Happiness is mentioned repeatedly at a wedding, but we suggest that marriage is not for happiness. Although happiness can certainly be a by-product, marriage isn't really what creates happiness! Couples try so hard, the honeymoon is wonderful, and then reality strikes. They get tired of each other or disappointed: "Where did the fun times go? I don't feel happy anymore." Then they divorce, only to cycle into a new relationship, perhaps a new marriage; and after a time, they begin to ask these same questions again. It's possible that the foundations for the marriage were inappropriate from the beginning. It's possible that . . .

Marriage deepens the commitment of relationship as a living process to encourage, grow, and mature two human beings to love more deeply, shine more brightly, exert more vibrant power, and enjoy life more.

Marriage can take relationship steps deeper and raise it steps higher, so that you have gone beyond happiness into communion. You revel in the bliss of your own awakening. You thoroughly enjoy the maturation of your partner. You grow yourself and you grow the other. The process demands everything you have, and the rewards match what you put into it. When you sign up for such a gig, it is a courageous act, and the spiritual world will notice. There is some kind of unseen, sacred support that shows up when you commit yourself to *anything* wholeheartedly. The commitment to the growth of your own awareness creates the biggest such opportunity. The angels celebrate, and become very attentive to you. (If the term "angels" doesn't resonate with you, think about the idea that positive intention creates an attractor energy that opens doors to growth and grace. If you like complexity theory better, then whenever we say "angels," think "more refined pattern." And see David's story on angels in chapter 5.)

A marriage can strengthen relationship in all its best qualities, and the wedding provides the ceremonial gate to that journey. With your focused intent to grow, you can create a wedding ceremony that takes you into partnership and then beyond, to communion. We believe that communion is possible, regularly and sustainably, between two partners. To get there, you must nurture this unified intention.

Marriage in Other Cultures

Around the world, in every country, the rituals and institution of marriage have played an important part. As we mentioned at the beginning of the book, every nation in the United Nations has marriage, between three and eight ceremonies per thousand people per year. Three to eight people per thousand may not sound like a lot, but when you consider that each wedding is an action that involves hundreds of members of the community, it means that weddings and marriage are on everyone's mind everywhere in the world.

Over time the basis for marriage has changed. As has been popularized in many books, movies, and television series, the arranged marriages of royalty in Europe until the twentieth century were based solely on political advantage, and on maintaining the bloodline of the ruling class. They rarely involved love and compatibility or resulted in happy, well-adjusted heirs! What happened in the twentieth century?

Marriage laws in the West altered greatly in response to the emancipation of women and the establishment of women's rights in the nineteenth and twentieth centuries. The economic status of women changed, and so did the female servitude that was acceptable up to that point. Marriages were more likely to be arranged, or forced, prior to women's liberation.

Arranged marriages are still found throughout the world today. In most cases, they are "endogamous," meaning that the marriage is within the cultural, religious, or ethnic group; often a third party has selected the bride and groom in order to satisfy cultural, family, religious, or social criteria. Arranged marriage is common in India, where the caste system remains a consideration. Amish people and Orthodox Jews also practice endogamous marriage.

A marriage becomes "forced" if either the bride or the groom is denied the right to decline the arrangement. This is a more extreme situation, and—while it still exists in certain countries to preserve cultural and religious traditions (or to preserve financial fortunes)—it is not relevant to our discussion here. Forced marriages and weddings are seldom conscious, in the sense that the constraints on choice undermine the ability to be awake and aware of spirit moving in the celebration of union. It's not impossible, though it is very difficult.

The idea of arranged marriages shocks modern thinkers who consider freedom of choice paramount. Let us describe the point of view of an East Indian couple with whom we became friendly and could speak about such things. Their marriage had been arranged twenty-five years previously. They were happy, compatible, and productive medical doctors. When we asked them how it had felt to have their parents, in consultation with a Vedic astrologer, make the choice of marriage partner for them, the man said, "It was such an important life decision, I would have been terrified to make it without guidance." Thus there was an element of "consciousness" in that marriage, though mostly on the part of the parents and the astrologer. The youngsters needed guidance from someone more experienced, more adult. And a key point: they both said, with eyes wide open, "Yes." It was not forced. Once the partner had been chosen, there was a courtship phase, and they could have said, "No."

That perspective has stayed with us, after observing so many marriages based on impulsive attractions or the whims of romance that rise and fall.

The three lowest divorce rates in the world occur in cultures that arrange marriages: the Amish, Hindus in India, and ultra-Orthodox Jews in Israel. That fact does not necessarily reflect stability, nor is it a commentary on happiness or soul growth. It is a reflection of the second ring of Concentric Circles, where the influence of the family and culture far outweighs any individual choice.

Where does this leave the culture of romantic Love? We have all been raised on the fairy-tale version of "happily ever after." That particular rosy-glow myth affects even the most sane and practical among us! Eva Illouz has written about the strong ties between the rise of romantic Love and the development of capitalism: it serves commerce to have expensive romantic dinners, flowers, vacations, and weddings. None of us is immune to the monetization of Love and the selling of it through advertising and the cultural spin of music and film.

As we seek to answer the question "Why marry?" we find ourselves at a choice point in the confusion of historic influences. Is the foundation of marriage in romance and Love naïve and driven by clever marketing tricks? We believe that there is another turn of the cultural spiral. From our observations of history and culture, we believe that fashions change, mores change, and, most importantly, human consciousness changes. There is something emerging that has always been there in part—something different from forced unions, something different from impulsive expressions of desire. This new development of consciousness reveals that something holy does exist at the deep core of the human commitment to choose, and to build, a Sacred Union in marriage. Romantic Love has been romanticized, sensationalized, and mercilessly manipulated by the media. Yet, it is our profound feeling that in the outer ring of the Concentric Circles, in the mythic, you can discover a strong foundation for union. It involves a true romantic Love, but is not limited to that. We prefer the phrase "Sacred Union." When your vision of marriage values romantic Love as an important phase that can resolve into Sacred Union, then you begin to see how a conscious marriage can have an important influence not only on personal development, psychologically and spiritually, but on the whole of the culture as well.

The Ideal Love: From Romance
to Soul Mate to Sacred Union

We visited the south of France in the late 1990s to understand more directly who the Cathars were, and what their connection was to the culture of the troubadours. They thrived in southern France in the twelfth and thirteenth centuries, leaving important traces behind. In the Gnostic faith of the Cathars, the true living example of Jesus was treasured as a healer and teacher—and they believed that he was a man who valued women. In that tradition, women were respected in Cathar communities, and generally in southern France, in contrast to the rest of Europe at the time. In the tradition of Courtly Love, or, as it is often known, troubadour culture—which overlapped with that of the Cathars—the *chevalier* was to conduct himself with "chivalry" in his *domnei*, or his devotion to his chosen lady—from which we have our term of respect, madam (*ma dame,* "my lady"). Poetry and songs in honor of the feminine, new forms of clothing, new forms of language, and indeed all of the arts flourished, a cultural renaissance based on "romance."

The Cathar faith was a powerful movement from the 1100s up until 1244, when the Catholic Church, in cooperation with the king of France, wiped out the last of their communities, completing the seizure of their lands and the suppression of their faith at the siege and bloody end at Montségur.

The persecution of the Cathars marked the beginning of the Inquisition in twelfth-century France. The damage done by the Inquisition is alive and well in the subconscious of many women and men today. In two books Arthur Guirdham demonstrates through hypnosis how deeply held these memories are. It intrigued us to realize that the world might be a different place altogether had these cultural expressions from the south of France been able to flourish. We had to lose those values and then reform them some centuries later in a new way.

What is the deeper meaning of romantic Love? Is there something threatening in true romance or Sacred Union to both Church and state? We believe that the empowerment of women is the foundation for Sacred Union—that is to say, the recognition by the partner and by the culture of the power intrinsic to the feminine.

From our research in southern France and other places, we came to a new understanding of the role of Mary Magdalene in relationship to Yeshua, and why the Church has been so threatened by the attempt to recognize her as a high initiate—a pinnacle of consciousness. We wrote together a full-length play on this topic, *My Magdalene,* produced a DVD about that process, *Remembering Mary Magdalene,* and wrote a long preface to a little book we found in France and had translated into English, *The Gospel of Mary Magdalene.* We worked on telling that story because we found in Mary Magdalene a model for something rare then and much more available now—the consciousness and power of the feminine.

Here, we will simply go with the question: what effect might the existence of true romantic Love have on our culture today if it were seen and known in its glory, as more than the vapid reflections we get in films, songs, and television shows?

We may be oversimplifying the trajectory a bit by tracing romance to the twelfth century. Surely romantic Love existed before the troubadours? Yes, of course it did, but it found its fullest expression in the West at that particular time. There follows a long, traceable history from the poetry and courtship of the troubadours through Western literature: some works supportive, some contradictory.

In late medieval times, a theme begins to emerge in which romance is at odds with marriage. That plot can be seen in great works such as Shakespeare's *Romeo and Juliet,* and in the tale of King Arthur, his wife Guinevere, and his best friend Lancelot. In a time when forced and arranged marriages were the rule, romance was shown to lead to tragedy. Many of the great operas lead with that premise: *Tristan and Isolde* is another example. True Love can only be resolved in death. But what was behind romance was rising in the culture. In the course of centuries, the notion grew that the attraction of soul to soul was more important than the rules of property, caste, class, or ethnic group.

There is a new conviction that has been growing over centuries in the cultural collective consciousness, a belief that deep romantic Love, a Sacred Union connection, holds the healing power we so desperately need. It is a belief, or an openness to the idea, that an actual engagement in relationship with the Beloved is what will lead us toward restoring wholeness, beauty, and harmony. We learn to love truly in our partnerships, then move the ideal of the Beloved into a much more vast expression of relationship to living.

Out of the ideals of romantic Love emerge modern phrases such as twin flame, soul mate, and Sacred Union. A little history on soul mates: Plato first mentions the principle in the *Symposium* (380 BCE), in relation to the fundamental androgyny of the human being who is split into male and female by the gods. The theory isn't found much in the centuries after Plato, other than perhaps in idealized philosophical thought. Yet it reaches an apogee in the nineteenth and twentieth centuries in Theosophy and the works of Edgar Cayce and Elizabeth Clare Prophet.

We suggest that this reflects something that is growing in world consciousness, and that widens the mythic realm to the reality of a deeper expression of Love. Based on their research on intimate relationships, the psychologists Susan and Clyde Hendrick of Texas Tech University postulate that true romantic love will play an increasingly important role in our culture. We wholeheartedly agree. When we are motivated to realize that our marriages reflect something core to the nature of all creation, we might find the high note that supports our will and strength to cocreate them as something truly extraordinary.

We recommend the ideal of soul mates and Sacred Union, as they reflect something in the cosmology with which we align. It comes from the pattern of the universe itself. The recently articulated model of the electric universe understands that masculine–feminine polarities (often termed positive–negative, though we have to take away the value judgments that seem to hang around all polarities) are fundamental to life and creation, at every level of consciousness. Certainly we see it in procreation. And it is relevant also in the truest sense to the mythic, to being-itself at Source, and to choosing to Love.

When we live in the full potential that we are spiritual beings having a human experience, and that all life in all forms revolves around the principles of masculine–feminine, then we can make a fundamental choice to penetrate the mystery of life. We can work with the Beloved to comprehend the true nature of Love, and how to craft a relationship that will be deeply fulfilling and of profound service to life itself. Perhaps both the Cathars and the troubadours understood the potential for this resonance with life, and that's why they were eliminated by those who wished to retain that power for themselves.

If we put romantic Love and Sacred Union in the outer ring of Concentric Circles and see these as healthy, magical, and numinous powers, how might that change the way we cocreate our relationships, and lead us toward ceremonies that can transform ourselves and others? This is an additional question to the list in chapter 9—given here because it took a chapter to introduce it. Ponder the question singly and together. Do a bit of journal writing about it. You may find more deeply the core reason for pursuing your Sacred Union.

We wrote this book because we believe that deep Love relationships are at the core of life, and at the core of all that is sacred. We can practice awakening to this awareness through our cultivation of the core of the wedding—and of the marriage that follows: the Sacred Moment, as summary and prescience of the Sacred Union.

The Sacred Moment:
Core of a Conscious Wedding

chapter 11

Aconscious wedding depends on a conscious partnership. You began to explore aspects of your relationship in Part One, and we urge you to continue with that exploration as we proceed. Since some people need to know where they're heading with all of this, let's go right to the core, to the very center, of a successful conscious wedding. We call it the Sacred Moment.

This is the moment, long or short, when everyone in the room witnesses that two human souls have come out of hiding, found each other, and, with the support of friends and family, are forming a divinely married couple. Communion—"coming into union"—occurs. The Two merges into the ONE. Energies swirl and combine—synergy. Everyone feels blessed. Philosophers use a wonderful Greek word for this communion—syzygy, pronounced "sizz-EE-gee"—and its sound suggests the sizzle that happens when two people get together and something powerful takes over. Bliss sizzles.

To get to that you have to be conscious, which means awake, aware, interested. What does a Sacred Moment look like? What does it feel like? How do we know it happened or didn't happen? Do you remember a wedding that brought you to tears, or where you felt a deep thrill that made you grateful to be alive? Or that reestablished your awareness of Love and connection to your partner, even though both of you sat among the witnesses? Or that reawakened the sense of expansive, compassionate joy, what you might call your Higher Self? That memory is a good indication that a Sacred Moment occurred in the ceremony. Maybe you can identify the moment in time when it occurred, or maybe it's more of a general feeling that grew over the course of the ceremony.

Perhaps you have memories of other weddings where there was a sense that "nothing really happened." There were no inspirational moments, no lifting out of the normal state of awareness. Even the places where it was "supposed" to happen, such as with the vows or at the declaration "I now pronounce you husband and wife," nothing special was felt. Everyone went through the motions and smiled, but nothing zinged through all hearts.

What is this mysterious Moment? How do we plan for it?

Ideally supported by, and certainly surrounded by, all the "stuff" of a wedding—the fine dresses, the omnipresent flowers, the decorations of the space, the food, the drinks, the clicking cameras, and on and on—the fundamental fact is that there are two souls who are seeking to bring their lives together, to marry, to merge, to deepen their commitment.

They are seeking to meet—and to speak—in soul speech. This can include words, or it can happen in thundering silence. It can include a sense of presence so intense that everyone feels it. It can include words sung or spoken, or wordless song. This soul speech can come at any time. When we facilitate weddings, we sometimes wait for the prepared words to be spoken when rings are exchanged—for instance, "This ring represents the circle of our eternal Love"—and then surprise the couple by saying, "Now, close your eyes and deeply look in your sacred heart . . . Is there something more you wish to say to your Beloved?"

The question can open a gap, allowing Spirit to rush through the form and Love to blossom into the room. Sometimes the sacred can permeate an entire ceremony. Sometimes it comes through a small gap of time.

The Sacred Moment may come unexpectedly. It might arrive when the rings are fumbled or another so-called "mistake" occurs, because the soul seeks to free itself from the restraint of a rigid order of events. In the "mistake," something leaks out that is genuinely soul-nature: a smile, a hand extended to support a fall, an unrehearsed comment. The soul comes out to say its piece, and then the witnesses in the room nod, as they know that the true ceremony has been fulfilled. The witnesses know that these two people really mean it, that they are on their way to partnership and communion.

After the "mistake," the engine of the formal ceremony can pick up again and continue, but the sweet and delicate Sacred Moment has occurred and the heart is satisfied in each and every person present. When friends and relatives witness such a moment, you engage a power of support that will last you the rest of your life.

That's one reason that we are very accepting of "mistakes" or "mess-ups" in a wedding. Maybe one of the rings can't be found. Or someone accidentally steps on the bride's train and pulls her sideways. Or a vase of flowers falls over. Or the best man—or, hey, the bride herself—yawns! If the witnesses giggle, the celebrant can explain that yawning awakens the centers of empathy, memory, and expanded consciousness in the part of the brain called the precuneus. Or simply smile. The point is that the content of these mishaps is unimportant. The rigid form has cracked, and the two souls can slip out and commune in the sight of all. It can be in the unexpected event and how it is handled that the most genuine feelings and communications arise. You can't prepare for the unexpected, and that's the point.

When the standard parts of a wedding ceremony are read aloud from a book, they may fail to leave room for the souls to come forth—yet that's what everyone is waiting for! The witnesses yearn to observe with their senses a happening from which they can conclude, "These two people really see each other, heart to heart; they have met soul to soul; true Love has flowed between them, and they will go now as partners into the great world, stronger in partnership and communion than as single people. I have seen it and I can support it." If your witnesses can say this, then you have used them well. They will stay true to their experience of truth, and support you in your conscious partnership through thick and thin into the future. For that, it's worth having a ceremony.

Ought we script the Sacred Moment? Let's try this:

Bride (smiling broadly to the groom): I see you.

Groom (genuinely nodding his head): I see you.

He begins to spin her around, the two locked in loving eye contact.

Bride: Heart . . .

Groom: To heart . . .

Bride: Soul . . .

Groom: To soul . . .

And so forth. It sounds so beautiful, but most of the time this wouldn't work. Your witnesses know acting from a script when they see it. They are waiting to experience something unscripted, spontaneous, authentic, lively, unexpected, a lightning flash in a clear blue sky. It might look something like this, but now that you've read the script, it can't be this.

In much of this book, we ask you to become more conscious of your relationship by tackling large issues head on, by becoming decisive about conflicts with your partner, and by taking control of many details. Now we ask you to consciously choose to surrender, to let go of that control. You will soon find that letting go, surrendering, is not a one-time affair. Your conscious, awake discipline will be needed to continue that surrender, especially during the core of the wedding, and ideally for some time before and after it as well.

How does it feel? When you have a Sacred Moment with each other, you feel wonderful. It can look or feel like any number of things: a great fountain of energy works its way up inside you; you see stars and sparklers; you hear heavenly music; you feel sheer, simple joy, the great pleasure of being alive; you feel that this is the reason you are alive; you want to dance; you want to smile; you nod with the feeling that this relationship is true and right; you want to shout, "I am in love with this beautiful being, and I thank the lucky stars that brought him/her to me!" You can feel the unity—the ONE—of everyone present and perhaps ONE-ness with all creation.

story

A Sacred Moment: The Ring

After the exchange of rings, the celebrant asked the groom, "Is there something more that you would like to say from your heart about what this ring means to you?" He was silent for some moments. Then unexpected eloquence poured through him. "This ring is the Sun come to rest on the finger of the woman I cherish. I forged this ring in my imagination, and had it made. It is a part of my Sun nature, shining to her all day every day, a message of my Love." As he spoke, he beamed at his wife and at the witnesses. The tone of his delivery was completely authentic. Later he reported how surprised he was at what he had said, and vowed to stand by every word. The witnesses commented on that moment and those words; they had beheld something extraordinary. ❀

story

Tying the Knot

Here is another, more subtle example of a Sacred Moment, which occurred at a wedding we attended. Sarah and Michael were married on the porch of a rambling old inn in New England, chosen because it had been the site of their first kiss. The weather challenged the wedding with cold and rain. The witnesses huddled together while the minister spoke in a low voice, which was not easy to hear above the sound of the rain on the metal roof. Sarah and Michael looked at each other and spoke no words. They simply gazed at each other. We could observe the life force flowing from each of them to the other. It streamed out powerfully from the energy centers of each body, mingling and intertwining like living knots. We understood then the term for marriage, "tying the knot." The rain drumming onto the roof above us became a drumroll for knots of strength, not of limitation, joining these two. ❀

What happens on the outside may look "normal"—people moving about and doing what they usually do. On the inside, however, in a Sacred Moment, time may completely stand still. You don't feel asleep; your senses are operating at full speed. You don't feel awake in the usual way because the light has become golden, the sounds are all precious, and the touch of your partner's hand sends tingles down your spine. Complete clarity. No thoughts. No planning—"this is what I should do next so I'll look good": that's gone. No worries. In short, bliss, awake bliss. The witnesses can feel it and will reflect it back to you for years to come.

Sharing such a moment together is a communion, a coming into Sacred Union, soul to soul. You feel naked before the gaze of the other. In a Sacred Moment, you feel vulnerable because you have shown up and all of you has come out of hiding, and anything can happen. You become a gorgeous trembling bird, completely beautiful and completely alive.

Some people actually recall a Sacred Moment when they first saw each other, even before they exchanged names. Across the room, you saw each other and something zinged for you. Remember that zing and find the way back to it, not by trying to capture it, but rather by opening to a new visitation.

To open to a Sacred Moment, you must learn to trust yourself, trust your body and feelings. Practice spontaneity, allowing imaginations, emotions, and actions to arise. All of the exercises in this book help you practice spontaneity.

Observe the wisdom in the body. You can watch it when you walk across a field of boulders. The body chooses the right place to step easily. If you had to think about each step, you'd progress very slowly. The body knows where to step and you jump from boulder to boulder, the mind amazed at what the body can do without direction. If not across boulders, then you can observe how your body negotiates furniture in your living room or other people on a crowded street. Your body tips and turns with sophistication. Were the mind to have to think about each move, you'd never make it. You can cultivate the body's innate knowing by putting yourself into a little training in the time leading up to the wedding. Exercises such as Mirroring (p. 108) can assist. Your body may lead you to a Sacred Moment while the mind reels from the swirls of energy.

In a Sacred Moment, the One (individual) speaks to the One (the partner, in a One-to-One that becomes Two) imbued with the ONE (communion). The ONE spreads out to nourish all present, a gift to everyone.

How do we integrate a Sacred Moment into a ceremony? So many times, we find that the marrying partners want to pull out 3 x 5 cards with their carefully chosen words—sometimes their own, sometimes quotes from famous poets or bibles. Then they nervously read these words and think that they've given the soul its turn. No, we're sorry to say, it's not that easy. The two souls need a space of time where nothing has been planned. Yes, that's right—nothing! Nothing except a space of quiet. That includes the respectful quiet of the entire group of the witnesses.

It can be frustrating when people say, "Be authentic!" Or, "Be genuine!" Or, "Be yourself!" So easy to say, and so difficult sometimes to achieve. It's what happens when a waiter spills your coffee. You could go immediately to anger, or you could use the tool from chapter 7: "How interesting!" In the end, how big a deal is spilled coffee? There may be a layer of anger in you, but we can say from experience that this is not your authentic, genuine self. You can observe the anger flash through, and then coax out the deeper layers of response.

exercise

Warm Interest 1

Take a moment right now to experience a truly quiet space and the focused awareness that can arise there. Pause, look up, and ponder some interesting visual point in your room. Let's say it's a corner of a chair or a square inch of a desktop—just a little area. Don't gaze at words on a book cover or on a poster. Don't drift without focus. Simply observe a specific form in the world. Entertain no other need than to examine that particular zone of space. Notice its color, shape, size, texture, and density. You don't need to do anything with it. You don't need to derive meaning from it. You don't need to write about it or even verbalize what you see. As you gaze at this place, let yourself calm. You don't have to do anything, just "be" in the exquisite awareness that you are awake. The process may take a few minutes—don't hurry. Focus your interest on this small area and you will notice warmth arising. The calmness that you develop becomes the ground from which great thoughts and great feelings originate. To begin with, simply examine this little piece of creation with warm interest.

In the conscious wedding, you demonstrate what lies at the basis of your relationship. Can you imagine practicing this moment of silent connection with your partner? If you are with your partner now, we suggest you actually stop and just "do it!"

exercise

Warm Interest 2

Focus on a very small part of the body of your partner, just a little area, not especially sexually charged. A small part of the back of the hand, or the place on the neck just below the ear. Breathe easily and slowly and let a warm interest arise in you for that area. Don't look for meaning or something special. Simply relax into observing this area with interest for several minutes.

Do you feel the beginning of a flow between you, a flow of warmth, as if it were a large, slow-moving river of warm attention flowing between you? That's exactly what you have with your witnesses: a river of energy moving toward you that you must care for and direct. Through the contagion of vibration, everyone is drawn into this powerful Love wave.

exercise

Warm Interest 3

Your life is full of opportunities to observe what comes up in the moment, before you've had a chance to put on your personality and respond from the habits of your past. Note those opportunities. A waiter spills your coffee. Someone trips on the sidewalk in front of you. You see it's raining outside, and you didn't bring any gear because the forecast didn't predict rain. A colleague tells you that another colleague has suddenly been taken ill and has gone to the hospital. You look in your wallet and find you forgot to bring cash to pay for something. All of these brushes with the unexpected afford opportunities to notice, in the milliseconds before the mind jumps in, what lives below the controlled life. Relationship calls out these capacities frequently. You notice how swiftly you react, and you notice when warm interest permeates each of these situations, including warm interest in the content as well as in the fact of the conundrum. Before you "fix it," take each opportunity to widen the zone of warm interest. "How interesting that this phenomenon happened, here and now." This is practice for greeting the unexpected in both wedding and marriage.

Communion 2

Sit with your partner, facing each other and holding hands, and simply gaze into each other's eyes. Take a couple of breaths together, close your eyes, and in the silence, connect to each other. No words. Just feel your energy reaching out and merging, blending, warm interest in the whole of the other. Fill each other with the intention of communion.

After you've given yourselves the time to settle into the relaxed feeling of each other, imagine how you might bring this feeling into a quiet moment of the ceremony. Even while surrounded by people and the sounds of chairs moving and sneezes, you can find this same connection. If you feel delicate, vulnerable, unprepared, realize that this is exactly what your witnesses would like to see. So develop this part of yourselves over time. It may be uncomfortable at first. Some people have difficulty looking deeply into the eyes of another, any other, including their partner. This should not be a source of embarrassment, as some people are much more sensitive to what lives in and behind the eyes. Begin with focusing on the point between the eyes of the other and relaxing your gaze to a soft openness. Rest in the knowing that this state is the source of all creativity.

Imagine creating a time like this in your daily life. It can be a moment of walking silently in nature, eating a meal in intentional silence, meditating together, or enjoying sensual touching. Dedicating some time to silence while staying connected is a practice worth developing. It will call you out of your normal habit patterns and into some enjoyable and sensitive places. It will water seeds of intimacy that might otherwise remain dormant.

exercise

Reflective Time

Either with your partner or in self-reflection, write a vision of how you might bring this kind of silence into your daily or weekly routine together. Create one image, and turn it into an experience that you are willing to enact. Decide on the time involved. Is it for ten minutes, an hour, or the whole evening? Then make a date with your partner. Practice! Simply notice what feelings arise between you when you are together. You don't have to say everything that occurs to you. Savor your feelings and your insights and then continue reflecting. Notice how your feelings and insights change.

Both reflective time in silence and soul talk focus attention on what streams naturally through your being, the latter opening to spoken words. Soul talk includes creating time in the daily or weekly routine for either a Heart Talk (see chapter 7), poetry reading, or some way you may have of expressing the soul qualities of yourselves to each other. Having a favorite book of love poems is a good start. Read the poem, pause, and then add your own words in the same theme. Not only, "I liked that," but something in the same theme from your own life. "This reminds me of . . ." Or, "The one phrase that is most appropriate to us is . . ."

If you write, or have always wanted to write, then assign yourself the task of writing a poem to your Beloved. This may end up being something you read or sing at your wedding, or it may be something completely private between the two of you. Don't let the notion of public performance push you toward printed poems by others and away from your own words. If you feel that "Rumi says it better than I can," then learn to say it better yourself. Start as students of painting do, by copying the great masters, in this case writing out the words of Rumi, and then inserting your own words one at a time. A simple phrase of your own heartfelt words is worth more than volumes of any brilliant poet. The poet intends to raise your awareness of yourself, and then give it back to you. Receive the gift, and write your own poetry.

In a conscious relationship, you must develop this skill of soul talk. It may start very small, with just a few words, and then grow slowly. It's like putting a seed into a flowerpot and watching it grow day by day. This is the way people grow, too—slowly, urged on by the light of the sun, until something quite beautiful comes of it, a blossoming of beauty and complexity.

When you can bring that slowly grown skill into these few minutes of a conscious wedding, you accomplish several things. You demonstrate to everyone in the room that your souls know how to talk. Very importantly, you get the support of everyone there, because they now know that you are more than "an item"—you are awake and in Love, rather than asleep and in Love, a state that never lasts long. You can feel the energy surge when the witnesses really get this, and you are in the center, receiving all their good wishes. You have demonstrated to everyone—spiritual beings included—that you are willing to go to the soul level of life.

Do you see how helpful the witnesses can be? They are much more than an audience who has come to enjoy a good entertainment. They bring energy to the ceremony. They are conduits for ancestors going far back into the past, all present through those in the room with you. With good direction from you and the celebrant, they contribute to the Sacred Moment and to the ceremony that is unfolding around them. Ideally, they will support you later, as members of your community. They will love you for loving each other. They will grow from having experienced a Sacred Moment with you.

To meet them, you have to be willing to plunge into beauty. Each invitation you send out should say—not on paper but in your mind—"Come see us vulnerable, fully in our hearts in front of you, making a magical event before your eyes that you can join!" You imagine that everyone will feel invigorated, more awake, and happier—during the Sacred Moment, and after it as well.

We've talked about spontaneity and allowing for the Sacred Moment to arise as a surprise in the wedding. That obviously doesn't mean that the whole ceremony should be unplanned. Indeed, a structure for the rest of the ceremony is very helpful, crafting a container in physical and social space for the preciousness of the Sacred Moment. But when these supports seek to take over and strut their stuff, you have to defend the quiet space for soul talk from the encroachments of "things." As soul talk cannot be bought, the merchants of wedding gear will not be able to sell it to you and may not mention it. Don't let the merchants' ignorance of the Sacred Moment belittle its importance.

Let's dive in again to the feeling of the Sacred Moment.

exercise

Create the Ideal

Find a place right now to look into each other's eyes, deeply gazing. If your mind wanders, bring it back. Put your hands on each other's hearts, and just sit there. Create the ideal relationship between the two of you—the most intimate moment—right now. Make it so. Simply the two of you and your willingness to be intimate with each other. Gently reach out and, one at a time, stroke the cheek of your Beloved, in silence. Gaze into the eyes of Love.

When you have this sense of the depth of yourself, you will find the depth in your partner. Beyond any personality quirks that he or she may have, you experience the brilliance, warmth, and Love that lives inside. It has always been there, and you just need to open up to it. We know how difficult this can be, especially when you're younger and less experienced, or when you're older and have been hurt too many times, but you must persevere. When you can look into his or her eyes and feel completely safe, at home, and uplifted all at the same time, when you can feel the thrill of happiness to be alive so that you can be with this person, when you can feel that you are Divinity looking at its handiwork in your partner and that your partner is Divinity looking at its handiwork in you—even briefly—then you are ready to make time for a Sacred Moment in your wedding.

exercise

Eyes of the Heart

Look into each other's eyes and say, each to the other, "I seek to know your inmost being. I seek to know the one who sparkles in your eyes." Then wait, gazing softly (not focused on detail) into the eyes, or at the space right between the eyes. Your entire torso is a sense organ—what we call "the eyes of the heart." Open the eyes of the heart, and breathe together. You develop the patience of a naturalist or a biologist in the field, for there is a lovely shy creature in your partner, and you are waiting for it to feel safe enough to show itself to you. And you realize that you too harbor such a creature—who would like to come out but first needs to feel safe. The quiet

Love of the patient naturalist creates a protective container inside which previously hidden essentials can be revealed to the eyes of the heart.

This space needs respect. This space has no fanfare, and you don't know what might arise. Words may arise spontaneously. Let them come with joy! Proper grammar not necessary!

exercise

Soul Meeting Soul

Once again, sit or lie with each other. Words may come, but don't force them. Communication without words has soul talk in it. You don't have to look into each other's eyes; in fact, when you get really good at this, you don't have to be next to each other. For now, though, be next to each other, with no goal but to experience your soul coming out to meet the soul of the other. Agree that you are exploring this area. After a few minutes, ask each other what you have experienced. The majority of the mind tends to think about the past—movies, appointments, the last meal. What you're developing is the capacity to speak about the subtleties of the present experience in mind, heart, and body. You might speak of sensations in your body: "I feel a buzz in my lower back," or, "I feel warmth increasing in my chest." You might report an image that arises: "I see us on a mountaintop looking out over the world." You might find something in your heart: "I feel a sudden wave of intense Love for you, and then it ebbs like the tide." Follow these soul movements with each other.

In the months leading up to your wedding, these exercises can help you develop the skill of creating Sacred Moments. You might ask, "You mean to say I'm going to present our most intimate moments in front of everyone?" Yes! "You mean even in front of my mother-in law?" Yes!

Everyone melts when something truly intimate happens, as everyone can feel it. Everyone has felt that special something that can happen in the presence of two people who are so in Love and connected that they generate a field of Love—in a restaurant, or on a train, even at a political rally. This is one way the world will transform through Love.

story

DAVID   A Sacred Moment

Before we entered, our wedding director had explained to our collected friends and family that our ceremony would include an unplanned moment, because we wanted something spontaneous to arise. The witnesses were expectant and respectfully quiet. Lila and I grew quiet also. Then Lila began to sing. She sang so beautifully, each word of the song coming down like a smooth pebble into a still pond, creating ripples that thrilled through everyone present. I had disciplined myself not to plan what I would do and simply took in Lila's offering. When she had made it, I paused, circled around Lila, and began to sing tones, pitches without words, all directed to my Beloved. Though a man of words, I found my soul speech in tones pouring out from my heart. We completely opened to each other, completely offering our life and Love to each other. Everyone in the room felt it. ✤

Do you sing? Many people are embarrassed about this and say, "No, not me, never!" But how about singing to yourself, or singing along with a tune that's on the radio? Can you imagine singing a song that you really love? Maybe in the shower? Can you imagine singing to your partner, just the two of you? Don't let embarrassment get in the way. You're a couple, intimate—you can share everything, even the places where you are shy and embarrassed. Often those are the places that have the most soul in them.

Intimacy through Song

Sit with each other and sing a little song to each other. "Amazing Grace," or "Twinkle Twinkle Litle Star," or "Let It Be," or something you create. Song excites the soul and encourages it to come out. You aren't performing, and you aren't being recorded. You are bringing out the tones of your voice, which are already there, so you are simply adding emphasis to something already there. Sing to your partner, words you know, words you make up, even just tones. If this is really too much, write a quick poem and read it aloud. Poetic words spoken slowly have song in them.

Now, can you imagine singing in your Sacred Moment?

As you prepare for the Sacred Moment, you will need one element in particular—something that surrounds the Sacred Moment and also reigns inside it. That something is, paradoxically, nothing—space, the absence of busyness.

Right up to the part of the ceremony set aside for the Sacred Moment, you can have photographs, music, wise words, all of the props, but when you step into the core of a conscious wedding, the central zone, you step in without the "stuff." The flowers, cameras, dresses, even the family dramas all disappear. You step in, soul to soul, in a kind of nakedness and simplicity that frankly forms the food of souls and the food of Love—for you and for everyone in the room. This is the reason they have come, to share in this moment with you, as their souls are fed then, too. The delicacies and drinks afterward serve physical and social needs, but the Sacred Moment feeds the souls of all.

Energy Leaks and How to Fix Them

To invite the Sacred Moment, you have to be present—"conscious," as the title of this book says. You have to cultivate the ability to be "alive, awake, aware, enthusiastic" (that's a chant we sing to each other when we need reminding). You need to fill a reservoir of energy that you add to over time through healthy living and through the exercises in this book.

You also need your witnesses to have energy. In conscious weddings, as in good live theater, you can feel the river of energy flowing in from all the witnesses to the center of attention: you. In that river are Love, good wishes, adoration, excitement . . . Perhaps most powerful of all, partly because people are largely unaware of it, is simple attention. People are watching you, and it creates a river of energy. That's the main reason that people are afraid of public speaking: the power of the audience is so strong; it's unfamiliar; it's unnerving. That energy—its empowerment in the moment and its promise of continuation for years to come—is the reason that you invite all these people. A recent study shows that larger weddings lead to more stable marriages. This is why.

We have encouraged you to feel that it's all right to be unnerved, and not your usual cool and collected and under-control self. Let the celebrant and wedding director and other helpers handle the logistical and normal way of relating. Let them guide you through. They have experience working with that river of attention-energy. Let it flow through you, and enjoy the unusual fruits of it in your wedding and marriage.

To take the full opportunity here, you need those witnesses at their fullest. So we come again to the issue of electronics! Studies are now very clear that, despite the long list of the wonders of technology, cell phones in all their many names and guises are bad for your health, physically, psychologically, and spiritually. We don't want to argue the general point with you here right now; you can find the research if you're interested. However, we strongly suggest that you minimize or eradicate—for the short period of time of your wedding—photographs and phone calls and text messages sent during the wedding. "Josie's getting married RIGHT NOW!" is an actual example of a text message typed out by an excited friend; was the friend's attention available for the actual event? Banish the phones and any other things that buzz or beep or otherwise distract. Because that's the key word: distract. Distraction of attention. Attention going off in all directions is energy that ought to be in the container of the wedding, but is leaking out. This is something that you need to try to corral like horses or herd like cats.

It's challenging enough for you two to reduce the various leaks—mobile phone time, texting time, watching television, watching movies, any massively multiplayer online role-playing game (MMORPG), any video game, any alternative life through technology, watching YouTube, other grabs on your attention—for the day or days of your wedding, both before and after. Though intensely exciting, these excitements occupy a small percentage of your full capacity, and we need that broader awakeness for reception of a Sacred Moment.

It is much more challenging to change the lifestyles of your witnesses. You can restrict the leaks for the core of the wedding ceremony fairly easily, which we recommend in this book. You can put out envelopes at the front door of the wedding ceremony, into which the guests can deposit their mobile phones (reminiscent of the "leave your firearms at the door" rules in some places.) If they push back, you can say, "It's the Yerkes–Dodson Law—hyperstimulation decreases attention—and we need your attention." That might work.

You can manage the energy of close friends and family by creating a bigger distraction, so to speak: ask your key people to do things for you and for your wedding that take time. If a friend is sewing placemats for the wedding dinner or stacking firewood for a large bonfire, she or he is building energy in relation to you and not leaking it outward to some hungry website. It's very important to have jobs for everyone. Those from out of town especially need guidance. When they say, "How can I help?" you or your director need to be able to answer. Some of the best moments of a wedding gathering can occur when the men from various clans of family and friends are told, "We need a hundred chairs moved from point A to point B." Or, "There are a hundred flowers that need to be trimmed and put in vases." People seek to be distracted from their usual distractions, because deep down they want to be there for you, which means they want to add to the reservoir of energy collecting for your wedding and marriage. Help them by directing that precious attention energy.

You could name a theme for your wedding, which you put into a "save the date" announcement, later into the formal invitation, and later into a reminder. Such a theme could be "Dress as for a midsummer night's dream," or, "Bring photos of your parents who produced you, to place on our memorial table," or, "Write a short poem about the best aspects of marriage, from your own experience, so you can place these poems on our head table." We have seen all of these, and they all worked to focus the witnesses for days and weeks before the wedding. The celebrant should pick up the theme during the ceremony itself. Then you will have that much more loving energy to support your Sacred Moment.

It may take time to do all we've suggested in this chapter. We know couples who have prepared for six months and couples who have prepared for a year. If a wedding is something that you schedule without allowing the time for preparation, it will be a challenge to find the "conscious" in a conscious wedding. Love nurtured matures into something superb and very strong. It's very much worth the work.

Synergy

We can summarize what we have said about the Sacred Moment in relation to other aspects of the wedding with a diagram:

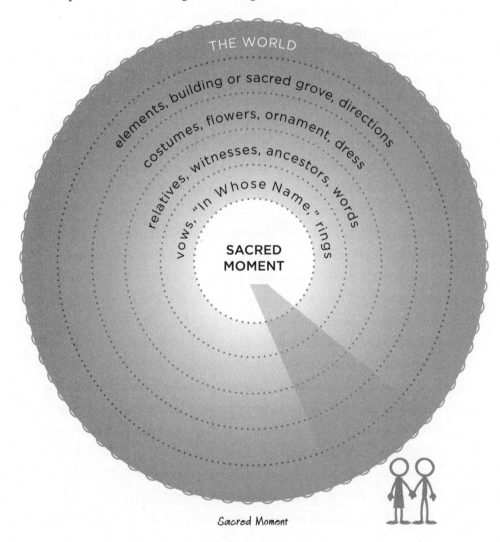

Sacred Moment

The Concentric Circles model has the story-drama at the center, where you're standing, and the ONE at the periphery; you climb Mount Maslow to find the mythic in the zone of the ONE. In a wedding, you start at the periphery, in the busy world, and travel together to the mythic in the core. Life asks you repeatedly to turn inside out. The point is: there is an inside and an outside to a wedding. At the core of the inside there lies a treasure, as engaging as the perfume of a flower, as delicate as the most perfect music that you have ever heard. The inner core is the blessing of the Sacred Moment. Around that core you build levels of container to hold and protect what lives in the center. The building, the flowers, the enactments of ancient rituals, the people with their expectations and special clothing, as well as the words of the ceremony, are circles within circles through which you will move toward the moment of transformation where true ceremony happens, where the merging is felt and something new and precious is born. The couple enters through this sequence of containers into the center. Those gathered around that core participate through witnessing. Afterward, you exit through circles until you are on the other side, a transformed person and a transformed couple. The rings on your fingers remind you of this circle. Every ceremony works this way, from aboriginal initiation rites to the coronations of kings and queens. It works better if you understand that you're going through exactly this process.

Now that we know where we are headed, we can step back to look at how the container is built, beginning with an overview of a wedding whose core was the Sacred Moment.

Example of a Conscious Wedding

chapter 12

Let's go over one actual wedding in detail. We put this here because it integrates what we've already discussed and prefigures some aspects of the wedding that we haven't talked about yet. Not all aspects of this personal account may be appropriate for your own ceremony. You get to choose what works for you. The story is written from David's point of view.

As we had attended weddings and practiced on a couple of our own beforehand, we designed a wedding ceremony that used the best of the past, with some new ideas. We chose a celebrant to manage the energetic flow and spiritual power of the ceremony itself. We chose a director to take over as master of ceremonies and to deal with the many logistical issues that would come up beforehand. We knew that these issues would be more challenging than usual because we decided to stay apart for the three days prior to the wedding. We asked for specific help in many areas, from flowers to dealing with relatives. We matched one of our friends with each of the relatives that needed assistance, and especially those relatives who were coming from out of town. This was a kind of buddy system that put younger people together with older people, to everyone's delight.

We wrote vows that formed a contract between us—a longer text than the more distilled vows we would speak in our ceremony. Having a background in theater, we knew that too many words would lose the audience, both the audience of people and the audience of unseen spirits.

We assigned many friends to take various parts in the wedding, giving directions on what was being asked of them but instructing them to contact the director if their part needed clarification. In other words, we delegated. We focused most of our attention on making ourselves as ready as possible for the core of the event, the Sacred Moment.

Three days beforehand, I moved from the house and took up residence in a small cabin. The first day, I called together ten men friends. I asked their advice about relationship and marriage. They took me on a walk into the woods. There they gathered around me and spoke sincerely and earnestly from their own life experiences. (Those same men met monthly for many years afterward to speak about the progress of their lives.) I spoke of my anxieties, past hurts, and ideals. They listened and reflected back to me what they had heard, relating what I said to their own life stories.

I hiked alone among the mountains of Colorado, marching for hours through an early autumn snow in high country. I used the time for solitude to prepare myself for the ceremony.

Lila gathered with her women friends for two days away, and shared stories and rituals. Women have a way of knowing how to honor threshold crossings. Marriage takes one over a threshold. Lila's women friends had her dance wildly in front of a bonfire to shake out past relationships and to express her yearning for the Beloved. When she had deeply released her stories of the past, the elk began to bugle loudly in the distance.

We both ate simply, and we were in a phase where we weren't drinking alcohol. Our preparation resembled that of athletes preparing for an event—this one not based on competition, but rather on running-with!

On the morning of the ceremony, I met with the men who had come early, about forty men in all. They asked me hard questions and showered me with gifts. In a ceremony, it is fine for an old friend to become stern and ask difficult questions in front of other people. The basis of trust exists already in the friendship. The men focused their questions on the most intimate details of my life, to awaken me and everyone in the room to what's important. "How will you take care of this woman?" "What does 'in sickness and in health' mean to you?" "How have you ensured that you have personal time?" In other words, how was I taking care to nourish my One? "You've divorced before. What makes you think you won't do it again?"

My answers were accepted lovingly.

At the same time, Lila met with the women who were coming to the ceremony. The women honored Lila, asked her questions to focus her attention on what this day was all about, and brought her into an awareness of the mystery and magic of the day. "Will you abandon your sisters in your women's work?" "Is this man good to you?" "Do you honor him?" "Do you nag him?" "How will you care for your own soul in this relationship?"

Forty-five minutes later, Lila and I exchanged venues, being led along different paths so that we did not see each other. I sat in the center of a large group of women, and Lila in the center of a large group of men, a first for both of us. The women asked tough questions of me, in loving protection of their sister Lila. The questions to me included: "Who are you to desire to marry our friend and sister? Present yourself! Reveal if you are worthy!" Then they honored me as representative of the masculine and of manliness.

The men honored Lila as representative of femininity, creating a thronelike chair and offering her their prayers and visions in a simple, powerful ritual. Men and women gave advice earned the hard way, through their own life experience. They did not bring books to quote from or poems to read, but spoke freely from their hearts about what life had taught them.

Then other guests arrived, and all prepared for the ceremony itself. The director had already given lists of things that needed to be done to family members and friends. Lila and I went in separate directions, first to change clothes, then out into special spots in nature, awaiting our cues to enter the ceremonial space. Lila wore a dress she had found some months previously, going back to the shop three times before she decided that this expressed what was most beautiful in her. It had dozens of chenille tassels ranging from turquoise to blue. I had had something made to coordinate with her dress.

When the guests had assembled, the director and celebrant explained to them what would happen, that photographs were not to be taken during the core of the ceremony, and that they would announce as a community at the end, "Now we pronounce you husband and wife, partners in life!" and sing "Jubilate Deo," which they then practiced. The celebrant told them about the importance of community, that by being here they were agreeing to hold two people in their hearts, in complete safety, Love, and also truth. There might come a time when they would be called upon to present strong questions and even interventions when they could see the couple going astray.

The celebrant asked for full participation through the gift of attention.

Then I was led in by a male friend, and took my place behind a translucent veil at one end of the room. Lila entered, wearing a translucent veil, and stood across from me. The celebrant asked, "David, are you willing to see your Beloved truly, and not through a veil? Are you ready to remove the veil of prejudice and ignorance and behold the soul of your Beloved?" I replied strongly, "I am ready!" The celebrant removed the dark veil from before my face and asked the same questions of Lila. "I am ready!" she said, and her veil was removed. Now we beheld each other for the first time in three days, and, in this new way, for the first time ever.

The celebrant asked, "In whose name do you marry?"

We both responded, "Love."

Various people rose to speak. An elderly scholar recited a sonnet of Shakespeare. I recall the sophistication of his feeling for the words. The poetry lifted the witnesses' awareness of the power of words. Pairs of people had been assigned to the twelve months (signs of the zodiac) and were arranged in a circle around the congregation. Each pair delivered a brief blessing from the heavens. Others had been assigned the elements of earth, air, fire, and water (placed to the north, east, south, and west), on whose behalf they conferred blessings. A representative of the fifth element, Love, which binds all elements, spoke. Two women performed a sacred dance with white veils in the style of eurythmy. In all of these ways the community participated and expressed their joy in the two marrying this day.

The celebrant announced that we were approaching the center of the ceremony. Cameras were set down. Everyone was attentive. The celebrant asked us what we shared. In unison we spoke a Shared Affirmation, "We joyfully live, love, and create in magical beauty, truth, and passion."

The celebrant guided us to state our prepared vows, which we did with enthusiasm. Then came the unplanned time, the space for the vows beyond what we had rehearsed—a time when we had pledged to be completely open to whatever happened. What would arise in this Sacred Moment? It began in silence as Lila and I stood together, permitting our shining faces to express our Love. Then from Lila emerged a beautiful song, and the words "I vow to hear the song of your soul!" I too poured forth a song, singing without words as I circled around and around my Beloved. Lila and I spoke in the simplest possible way—through tones, a few words, each a vehicle for the Love we felt for each other. The angels came, as shown by the joy in Lila and me, and as shown by the smiles on all faces and by the increase of light in the room. My whole body tingled. I felt my boundaries expand to include every shining face and golden heart. As a unified couple, we felt gratitude for each and every one present, giving freely of their attention and Love. We mirrored back that Love and attention from a dynamo of energy surging through both of us.

After a pause to savor what was living so strongly in the atmosphere, the celebrant organized the exchange of rings with a very few words about what this meant. Our rings had been made specially by a goldsmith and contained gold from our previous wedding rings, demonstrating our thanks to those who had taught us to be better partners. Lila's beloved dog, Willie, came forward with the rings hanging from a ribbon tied around his neck. We placed them on each other's hands.

The celebrant said, "As we have all perceived, you have committed yourselves to the divine relationship of marriage. As a community, we now declare . . ." That was the cue to the witnesses. In unison everyone shouted out, "We now pronounce you husband and wife, partners in life!" Then applause, the clicking of cameras that had been silenced until then, and general merriment while singing "Jubilate Deo."

We kissed, also to enthusiastic applause. As Lila and I began to leave, the celebrant asked everyone else to stay behind. After we left, the celebrant asked the guests to follow to a space outside the building, where a ceremonial dance would occur. Meanwhile, we walked to a prearranged place in the forest, where for ten minutes we spoke some but mostly gazed into each other's eyes. This had the effect of firming and integrating the event that had just occurred. We could feel the buzzing in our bodies, the dryness in our mouths, and affirm that extraordinary energies continued to surge through us.

A dance had begun and we joined it. All participated in the simple song and gestures in unison, moving as one organism in the golden light of the autumn afternoon. Afterward everyone walked to a reception hall, where an excellent meal had been prepared. Instead of champagne, a single rose was given to each person. Toasts—the wishes to the wedding couple and to everyone present for health and life-power—were made by raising the roses high into the air. The music in the background was a small string quartet, playing chamber music, rhythmic and soothing, no competition for conversation. Cakes were served. People mingled, and gifts were given to the newly wedded couple.

As the party drew to a close in a few hours, the director had arranged that some people stay behind to clean up the space. We had gone by that time, to a specially prepared cabin, to spend the night together in undisturbed peace.

A wedding does not end on the wedding day. A wedding marks a passage that one has prepared for in the months ahead and that continues to unfold in the months after. The wedding is a model for what every day can bring—celebration, smiling blessings, hard questions and sincere answers, appreciation of food and drink, appreciation of one's friends and relatives, and, most of all, an affirmation of Love in all its forms, from the most basic to the most refined.

Each wedding is unique, yet all weddings share common elements. When designing your own wedding, you can pick and choose the elements you like, and avoid the ones that don't seem to work for you. In the next chapters, we will examine the common elements and directions for creating your unique wedding.

Contracts and Vows

chapter 13

In order to arrive at a wedding ceremony as ready as possible, you have to make some important agreements with each other. Each couple makes different kinds of agreements, which ought to be unique to their situation. Because these agreements are unique, we won't be able to spell them out for you. We can, however, put the various kinds of agreements into a context that will help make sense of them all.

In the old Tarzan movie starring Johnny Weissmuller, at the end of his first lesson in English, Tarzan says simply, "Me Tarzan. You Jane." Yes! The first simple agreement! "You are you and I am I, One-to-One; now we'll swing through the jungle together and perhaps discover Two. And, if things go well, we'll experience the ONE." Your agreements will have acknowledgment of the individuals and acknowledgement of the couple, as foundation for communion.

Words are powerful. "In the beginning was the Word," proclaimed the Gospel author John, writing long ago in Ephesus. The word, spoken or written, can have great power to make something happen. You are about to "give your word" to each other.

We'll approach this through:

1. Your "Credo": what you believe about yourself.

2. Shared Affirmations to remind you of your strengths as a couple: simple, brief, and powerful foundations.

3. The "what if" scenario, leading into the legal world of prenuptial agreements: complicated, lengthy, challenging, and important.

The first two provide the beginning for social and spiritual vows that should take most of your attention. The third covers the end—the exit strategy, the retreat. Together they prepare you for the actual contracts and vows.

4. A practical and heartfelt contract that you may choose to write together, which can be lengthy and is not recited at the wedding ceremony.

5. The vows that you prepare ahead of time to say in the center of your wedding, memorized or read aloud.

6. The vows that come spontaneously in a Sacred Moment.

These are all explorations of your rules of engagement, a definition of what's fair, the good housekeeping of your relationship and marriage. We recommend that you master each of these before your wedding, and review them after your wedding—annually. Or, if there are many pieces here, review one item every month until you need to change them (in which case, consider rededication, chapter 18).

Credo

Before you engage another in vows, you have to come to know yourself—your One—a bit better. How do you define yourself? To others? To yourself? You've likely written a résumé or curriculum vitae or short bio. Those facts are true, and now we're looking for something that goes to the heart of you, a mission statement of your heart and soul, from whose foundation you can then make agreements with your Beloved. Some people have learned to write a résumé that includes beliefs, values, and goals. That's a good beginning.

We know that the human being is infinitely deep; you could answer the repeated question, "Who are you?" for hours. All the things you've said in response to the questions we've asked form part of your answer. We're seeking here that you come to know the strength of what you stand for.

Some say, "Oh, I can't do that—I need to keep my options open." Then you can say, "I am flexible."

Be patient with yourself in this. Filling in the blanks for the Credo—"What I believe is _____"—can occur at any time. Knowing yourself will assist you in making vows to another.

You can also begin to work actively with what you believe about yourself and about life. These are simple affirmations, a technique pioneered by Émile Coué, Ernest Holmes, Rhonda Byrne (*The Secret*), and others. Though shadows, knots, and thorns (see chapter 4) can block the way of a positive affirmation, they should not prevent you from voicing your ideals. At the least, use the Cherokee advice: "Be of good mind."

Shared Affirmations

We recommend a very old technique, the crafting of a Shared Affirmation, which we introduced in chapter 7. From the beginning of our relationship, we, David and Lila, have used a Shared Affirmation. This is an agreement you make together, which includes *remembering and reciting* the affirmation when things go sour, when life gets challenging. It can be as simple as "We create easily and masterfully together." Or, "Our wedding ceremony flows with grace." Or, "We are Love!" Whenever the going gets tough, you look each other in the eyes and speak these words to each other. As you've practiced these words together many times before, they cut through the obstacles of present tensions and help relax the situation.

Shared Affirmations can be more comprehensive as well, and can grow over time. The Shared Affirmation we crafted months before our wedding has tripled in length since then, every new word added after discussion, sometimes a great deal of discussion. When we say these words, all those discussions come up in our minds and hearts:

> We joyfully live, love, and create, in magical realness,
> beauty, truth, and passion. By Divine Grace, we create

ourselves—husband–wife, spiritual partners, soul partners, and earth partners—and Love-makers in joy!

You might see here dangling phrases, repetitions, and odd combinations of words. You don't know what some of it means. The best part is this: that doesn't matter! The affirmation has meaning to us, and yours should have meaning to you. After twenty years of marriage, we speak this Shared Affirmation with each other daily in complete enjoyment of the nuances and power that we have built into it. Daily? Well, all right, to be honest an average of five days every week. We recommend you begin with a much shorter Shared Affirmation and let it grow with your relationship.

When the stresses of life surge strongly and threaten to drive a wedge between us, we pause, breathe, look each other in the eyes, and say these words. The worry of the temporary storm diminishes in relation to the much greater importance of the power of our relationship.

Do you see how you can use the work you've done on social and spiritual agreements to craft a Shared Affirmation that reinforces your commitment to each other? We go through this process with each couple we work with, and recommend it to you.

One hint: Avoid "eternity," as in, "We are together for eternity." That's a long time. Leave time out of it and make your affirmations passionately in the present.

exercise

Building a Shared Affirmation

Sit with each other and speak words that have meaning to you (using what you've written in response to the "Big Why" questions in chapter 9). Just start collecting words, as you might collect seashells from the beach, one at a time: verbs, nouns, adverbs, each a different type of word. When you bring the shells home, then you can arrange them into some kind of pattern. Same with the words—you can arrange them into the pattern of a phrase or a sentence. Start simple. Both of you should participate; take turns contributing. Craft one declarative sentence. Try it out, saying the Shared Affirmation at the same time, to each other. Settle on something poetic and easy, and then speak it to each other a few times, over a few days. Add or subtract a word or phrase. Discuss it with each other. Savor the words that are now a sacred tool serving your partnership.

The "What If" Contract: Prenuptial Agreements

This next section is challenging to many. It can seem like a minefield. However, begin with the attitude that this is foundation work for creating really great vows in your wedding.

Divorce rates show that there are many couples who realize that, no matter how rosy the glow may have felt at their wedding, a time has come when they can no longer be together. We would like to help you create a relationship and a wedding so conscious that this outcome is unlikely. However, statistics indicate that the majority of adults in the West will have more than one significant relationship or marriage in their lifetime. Preparation for this possibility—when the ONE devolves into the initial One—can help you build a stronger partnership next time, and with gratitude to your teacher in how to become a better person and better in relationship—namely, your present partner.

Creating a prenuptial agreement can feel like a confrontation, and we suggest you speak openly during the process. We intend, by mentioning it here, to bring it up as a topic for you to consider. It is complex territory, and this is not the place to reach conclusions in detail, but it may be the place that helps you decide on a course of action. Heart Talk proves a dependable ally.

A prenuptial agreement basically asks many kinds of "what if" questions, such as, "What happens to our possessions and our money if the relationship changes, transforms, or completely dies?" Especially for men and women who come into a marriage with considerable material assets, this process may well be necessary, and it is usually challenging. But it is valuable for everyone, no matter what the quantity of assets! We know people for whom Granny's old desk was much more important than the bank account. It takes a great deal of maturity to entertain the possibility of dissolution at the same time as you are planning a marriage. You have to find a way to do that in such a way that you experience the discussion as constructive to the relationship, not destructive.

A formal prenuptial agreement does not address the important complementary question: "What happens to our emotions and interconnected energy if the relationship changes, transforms, or completely dies?" Not addressing the emotions, while concentrating only on the *things* in your life, often seems bizarre. You need to do both, and we give you some suggestions in Part Three. When you see the mediator or lawyer, the meeting will be about things and money. You will have to do the rest, or find a mentor or counselor who can help you with the realm of feelings.

Couples often say, "We're in love. We'll never separate. We'll never sue each other." Let's accept that those promises are true. However, let's examine a parallel situation. People have come to us saying, "I know you need some yard work done and I'll do it for you. You can pay me cash under the table and avoid paying taxes and worker's compensation. If something happens to me, I won't sue you. I swear it!" We believe that's true—if an accident happened, the person wouldn't sue. But his family—the spouse, parents, children, and lawyers—would be seeking financial support for medical care wherever they can find it, and understandably so. Accidents happen that aren't anyone's fault. As we value the people who work for us, we use the worker's compensation program every time and pay them above, not under, the table.

Marriages don't come with worker's compensation insurance packages. If an accident happens, the ex-spouse may stand by the pledge not to sue, but the family and others will come looking for "what is fair." The prenuptial agreement is the closest thing you have to a worker's compensation package. It ought to work to everyone's benefit.

Lila is a trained mediator, and is very supportive of this emerging profession as a way of creating agreements that can serve a couple considering marriage. The beauty of mediation is that it will assist the couple in discovering for themselves what is best for them, rather than relying on the opinions of family, friends, or lawyers.

Mediation focuses on the values that the partners share, and takes a less adversarial approach than many lawyers take in considering the many "what if" questions. The mediator's environment can provide support and safety for a couple who choose to enter a prenuptial agreement. The end result through mediation is most often a Memorandum of Understanding. The document can be a legally binding agreement created in consultation with lawyers, which you sign and have witnessed. The marrying couple can also create an understanding between them that they pledge to honor. There is a great deal involved in crafting a prenuptial agreement, and you'll need to determine the specific intent and content for yourselves. It can help a great deal to have a professional lead you through the steps so that you don't wound each other.

Some questions will be covered by your will, which is often neglected or overlooked in marriages between younger people. An agreement at this level is worth taking some time to consider, especially for older couples and those entering into second or third marriages, since more assets may have accumulated. The questions can be demanding, but you explore them more easily when the relationship is healthy and you intend to create a life together.

"What if a brick falls off a building onto your head?"

"What about your partner's head?"

"What if your partner runs off with someone else?"

"What if your partner doesn't tell you about an affair?"

"What if your partner begins to mistreat you?"

"What if you decide that things just aren't working out?"

The "what if" scenarios can go on like that. It may seem as if the mediator or lawyer calls into question every foundation of your tender Love for each other—indeed, dismantling and destroying them methodically, one at a time. The lawyer can cite case after case in which people have treated each other in the most appallingly cruel ways. We would imagine that the cruel couples didn't have a conscious relationship, but this need not be true; divorce can bring out the darkest of shadows, thorns, and knots in unexpected ways in people who otherwise have been apparently communicative and warm-hearted. Nearly every "messy divorce" comes about because two people who once came into union have changed in ways that they did not anticipate, and they had no road map for this unwelcome territory. Part of that map is the prenuptial agreement.

For some couples, an informal agreement can include the commitment to address some of the above eventualities by stating something like, "If one of us is attracted to another person, we agree to speak about it with each other honestly, and to see a counselor before taking any damaging action." There are ways to create levels of agreement without involving lawyers. Our culture jumps into litigation very quickly, and we have lost some of the wisdom-ways that tribal cultures have used to deal with these situations. Agreeing to having friends and family support you in a Council Circle—basically a Heart Talk with a group—would be one way of seeking support if tensions arise that are greater than you can handle as a couple alone. Professionals trained in psychotherapy and couple's counseling are there to help you before you abandon the relationship.

We speak more about the end result of divorce in Part Three. A well-thought-out prenuptial agreement can be a safety net that actually helps prevent divorce from happening, or, if it does happen, helps make it smoother and less damaging.

We had our own drama about our prenuptial agreement. We are able to laugh at the story now (told below), but it made us both anxious at the time. Making these agreements on the healthy side of a marriage can save much heartache if changes do occur down the road, as it can be very difficult to come to an agreement if you have become estranged. We offer some suggestions here to help you recover from the strain of designing a prenuptial agreement. They are based in the questions you worked through in chapter 9, supplemented with the Heart Talk process described in chapter 7. If you are really stuck, you may need to go through the release and rechoose process of Part Three.

story

LILA   The Prenuptial Trial

David and I decided to create a prenuptial agreement. I had very little financial complexity in my life, and he had rather a lot! He had also been through two divorces, and it was essential to him that he feel "safe" going into his third marriage.

I was very easygoing about the whole thing, and worked with a lawyer of my own to sort through the agreement that David's lawyer sent us. We talked it through, and I signed it . . . then came home and, totally unexpectedly, went into a rage. I was seeing double at the awareness that I had just planned the "demise" of our relationship and, in so doing, had given away much of what "might have been mine" if that demise had come sooner rather than later. (Our design stipulated that at the end of ten years, our marriage would hold all assets jointly, but not before then.)

It was a big double bind, because I was furious over a failure that I had no intention of creating but had agreed to imagine in order to help David feel safe in the present. Rather than fight, we worked a few of the exercises in chapter 7. In fact, that's how some of them were invented. At the end of the process, David was ready to let the contract go, and I was clear that it didn't matter. I knew my trust was truly being placed in a higher frequency, and I needed only to have my emotions heard and felt. I didn't need to change the contract. We emerged from the whole experience much stronger and more aware of the complexities of our union. And I learned that this man could hear and appreciate my emotions without being scared off. I also saw that it was more important to be heard than to make a legal change in the contract itself. 🌼

There is one more important opportunity in the prenuptial process. Most states and countries say that, at the termination of your relationship, you split whatever assets were generated between the time you married and the time of the termination. What was owned before the marriage isn't split, but belongs to the one who brought it into the relationship. (States and countries differ in their laws about divorce, so you have to check this point.) If you find you are anxious about splitting what is earned and built from the wedding day to the termination of the marriage, this is an excellent time to ask yourself how you have not been including your future spouse in your life. We suggest you consider that, in a conscious partnership, there is so much mutual support that each party readily agrees that the other has shared in his or her accomplishments.

An interesting situation occurs when one person, let's say the man, has invented something or started a company, while the woman has helped by tending the household and raising the children. The invention or company has not realized its potential. The woman has skimped to support the process. From a purely financial point of view, a settlement would seek to include future possibility, in the form of ownership of stock in the company. However, the emotional cost of continuing to relate to an estranged partner over many years is immense. We recommend settling for the present value of any assets, or a fixed percentage of a future sale. Alimony (payments to your spouse) can encourage the worst consequence, not letting go. We know a man who divorced his wife thirty years ago and has not spoken with her since that time, who nonetheless sends her a goodly amount of money every month. Developmentally this arrangement pulls both of them backward.

When children are involved, the rules change. Not every young couple realizes the immense responsibility that they undertake in having children. You have to take the time to imagine what it would be like to bear and nurture children. We ask about that in the questions in chapter 9. Use any of the other tools we've presented to ask the question, "What would our life be like with children?" Only then can you contemplate how you would care for those children if life circumstances were to pull you apart. Single parents have a very hard time of it, and you need to make sure that this is discussed beforehand. You're writing a contract for young ones that may not exist! This is where a mentor can assist you in understanding what life is like with children.

Make sure that you both understand the reasons for any provisions in a contract that you sign.

The prenuptial discussion, while uncomfortable, can reveal hidden fears that may lurk in the marriage, and these are best faced, armed with your Shared Affirmation, early on!

exercise

Playing with Imagined Fears

Play with the whole drama, asking "what if" questions and then trying on a possible outcome and saying what feels best. You could begin, "I meet Prince Charming and feel a deep unstoppable urge to go off with him." Develop the story into a playful piece of theater. The "Yes, and . . ." platform is perfect: "Yes, and we ride our white horses to a grand castle!" "Yes, and the castle gates are closed because the Prince has been behind on his tribute to the King and we have to camp out under an oak tree." What happens next? What arises in your imagination?

Rather than your fiancé becoming hurt by this imagination, you can frolic together: "Where are you going—I want to come too!" or, "I'd hope for your sake that the reality was as good as the fantasy!" or, "I know you'll soon get bored with riding white horses and always dressing in evening gowns." Play. Engage with territory that might really be a fear for you, but attempt to be lighthearted about it for the sake of exploring it. This exercise will help you both to identify any fears that you have been avoiding speaking about. You can then address these fears in a prenuptial agreement.

Why do we talk about prenuptial agreements and imagining the worst in a chapter on wedding vows? Because you will discover in this process some things you will wish to add to your vows, likely to the long vows which you write but don't speak, and perhaps to the shorter ones, the ones you speak at your wedding. Locate the landmines now, and defuse them. Then it's safe to walk anywhere.

The First Step in Creating Vows

In between the simple technique of Shared Affirmations and the complicated trial of the "what if," there is the realm of the practical agreements you will make with each other. These can be stated in your wedding vows, or they can be spontaneous statements made in a Sacred Moment. Or they can be written down in a contract between the two of you, witnessed by your closest friends. In chapter 9, you had a preliminary chance to get clear about what those vows might include—indeed, they include every aspect of your lives!

How much comes into the actual ceremony? The essence of you ought to be there in the ceremony, not all the details about your agreements. We recommend working this out beforehand. Whatever format this takes, we'll refer to it all for the moment as "vows," saving the term "wedding vows" for the distillations that show up in the ceremony. Some people have said to their partner, "You take care of the wedding—I'm not very good at that sort of thing. I'll say whatever you like." "Taking care of the wedding" might make sense for the secondary items like the flavor of the cake or the number of flower vases, but it's never true of the vows.

Vows that promise the sky are not very useful. You can tell that people who make all-and-everything-forever vows have not gone through the process we're about to outline.

You have to start from the realities of where you are right now. Don't promise something that you can't deliver. Fantasies are fun, but they won't convince your witnesses, or your own souls, that you've really shown up for the ceremony.

Vows are sacred promises. Often they are spoken in the context of a deity of some kind, the one who oversees the vow, who helps you hold it and lets you know when you've failed to keep it. Remember a time when you said something like, "I swear to God . . ." and then followed it with a statement of some kind, quite possibly something impulsive. Be careful what you invoke (recall the "In Whose Name" exercise) and what you are swearing.

Vows use words. It's easy to say, "Words can't express . . ." or, "Words fail!" But find the way to say the words. Recall what Rumi says: "Tender words we spoke to one another are sealed in the secret vaults of heaven. One day like rain, they will fall to earth and grow green all over the world." The words become carriers of a tenderness so potent that they hold life force itself.

Vows can be thin filaments of wispy intention or sudden reactions to life's challenges, not worth remembering. Or vows can be strongholds of your firmest visions and values—practical, grounded, backed up by your heartfelt intention, and supported by the name you invoke.

We are going to recommend something that certain traditions always took for granted, before "romantic love" became the norm. Marriages based solely on romantic love do not have a great track record. The flash-fire of hot-sex romance can easily be extinguished, while the well-crafted relationship will endure and keep the embers glowing through many attempts to quench them.

We suggest that you create a contract between you. This contract would be too long to recite at the ceremony; you would write out and keep a copy of it. In the Jewish tradition, the couple crafts such a document over time, then frames it and places in a prominent location in the home. Making it public helps to keep these agreements in the foreground. It provides an "organizing principle" for you to work with in the face of many relational issues that will arise over the years. And it may be something that you need to renegotiate consciously every five years.

If you have read this and said, "Oh, no, we don't need any formal stuff; our love will smooth out all these details and take us through any conflicts," then you need to take some time with the questions in chapter 9. Those will remind you that relationship is more than rosy glow, that there are many areas of life that need to be discussed and agreements that must be made. The very people who drift on pink clouds of love are those who later argue about whose dirty dishes are now in the kitchen sink. All human beings love the pink clouds! That's fine. In addition to the pink clouds, however, we recommend working all the levels of relationship. That includes mundane details on the one hand and spiritual intentions on the other.

Pause to Make Some Decisions

You have choices to make in this process of contracts, agreements, and vows. Consider now what your needs are, as it will make going through this material a bit easier. We recommend that you use all three of the following.

1. Do you wish to have a written contract that you keep somewhere? If so, make the commitment to take the time to craft it carefully. (We'll talk more about that in the next section.) This will involve writing up all the points that you've agreed upon, social and spiritual. There will be times when you will want to refer to these words. Remember that marriage is a fast road to personal development, and this document can be a lifesaver in times of stress.

2. Do you wish to pronounce a shorter version of this contract at the ceremony? These will be your wedding vows, in whole or part.

3. Would you like the ceremonial vows to be words from your heart only, as spontaneous words spoken in a Sacred Moment? You can still create a written contract that makes you feel secure, while leaving space for your wedding vows to be created in the moment.

4. Are you ready to create different sets of vows that you agree to review every year or five years?

Creating the Contract Together

Go back to the words that you wrote in answer to question 1 in chapter 9 (which are supplemented by the second round of "The Big Why," question 30).

Sit together and highlight the words, yours and your partner's, that are strongest and brightest for you. You may wish to edit and embellish ideas that were just beginning there. What do you agree about? Cocreate a contract, using the same categories as the questions, from the Physical through to the Spiritual, and don't forget the Sexual. This document may end up being several pages long. You may call it something like "What Being Married Really Means to Us."

Imagine for a moment that you were about to go into a fifty-year business partnership that would affect hundreds of people's lives, and potentially involve millions of dollars. Well, guess what! You are doing just that, and this exercise is really worth the time and attention it takes to produce a document strong enough to last through the years ahead. We recommend that you make it beautiful, with calligraphy, photographs, and artwork. Hang it somewhere in your home, and agree to read it every year on your anniversary. Agree also to change it if it has become outmoded.

Here are some examples of statements you could make. Obviously, of the first group, only one of the three can be chosen:

- We will share household responsibilities, including cleaning up the house and yard every Sunday afternoon.

- While Ann is in medical school, George will take care of the household chores, including shopping, cooking, and cleaning up.

- Fran will do all the cooking, and Dan will do all the dishes.

Other examples include:

- We agree to respect our different spiritual orientations, and will not interfere with religious ceremonies or festival days observed by the other.

- John does not have to be present at Jane's family reunion but will support Jane's attendance by covering her household chores. (Or, John agrees to attend Jane's family reunion every second year.)

- We will do everything possible to ensure clean air and water for our children.

- Arthur has the car on Mondays, Wednesdays, and Fridays, and Sally the rest of the week.

- I will look at you, and you at me, with a sparkle in my eye, and I will beam appreciation for the whole extent of your being.

- I will protect you in public and private.

You see, these agreements can be very broad or very specific.

You will notice that there are social and practical vows in what you have put together: how you agree to relate to friends and relatives, how you agree to use physical spaces, how you agree on your "responsibilities" in the world, and that sort of thing. Put those on one side of a piece of paper.

You will also find spiritual vows to each other—what the souls agree on. The spiritual agreements can be very large and inclusive. They can be vague to others, but as long as they are clear to you two, that is acceptable. They can include what we called the nonnegotiable vows—what you would agree soul to soul no matter what else happened—and they can include the life of feeling in everyday terms. Put those on the other side of the paper.

The social and practical side shows how the two Ones can work as Two. The spiritual side shows how Two can become ONE.

What is it important to agree on? Does he like to read passages of Søren Kierkegaard aloud to himself each Sunday at noon? You may not need to come to an agreement about this, because it doesn't really interfere with anything. Does he like to watch action movies at high volume late at night? You will have to come to an agreement about this. Practical things, details and more details, build to whole ways of desiring to live. Work these things out ahead of time. These agreements become a great strength in a couple.

Let yourself be guided by your search for "This I believe, and this I stand for!"

exercise

Coming to Agreement

Let's have some fun with the fringe items. That gives you some practice for the big ones. Even if you don't have these particular quirks, talk about them anyway—what would you do if you split on these issues?

- Does one of you watch the Super Bowl every year? With beer and popcorn? Does the other one watch too, or prefer to be far away? Who cleans up afterward? Work it out as an agreement.

- Is there a difficult relative? We'll call him Uncle Robert. Describe Uncle Robert's traits—what is he like? Do you share the same view of him, or do you differ in your perceptions? What are the expectations for dealing with Uncle Robert?

- Have you noticed any personal habits in each other that you should talk about now? Chewing ice with loud crunching noises, leaving dirty laundry in a heap at the top of the stairs, or something like the following story?

story

DAVID   Juicy

Early on in our relationship, I observed that Lila often ate with her fingers, and made loud chewing noises. I used a fork, knife, and spoon and wondered if Lila had been brought up by hillbillies. I didn't talk to her about this for the longest time (meaning, in this case, three weeks). Then I finally confessed this great difficulty with her behavior. She laughed and laughed. I thought my observation would be a big blow to her, but she found it greatly humorous. She thanked me for my observation and said she would agree to notice this more about herself.

The next day Lila invited me to dinner. When I arrived, she had made a bright, warm fire in the fireplace, spread a blanket and some towels on the floor, and laid out a meal of poached salmon with fresh mango and papaya slices on a platter. She suggested we disrobe and sit opposite each other on the floor, and then feed each other with our fingers. She fed me pieces of salmon and then dripping pieces of ripe mango. Then she invited me to feed her. The juices slid down my wrist onto my forearm, and down my chin onto my chest. Juicy! It was a glorious sensual experience, and at the end I felt initiated into the joys of food and this beautiful woman in a completely new way.

Though Lila ceased smacking her mouth when she ate, she continued to eat with her fingers when it moved her, and I enjoyed her thoroughly in her sensual love of food through touch as well as taste. This became a vow. I vowed that I would appreciate Lila's deep enjoyment of eating, and learn from it. I confess that in private I now sometimes lick my fingers and my plate, lapping up all the juices. Life has become much more juicy. ❁

The vows that are more serious often have to do with large demands on your attention. What about children? Who will care for them? Perhaps more important, what is your way of making decisions about who will care for them? You could take all of the questions in chapter 9, one by one, and create agreements around them. This can be a long document! And—good news—you've done most of it, although likely with a wink and nod rather than writing down your agreements. We recommend that you write them down.

We suggest that one of your agreements be as follows:

We agree to support each other in our growth as full and complete human beings, through all the changes that may occur.

That is an alternative version of the "in sickness and in health" phrase of the standard Christian wedding.

We have supervised weddings where the bride and groom are so proud of the accomplishment of this list that they would like to read it to each other. We recommend against that because it taxes the energy of your witnesses, whom you need for the remaining parts of the core of the ceremony. In one wedding we attended, the couple did read their list, ten minutes each—justifiably proud of what they had crafted. After a while the witnesses became restless and their precious attention wandered.

Print these agreements, and display them on a side table or altar at the wedding or at the reception. Post them in your house and agree to review them once a year.

Crafting the Wedding Vows

Now you distill the longer document you have created into something that can go into a ceremony. Condense; essentialize; articulate the nuggets.

exercise

Choice

Reference the larger contract, if you have written one together. Reflect on all the content, and on the power of these words that you have created together. You are vowing to share the adventure of life with this person, to the very best of your ability. Imagine that you are alone with him or her for this wedding; no one else is around, and you are pledging your life, expressing your love. Take up a pen and simply write to him or her, two to five sentences:

"My Beloved _____ , I choose to marry you! As for myself and my life and my values, I also choose . . ."

Let the words flow, and don't worry about perfection. Go for feeling. What does your soul wish to say to the soul of your Beloved about your choices? Don't wait for the wedding for these words to come. Practice now!

Vows to Be Spoken in the Wedding

We recommend that people not read in the ceremony, if at all possible. The reading part of the brain seems to cut off the heart energy of the words, and the warm connection to those listening to the reading. You can train yourself to read aloud in an alive and interesting way, but it takes training—it does not come naturally. If you decide you must read, we suggest you ask for very honest feedback from your friends—or, better, a voice coach—about how interesting your reading voice sounds. That also goes for those you may have asked to read an important passage from a special book.

Here is one recommendation for the moment of the Vow:

1. Write out the words that you really wish to say.

2. Come close to memorizing them.

3. On a 3 x 5 card, write a word or two that represents the whole thought to you. People sometimes bring 3 x 5 cards covered in small print. That's the contract whose design ought to have preceded the wedding. It's not for the wedding itself. A few key words or phrases should be enough.

4. Ahead of time, ask the celebrant to remind you, at the moment of the vows, to take a deep breath and speak slowly. You can also give the celebrant your 3 x 5 cards, and ask for prompts to remind you of a key word or the beginning of a sentence.

5. Look at those words, then speak from your heart. The energy and language of the heart will glow in the memory of everyone present—in yours most of all.

Often someone who has just been married will fret, "Oh, I forgot so much of what I wanted to say!" Now is the time to plan for that—beforehand. You negotiate now the terms of the marriage, and write down all the words that you might "forget."

You might also ask the celebrant to read the words you've written, preceded by "Repeat after me." The celebrant reads one phrase at a time, and you repeat the phrase. That way you can make sure that the words you wished to have in the ceremony show up there.

Do you see how you're creating a foundation for the spontaneity of the Sacred Moment? The wedding vows may be wholly or partly scripted. They are not the Sacred Moment. If you have memorized words to say, you can be proud of yourself for remembering; however, that isn't the complete openness of the Sacred Moment.

The Sacred Moment

The opportunity of the Sacred Moment is too important to miss. We've spent an entire chapter defining it (chapter 11), and need only mention here that it ends our discussion of the types of vows that you could craft.

The Sacred Moment defines the core of a wedding. Everything else has been there to support this expression of heart and soul. For this the witnesses have been waiting. Amid all the preparations jammed into the days before a wedding, it is always a miracle that the souls can find each other and proclaim their Love strongly and clearly. Each time it is a victory, a victory to be the one expressing this Love, and a victory for the witnesses to behold.

Broken Vows

Many of us have daunting memories of vows we have taken and broken—or of promises given by others that have been broken. Such betrayals are so commonplace that one wonders why we try again and again. Where would the movie industry be without story after story of betrayal?

The contrast of vows far too large for any human being to fulfill, followed by the crushing pain of betrayal, is not to be underestimated. We suggest you look closely at the vow you are about to speak in sacred space, and determine if it is one you can honestly make with the intention to do your best to fulfill it. In Part Three of this book, we speak briefly about ceremonies to release one another from vows. There are vows you will make to the soul of your partner that perhaps you would never break or release. And there are vows that you need to let go if the situation changes.

Make your vows honest and appropriate. Be careful even of playful vows—"I vow to honor your Sunday morning private reading time forever." So simple to say at the time, but what happens twenty years down the road? You don't need to say it that way. You can say, "I honor your passion for private study," and stand by this promise—but not give away all your Sundays forever. If Aunt Marge has an accident on a Sunday morning, you won't have to feel like you're betraying a vow by asking your spouse for help.

Let your vows emphasize the feeling between you. The specific agreements can go into the "What Being Married Really Means to Us" document, the one that you get to amend every five years.

Review of Contracts, Vows, and Affirmations

We have distinguished several agreements that could be called types of vows. They are all important—important enough that they need to be reviewed every year or five years.

1. Your Credo, what you believe about yourself, when made consciously, becomes a kind of vow to yourself.

2. Shared Affirmations that you can use at any time to recall the strengths of your relationship. You can say these in the wedding, now, or at any time. This is the minimum daily nourishment for the relationship.

3. Contracts you make with the "what if" professionals, either lawyers or mediators. The prenuptial agreement can be a minefield that you defuse, and an exercise that helps you better understand your vows to each other.

4. Promises and intentions that you make in a private contract written between you and your partner, to be reviewed every five years, covering the many areas of life mentioned in the questions of chapter 9. We call this document "What Being Married Really Means to Us." You can title it whatever you like. It can be one page long or many pages long.

5. A prepared set of words to deliver in the wedding ceremony, what we call the formal wedding vows. We recommend that you not read them, though you can cue yourself with a card with one or more words on it. If you must include a certain set of words for the sake of your religion, you may choose to do so here.

6. A vow that may arise spontaneously in a Sacred Moment, something unrehearsed and packed full of life energy, popping up anywhere in the ceremony! This doesn't substitute for the formal wedding vows (or the contracts in items 3 and 4 above). In the core of the wedding, you make space for the Sacred Moment, and it may come there . . . or at another time.

Congratulate yourself and each other. You have just completed the foundation of a grand building. As with all foundations, you don't see them except when they're being built. There will be times when you are very grateful for the solidity that you feel beneath you.

Building Materials for the Wedding

The previous chapters have all been important foundation work. Now that you have a foundation, you can begin to build the structure of the wedding itself. You could add boards and nails. You could add ropes for tensegrity structures, such as Buckminster Fuller's grand domes. Or you could combine grand logs, large lumps of clay, and balloons! The point is that you sculpt an event in the creation of physical spaces, and in what occupies those spaces. What you create will combine powers of tension (ropes) and compression (logs). In other words, some aspects you can pull on and they will hold, and some parts you can stand on, and they will hold—all holding because you have created a strong foundation.

We are fanciful in this picture of the architecture of your wedding because we invite you to think about your wedding as something that you sculpt. There are many layers of a structure that can house a Sacred Moment. You can build the experience from a variety of architectural materials. These materials needn't be expensive. Recent studies suggest that lower-cost weddings lead to marriages that are more resilient over the years. The best parts cost only your time to fashion them into the shape that will serve the wedding experience and the marriage beyond.

Planning the Ceremony

The Intention

What is your specific vision for the ceremony you are about to create? It is like the mission statement for a company. Example: "We wish to cocreate a ceremony of our marriage that reflects the love, joy, and commitment that we feel as a couple." Or, "We cocreate our rededication of relationship through a joyful and inspiring ritual that releases the past and opens to new possibility for the future, to be witnessed by those whom we love." Some people don't prepare and, when asked, answer, "We want to have a good time!" You can do better than that. An intention uses a Shared Affirmation for the wedding.

exercise

"Yes, and . . ." for a Wedding

This extends the "Yes, and . . ." exercise that we gave in chapter 7. What is the intention statement for your ceremony? This is a cocreation, involving both of you. Greet your partner's ideas with a "Yes, and . . ." rather than a "No, but . . ." This will keep the energy flowing and fun! If too many intentions pour out, fine—go with the exercise and do the pruning later. For now, write them all down. You could begin with "The morning of the wedding dawns with bright red and orange in the sky." "Yes, and . . ."

In Whose Name Are You Being Married?

In chapter 5, we recommended techniques to determine the vibration, breath, or name of the power that stands behind your relationship. Your ceremony derives its focus and strength from this name. You may choose more than one name. When the celebrant invokes a presence for the whole room, she or he will invoke this name or names.

David and Lila work with clients on "In Whose Name" from the very first meeting. It often takes a few meetings to discover those powers or principles upon which the couple agrees. We often wonder why people have not done this work before. However, practically speaking, these are powers that you must identify and call in for your wedding. They ought to be part of at least three of the six forms of vows that we reviewed in chapter 13.

Who Serves as Your Celebrant?

There are individuals within every religion who can lead you on a path toward a meaningful wedding. They can make space within the traditional form to discover the Sacred Moment, and include all the important features that you discover in this book. However, a spiritually powerful person may not accept you as a client. "What?" you say. Read on.

story

DAVID   Rejection by the Expert

When I was first married, at age twenty-two, my prospective bride and I happened to know the daughter of the Episcopal bishop of the Eastern United States. We thought with satisfaction, "How easy is that? Now our wedding will have a charismatic authority and power that will impress all our friends!" When we approached this man to ask if he would supervise and sanctify our marriage, we were fully confident he would agree to guide us and bless us.

His first question surprised us. "Are you members of the Episcopal Church?"

"Well, no, we aren't." Why should that matter?, we thought.

"Then I won't be able to help you."

Stunned, we left. This was a very good lesson. It pointed up the fact that my young bride and I were seeking a stamp of approval from "someone spiritual" and "someone impressive and an authority figure." We realized that this man served those who had made a commitment to a particular brand of religion—a commitment we were not ready to make.

We ended up with a very good man, a Christian who was open to all religions, who was happy to plan our wedding with us and then stand before us to pronounce us husband and wife.

What David and his bride wanted the bishop to bring to their ceremony was a sense of tradition without the details of that tradition, the power of a doctrine of faith without responsibility to believe that doctrine, a blessing without obligation in the other direction. They wanted a Guiding Hand to take them through a conscious wedding to something buzzing, light-filled, and holy. The bishop might have been able to do that. But his time was full with the good Episcopalians who wished to marry, following the exact order of service laid down in the Episcopalian Prayer Book. David and his bride wanted something outside the specific formality of the Episcopal wedding. They didn't know it at the time, but they were looking for guidance toward a Sacred Moment.

Do you need someone official? In fact, do you need a celebrant at all? We think you do. Beyond the usefulness of having someone to sign a marriage license, it is very helpful to have someone lead the two of you through the steps of the ceremonial process. That way, you don't have to think too much in your logistical mind. You can tend your vulnerable heart, which is meant to blossom in the Sacred Moment. Being told what to do, and trusting the person who tells you, permits you to open to inspiration rather than having to be in charge.

If you do not find someone in one of the formal religions, there are now celebrants who are not affiliated with any denomination. We have used the term "celebrant" to define the role fulfilled in various traditions by priest, imam, rabbi, pastor, and minister. Some will understand the approach of celebration and Sacred Moment that we present in this book, and some will not.

A powerful celebrant will help you draw the powers of light, and the powers of spirit, into the ceremony. Perhaps a friend can do this, but better to rely on someone who knows how to manage energy, ceremony, and groups of people.

Before the actual ceremony, we like to work with people for three full sessions, in which we become very clear about the ceremonial tools in this book: "In Whose Name," the Shared Affirmation, and, of course, an understanding of the Sacred Moment and how to prepare for that. As celebrants, our job is to help the couple decide what building materials are appropriate for the ceremony. Does Uncle Robert (our name for the high-maintenance relative) have to deliver his favorite Kahlil Gibran passage in the ceremony, or is that best done at a gathering afterward? Sometimes we've been asked to speak to Uncle Robert, because the marrying partners know that to them he will insist on his contribution.

That's a positive function of a celebrant for you—to take on the strong-willed relatives. It's not the function of a celebrant to arrange for rooms for the reception and work out the menu. That's for the director (see next section).

We will also question where importance is being placed—what seems to be taking most of your time? If we find out that the bride-to-be and her mother have tried on twenty dresses and still haven't found "the right one," we as celebrants will ask what's really going on here. Not that we would necessarily disagree with this use of your time and resources—in fact, this may be the very best forum for conversations between mother and daughter, in between the fittings and the "oohs" and "aahs."

Primarily, the celebrant is there to remind you over and over again about the importance of preparation for the Sacred Moment. Secondarily, their job is to lead you through the many steps of a wedding ceremony. Perhaps most important, the celebrant is there to bless you—but let's discuss what that means.

Blessing in this context means:

- Organizing the warm flow of attention of the witnesses to focus on support and Love for you.

- Organizing the flow of attention from those beings and principles that you named to focus on support and Love for you.

- Organizing all the structural elements of the architecture of your wedding so that they serve these flows of Love and goodwill.

You will likely not take the celebrant into your future life. You will take the witnesses and those "in whose name" you were married. The celebrant serves as a catalyst, through word and through touch, for these relations to your future.

Who Is the Director or Wedding Planner?

Who should be in charge of your wedding? You are, up to a point. After that point, which might be several days before the wedding ceremony or even sooner, it's not you. You have a different job. Many couples raise their eyebrows at this proposal, and a kind of panic sets in. Who will put everything in place in just the right way? Who will make sure that everything on the list gets handled? Who will handle Uncle Robert or Aunt Marge?

We have come to a wedding ceremony an hour ahead of the scheduled time, as we were officiating, and found the bride hard at work on the floral arrangements. She had boxes of flowers and was trimming their ends, putting them in vases, and rushing—actually running—from place to place to get everything perfect. She hadn't dressed yet, and there was so much to do! Even after everything we had said concerning calm and openness before the ceremony, there was the bride running about, panicked. We learned right there to insist that you have a director.

Every performance has a director. Even a one-man or one-woman theater show has a director who helps the actor take a script from the page into action on a stage. Sometimes a celebrant performs parts of this role. But we're talking about something else. We're talking about a friend or a sister or a brother or a cousin, or perhaps someone you hire, who literally takes charge.

The director receives all the phone calls. The director deals with the problem relatives, or knows whom to call to deal with them. The director finds rides to and from the wedding and the reception and the various houses where people might be staying. The director makes sure that someone else is doing the flowers at the last minute.

Most important, the director becomes the protector of your spaciousness, which is the foundation of your Sacred Moment. We sent the bride who was fussing with the flowers away and found someone else to finish that job. We reminded the bride that she had a larger job—to get ready for the Sacred Moment. She let go of the flowers being perfect, and worked on the perfection of herself and the core of the wedding—and in the end she did fine.

This job of director or wedding planner or organizational whiz or facilitator can be large, depending on the size and ambitions of the wedding. That's why you may shy away from asking someone for this kind of help. But the job must not be done by you. You have to ask for help. If you show up at the wedding frazzled, all the flowers in the world will not help you find your composure for the Sacred Moment. So we say again, what's really important? Flowers, or your conscious wedding? You choose. At this point you will hopefully choose the conscious wedding. Know that pressures will arise nearer to the date to force you into caring more for the details than for the core. It is best to be prepared. Find a director.

One of the director's jobs may be to speak to the gathered group before you enter, to alert them to the fact that this is a conscious wedding and they need to stay awake. The celebrant can do this too, but the director may have more of the logistical facts at his or her command. About logistical matters, it may be easier for the director to announce the order of events to your witnesses at the beginning of the wedding.

Who Is "Giving the Bride Away"?

If there's not a father, you can consider mother, other family members, even previous husbands or partners! A bride might not feel the need to be given away and decide to walk alone, giving herself. Or you might have two older chaperones, one for the bride and one for the groom, who escort them to the center of the ceremony. Some people bring their friends into this role, especially in rededication ceremonies and in weddings of older couples.

If you have a father bring the bride, we suggest the following procedure. The father brings the bride down the aisle, with bride on the left and father on the right. The celebrant asks, "Who brings this bride to this man?" The father answers, "I do, as her father," or something like that. Then the father takes the right hand of the groom in a handshake, looks him in the eyes, and they make a silent agreement right there to support this relationship, one that the father has tended for many years. With his left hand, the father then takes the bride's left hand and places it into the right hand of the groom. This exchange makes a very powerful and touching statement. In a few weddings, the mother has come along as well for this blessing of the hands. With bride's left hand in groom's right hand, they can now stand together, side by side. (Be sure to rehearse the hand movements.)

If you wish, your celebrant could then create a symmetry by asking, "Who brings this groom to this woman?" Then the mother of the groom—or a daughter from a previous marriage or the best man or someone else—could place the left hand of the groom into the bride's right hand.

Who Else Is Involved in Your Ceremony?

Those you invite to your wedding ought to be asked by the celebrant to support your union. They have a job: to be present at the ceremony, and to follow that up with presence. Recent research by Andrew Francis and Hugo Mialon (and corroborated by another study by Galena Rhoades) has shown that divorce rates are lower after a larger wedding. Compared to the couple marrying before a justice of the peace with no one else in the audience, a wedding with eleven to fifty people present is 56 percent less likely to end in divorce, and even less likely if more people are present. This demonstrates the importance of witnesses, the energy of the audience, that is available to your wedding and your marriage.

Some of these people will be present in the days and weeks before the wedding, and can have a role in the ceremony itself. This includes parents, children from previous relationships, friends and relatives, or voices who may represent an important spiritual or social tradition. Some very old voices can come into a ceremony—voices that you find in poems or scriptures from ages past.

Are parents speaking or doing something special? Is there a ring bearer? How many attendants, bridesmaids, and groomsmen? Would you like certain important people to speak during the ceremony? Will you decide what they say, perhaps a special reading, or would you like thirty seconds of extemporaneous blessing from each? Emotions about who is asked to do something and who might feel overlooked, who sits where, who stands where, can be delicate. We include more suggestions about how to deal with them toward the end of this chapter. One fact to consider: people love to be asked to do something, to contribute in some way. This means a list of jobs as long as your guest list—a large task of delegation for your director, but one that strengthens community. We have found that brides and grooms often forget this. They say, "Uncle Robert has traveled so far. We just want him to relax and enjoy himself." Chances are that Uncle Robert, not at home with his usual routines, is aching for something to do. You will make a much stronger bond to your wedding if you find all sorts of little tasks to do. However, you don't want to be the one coordinating all of that. The director, or someone given the job of coordinating jobs, coordinates.

What Kind of Music Would You Like to Include?

Live or recorded? Name some specific pieces. At the outset we recommend that one kind of music be turned off: the ringers, the buzzers, and the vibrators.

Some people insist, "I have to play 'You Light Up My Life'—I can't have a wedding without it!" Some people have a list of songs that they feel compelled to share with everyone who's coming. Realize that at the beginning, when people are milling about and interacting socially, your favorite song will be drowned out. No one will hear it. Also realize that if you make a big deal about it and put it into the center of your wedding—the celebrant announces, "Now we will listen to 'You Light Up My Life'"—it may go on and on for longer than you ever remembered that song lasting, stretching the patience of your witnesses. And you may find that recorded music in the middle of a live performance seems out of place.

Sometimes these favorite songs work; you will have to test them out. Try weeks ahead of time staring into the eyes of your partner while the whole song plays once. Can you hold the energy between the two of you? Now imagine doing that with a room full of people staring at you. Maybe it's that important. Maybe not. It's not the Sacred Moment that the witnesses and your souls are waiting for, though it may prepare you for that in a good way.

If a particular song is that important, we highly recommend that you sing it yourself. Next best is to find someone else to sing the song at the wedding. We are not looking for perfection here—your attempt to sing will be so completely endearing, and the warmth of a living singer will add so much to the setting, that it's worth doing it live. Overcome your shyness and sing your song to your Beloved! Live music, even a few chords on a guitar, far surpasses recorded sounds in a ceremony where living forces are moving about.

How Long Would You Like the Ceremony to Be?

It's valuable to ask each other how long you imagine the ceremony will take. Often one partner envisions a fifteen-minute ceremony, while the other has listed ninety-nine things that need to be included. Realistically, the length depends entirely on the complexity of the ceremony and the number of people involved. Your celebrant has the experience to help you understand the parameters for answering this question.

Be aware that estimates tend to be shorter than the reality! "Oh, that will only take three minutes" seldom turns out to be true. Most people attending weddings are not expecting a long event and don't expect the ceremony to last more than an hour. Keep this in mind as you plan, and remember that the Sacred Moment, the vows, and the rings take precedence. Everything else is secondary. If you say, "I must have everyone experience together a-certain-wonderful-experience," replace it with, "I realize that they have come to experience us, to feel Love pulsing in the room."

story

"Make It Short!"

The couple decided that during their ceremony each would go to his or her own parents, who were sitting among the witnesses. In doing this they wished to thank their parents for all they had given over the years, which now had come to this consummation of marriage. It would be a lovely surprise to the parents.

The man went to his mother, as his father had passed away, and began to sing her praises to the assembled witnesses. Everyone was touched by his display of gratitude and its reception.

The woman walked to her father and mother, smiling broadly. Under his breath her father uttered sternly, "Make it short!" That really hit her hard, and she did not recover from it in the remainder of the ceremony.

It's a lesson about caution in what you set yourself up for, especially before the Sacred Moment. Something like that can undermine the preparations you've made over the course of the weeks before. ✤

Perhaps you have sat through a ceremonial function of some sort and wondered, "How long will this last? I've had enough—get me out of here!" At your wedding, you don't want to arouse such a reaction in your witnesses, because you need their interest, their warmth, their attention—in other words, their energy—to support your Sacred Moment. That means you have to manage your timing well.

So be careful about the components you select to include in your wedding. Have you ever felt really hungry and finally found a restaurant, looked over the menu, and exclaimed, "I could order one of everything"? But you know you couldn't eat one of everything. Your hunger is gone after the first few bites, and then you have course after course in front of you, and you begin to tire.

These days, you can depend on your witnesses' focused energy for an hour. That means a great deal of efficiency at the beginning to get them seated. The first ones there might wait for the stragglers for a half an hour, and will approach their limit of endurance much sooner than the latecomers.

A long concert of music beforehand, or a long recitation of meaningful words, may not serve the point of the ceremony—the Sacred Moment! We have attended weddings that went on for two hours, one that went on for three hours, every moment and activity sacred and meaningful. It's like icing on a cake: you can't sit down to a plate full of icing. You need the cake too, and vegetables, and pauses . . .

Using the example of a wedding due to start at 2 p.m., your invitation could say, "Music at 1:45 p.m. Final seating at 2 p.m. We ask that you please be seated when the music starts." Most people will arrive when instructed. Some, usually older relatives, will arrive very early, so have active greeters ready from 1:15. Some people will arrive ten to fifteen minutes late. And a very few may arrive as much as forty minutes late; these are the ones who could disturb the core of the ceremony.

The ushers on duty after 2 p.m. must have a prearranged place to put latecomers that won't be disruptive. Some people actually close the doors at the beginning of their ceremony, but what if Uncle Robert arrives at 2:10? You can't not let him in. Still, we recommend that you not let *anyone* disturb the space during the core of the ceremony: the vows, rings, and hopefully a Sacred Moment. This may mean closing the doors and posting a very clear sign (such as, "Please wait during this most intimate part of the ceremony"), or stationing someone at the door at around 2:40. If you establish such a boundary as a certainty, then you can work backward from there about how to place latecomers. To support you in the Sacred Moment—which supports everyone else—you may have to keep late arrivals out for the ten minutes of the core of the ceremony.

Try out the elements you're considering for your ceremony by practicing live, with your partner and with your celebrant. Empower your celebrant to speak to those in charge of the features of your ceremony, asking them to be brief. Even to the extent of interrupting, "Thank you, Uncle Robert, you may need to speak the final part of that poem to the wedding couple in private. Let's move on to the vows." The director cooperates as the backstage manager of the many pieces of your ceremony.

Remember: your wedding is a form of theater, in that it engages the wonderful power of the community in service of your long-term relationship. You might study how theater moves along. There's even a saying in theater, "You have to get the audience on your side in the first five minutes." People attending a wedding will give you more time than that, but their patience is not infinite.

Great Quotes, Wise Words, and Famous People

Many people like to bring in famous quotes as a way of sanctifying the experience. Of course, we think that whatever you say—or don't say, but rather feel—during your Sacred Moment has far greater importance. But some people will insist on this element, and early on in the ceremony, it can help draw in traditionally minded relatives.

Our hint: make the words your own. What do we mean by this? Study the famous words beforehand, take them apart and put them back together, and then you can say them with genuine conviction.

story

The Most-Read Quote on Marriage

Let's take an example of words that you must understand before speaking them. Probably the most-read quote on marriage (in Christian or quasi-Christian settings) comes from Paul in his first letter to the Corinthians, chapter 13, beginning with verse one:

If I speak in the tongues of mortals and of angels . . .

This refers to people who are so attuned and so spacious that words come through them that originate from angels and from advanced human beings.

. . . but do not have Love, I am a noisy gong or a clanging cymbal.

Those who have these powers but are cold and impersonal do not actually hold anything useful for the rest of us. What they are missing is Love. It is always interesting to hear a serious professor of theology speak these lines, because he drones it out as if the Greek word for Love that Paul used was *philia* (a root of the word "philosophy")—that is, an intellectual attraction or friendship. But that was not Paul's word. He uses *agape,* which means abandoned, fully embodied, indeed wild, Love. What tone would you use to pronounce a word that means wild, boundless Love? Try it, even if you don't use this quote.

And if I have prophetic powers,

Many would like to have the power to see into the future, to see, as with x-ray vision, into another in order to diagnose a medical condition, that sort of thing.

. . . and understand all mysteries and all knowledge

Now we have the greatest of all professors! This is the aim and desire of all scholars, scientists, and mystics. All knowledge!

. . . and I have all faith so as to remove mountains

Now, this is a powerful magician, indeed. The faith in the power of Divinity is so strong that one can command whole mountains to move, and the mountains move.

. . . but do not have Love, I am nothing.

From a great buildup, a great letdown. Worldly power is not what it seems. The princes of the world have nothing. Those who seem high are actually very low.

So what is this Love that he recommends? Let's skip to verse 4 now:

> Love is patient; Love is kind; Love is not envious or boastful or
> arrogant or rude.

This list goes by so quickly, too quickly. You have to take the time with your partner to find the instances in your life when you were impatient and patient, unkind and kind, envious and unenvious, and so forth. You can only know a virtue if you have experienced its opposite. Such is the power of human experience.

You see how complicated this quote is? Don't use it unless you can explore it and understand it fully. If you use it, speak it slowly and with understanding to share with others what you have learned by exploring its meaning. Then it has the power of a repeated affirmation, which is far more powerful than the way in which it is usually used.

Perhaps first you ask yourselves, "How can we say all this in our own words?"

We could continue our elaboration of Paul's quote, which does go on, and shows in the end of the short chapter that he is speaking in tongues himself, in a kind of bliss-filled ecstasy. If you use the quote, don't drone it out. Speak it the way Paul might have spoken it as he stood on the Speaker's Stone outside the Parthenon in Athens, or on the stage at the great theater of Ephesus, both places you can visit even today, and shout out these words again to the gathering populace.

exercise

Wise Words

Summarize in your own words what Paul said. Do that first without rereading the content above. Summarize simply from memory, that is, what stuck with you from your first reading. If you have chosen another "favorite quote" or "favorite poem," do the same with it, right now, without finding it again to read it. What's the point of the quote? What do you leave with, and what do you intend your witnesses to leave with?

If you intend to use a quote in your wedding, then go over with your partner what it means. With the Paul quote, review the times that you have been impatient and patient, kind and unkind, envious and unenvious, boastful and modest, arrogant, rude, all of it.

Use famous words by famous people, yes, but make them your own through study and intimate experience of them. When you actually understand the words, you will see that you read them much more slowly.

If you're looking for a great quote, you could also try this one from Henry David Thoreau:

> Love is the wind, the tide, the waves, the sunshine. Its power is incalculable; it has many horsepower. It never ceases; it never slacks; it can move the globe without a resting place; it can warm without fire; it can feed without meat; it can clothe without garments; it can shelter without a roof; it can make a paradise within. . . . But though the wisest men of all ages have labored to publish this force, and every human heart is, sooner or later, more or less, made to feel it, yet how little it is actually applied to social ends.

Would you use that final bit beginning with "But"? No! In the same vein, you can cut and paste any part of this quote that you like. Put spaces between the phrases, and first study them to know what they mean.

From our point of view, it is more successful to get the meaning and speak your own version of Paul or Thoreau. To repeat: we feel that you two are the most "famous" people on your wedding day. Quote others only *after* you've really looked at the words and know what they mean. Otherwise they become distractions rather than aids.

Calling In the Directions and Elements

In the traditions of many indigenous cultures, the directions are honored, each with its own element. We use the Celtic cosmography: air (east), fire (south), water (west), earth (north). We then include above, below, and within, making seven in all. Some people use only the four points of the compass. Other traditions may associate the elements with different directions. It doesn't matter, as long as you're clear what you're doing.

Sometimes the parents of the bride and groom may feel uncomfortable about what they consider to be pagan ceremonial elements, and would prefer to have a traditional ceremony in a church. We like to point out that churches are always constructed with orientation to the compass directions, as well as above, below, and within. Look at the architecture! Study how the elements and directions have all been conscientiously set into the space of a church. The directions and the elements are implicit. In a conscious wedding, we like to make the implicit also explicit.

"Pagan" comes from the same root word as "peasant": those people who knew the lay of the land and how to work with it, knew the directions and how to work with them. Pagan knowledge has not been done away with in modern religions—it has been incorporated, and can easily be found if you look for it. For example, Ezekiel and John called in the directions; indeed, they invoked the four fixed signs of the astrological zodiac, so you are in good company if you also call in the directions.

Sometimes when people "call in the directions," it can go on and on, listing all the attributes of the directions. Investing ceremony with life force takes practice and must also be sensitive to the needs of the witnesses. A long form can be used for blessing the space when the setup crew moves in, while ten people are there. Compress to a much shorter form in the wedding itself.

If you choose to honor the directions in the ceremony itself, having a person stand at each of the four true directions (which may vary from magnetic compass points by a little bit) is a great help in establishing a sense of safe space, that is, a space that is held. Long churches make this more difficult, but it is still feasible. A certain color or fabric or item that symbolizes each direction can also be helpful.

In Part One, we gave exercises to make you more familiar with the four classical elements: earth, water, air, and fire. You can bring these into your ceremony in an abbreviated and symbolic—yet quite real—way. Get familiar with the elements, right from the beginning, even in the planning stages.

Earth: In an architectural structure on the ground, you may be standing on old stones, firmly founded in the earth. Stone pillars may tower up around you, orienting you to the weight and profundity of earth. If, instead, your wedding venue is perched on the twentieth floor of a glass-and-steel building, then you may wish to bring with you a bowl of soil from a place that has meaning to you. Or bring a crystal or a potted plant. A metal ring comes from the earth realm, as do the precious stones set in that ring. Though the refined metal and the gemstones represent the pinnacle of the earth realm's creativity, don't let it be the only representative of the earth element at your ceremony.

Water: A cup of water—either from the nearest tap or brought from a fresh spring that has meaning for you—can represent the whole world of water. Sometimes a special glass of wine is used, sometimes a drop of blood. In these and other ways, you can bring in the element of water. The studies of Dr. Masaru Emoto in Japan demonstrate that water can pick up imprints of thought and feeling directed at it. The water at your wedding can likewise take on the impression of this beautiful experience. If you're using water in this way, don't throw it out at the end. Save it, to water the earth in front of your home, or to anoint each other's foreheads, for it contains a patterning of the joy that you create together.

One couple kept a jar of water through the entire preparation process, including their Heart Talks and many of the exercises in this book. They brought this with them to the wedding, and afterward anointed each other, their friends, and the earth.

A friend who is a celebrant collects waters from the sacred wells of all the continents. She mixes them for the weddings she supervises, and applies them to the foreheads of the marrying couple.

Air: In their fine and strong structure, feathers indicate the essence of the air. They bring the feeling of air wherever they appear. Banners and flags indicate the air. You can create a design that has meaning for the two of you, and make up little flags one hand-width square. Have them around the wedding site, and give them to people as they exit. Perhaps your banner has a golden sun on a white background, or a silver crescent moon on a dark blue background. Printed words invite thinking—usually an airy phenomenon. However, don't use too many printed words, as they can distract your witnesses. The sounds of song and the sounds of words during your ceremony affect the quality of air for your marriage.

Fire: Invite a representative of fire to warm your ceremony. Candles are one possibility. One couple had a cast-iron hibachi stove with rock salt soaked in ethyl alcohol, which makes a smokeless fire. Don't put too many candles close together, as they create a towering flame, a communion of fire that can be dangerous. We speak from experience. The little flames of a hundred candles joined together in a tower of flame that rose three feet high: dramatic, dangerous, one of the Sacred Moments of that ceremony, yet not something we would repeat.

The elements can help you craft a brilliant wedding.

story

DAVID ~ Invoking the Elements

We asked good friends to stand at the four directions and open them for our ceremony. The one in the east spoke aloud, "I call in the East, direction of new insight and the rising sun. Join us and bless this ceremony, East!" The representative of the East brought in the element of air, feathers from many different kinds of birds. Then came the South and fire. The one in charge of that invocation actually lit a small fire in the room, using high-proof grain alcohol, and called in all the fire beings of the volcanoes around the world. The person in the West brought in waters from sacred wells and springs from around the world. The earth person in the North brought in rocks and crystals. They all did a fantastic job, coming up with ingenious ways to express the element and the direction. We felt that the essences of the elements were present, and that we had the opportunity to thank even the elements as our oldest ancestors for supporting our Love.

When you acknowledge the directions in this way, you have four people in four directions. They enclose the space. Add four people in between the others and you have a very strong container for any ceremony that takes place within.

Memorable Stunts

Every so often one reads about stunt weddings. One couple was married underwater, everyone wearing scuba gear and writing the words of the vows with grease pencil on plastic slates. One couple was married while skydiving, that is, free falling ten thousand feet above the earth, all holding hands and mouthing the vows. Some have said, "I do!" while dropping from a bridge on bungee cords. Some have gone to Disneyland and dressed as Mickey Mouse and Minnie Mouse. And so forth.

You probably have guessed how we would respond to an idea like this. Does it make it more possible, or less possible, or indeed impossible, to realize the mystery of the Sacred Moment? Will you remember your wedding not for the spirit that moved but for the oddity that temporarily grabbed your attention?

Other Traditions: Breaking Wineglasses, Tying Hands, and So Forth

Each tradition has little eccentricities. The Jews wrap a wineglass in a cloth, then set it on the ground; the groom smashes it with his foot. The Celts have hand-fasting, which means tying one hand of the groom to one hand of the bride to signify their joining. There are many traditions to choose from. You can joyously participate in the specific demands of the tradition to which you are closest, as long as you see these extra bits as supporting your Sacred Moment.

Themes

Sometimes people pick themes around which to organize the costumes, venue, drinks menu, and so forth. Much of the time themes detract, and you have to ask whether this is helping or hindering your witnesses from being fully present for you—or hindering you from being present. Does dressing up as cowboys or cowgirls—unless you really are cowboys and cowgirls!—help or detract?

In our experience, an exception was a wedding that used the theme of *A Midsummer Night's Dream*. Shakespeare's play features the knots, thorns, and mix-ups of four couples, and ends with the right people marrying (and, in the case of Oberon and Titania, remarrying). Before the wedding couple arrived, the celebrant (David) spoke lines from the play to set the tone:

> Over hill, over dale, through bush, through brier;
> Over park, over pale, through flood, through fire;
> We do wander everywhere . . .
> And we serve the fairy queen.

For indeed, the bride soon appeared as a queen, her dress covered with white feathers and her hair in a dazzling crown.

In the celebrant's instructions to the wedding couple, other lines were spoken:

> Things base and vile, holding no quantity,
> Love can transpose to form and dignity.

After the rings were exchanged, other (slightly adapted) lines were spoken to affirm what had just happened:

> Your heart unto hers is knit,
> so that one heart you can make of it.

At the very end, these words were spoken to the witnesses, after the bride and groom had left:

> . . . you have but slumbered here
> While these visions did appear.

How lovely to understand that the mythic realm can feel as dreams and visions, and brings on a kind of sleep. And finally, though from a different Shakespeare play:

> Our revels now are ended.

Thus, the play offered poetic summaries of various parts of the ceremony. The words were more effective because the costumes of the groomsmen and brides-maids were fanciful, medieval, and beautiful. The theme worked because it enlisted the help of grand archetypes to make the core of the wedding deeper. (This particular wedding is outlined in the appendix.)

Archetypes, Stereotypes, and the Mythic

Throughout this book, we have emphasized the power of a greater story in which you participate, most formally presented in the Concentric Circles exercises in chapter 5. We have repeatedly referred to the "mythic" and how it provides an immense power that is available to your wedding and marriage. But how do you know when something engages powers of invisible realms, and when it is simply parroting superficial stereotypes?

Recently, a group of gender-equality guerrillas took many boxes from a toy store—Barbies and G.I. Joes. They carefully unpacked the boxes and exchanged the little speaking devices inside the dolls. Now the Barbies said in gruff shouts, "Ho, guys! Weapons ready! Let's go!" The G.I. Joes said in a high-toned singsong, "Oh, Trixie, let's meet for coffee!" The activists repacked the boxes carefully and returned them to the toy store and imagined the impacts on parents and children. Exaggeration of stereotypes, in this instance through reversal, sometimes makes it easier to see them all around you.

In the 1970s, we both participated in the women's liberation movement, which at that time seemed often to mean something more like "women's same-ness to men." Weddings in that era often featured bride and groom dressed in the same clothing. Some social scientists tried to prove that women and men were not only equal but the same, and that the only differences came from the biases of cultural training.

That hasn't held. There's something different, but what? And how can you possibly know what is intrinsically male or female when there are so many dif-ferences between individuals? At a time when human consciousness in general is expanding and changing, when individualism is on the rise, how do you appeal to greater powers? You will know a stereotype when it feels shallow and superficial, and often insulting; let it go. You will know an archetype when you feel intrigued, engaged, and met in some way that is unusual; pursue this one, as it may lead to resources that will support your wedding (as a candidate for "In Whose Name") and marriage.

Symbols

The further reaches of the mythic have a language that doesn't include words as we speak them. Special words can be spoken there, thus the importance of "In Whose Name" the ceremony is being held. When spoken correctly, such names have in themselves an invocative power that moves the entire room into a special refinement. Words used in this manner function more as symbols than as daily communication.

Symbols can also be used. Here is an example, showing the One-Two-ONE progression:

Simply having this graphic present, even if unexplained, draws people into the mythic realm. However, don't pile on the symbols. Use only one or two, something that relates specifically to your wedding or to what you hold as important. "In Whose Name" can include a design or a principle expressed in symbolic form.

Logistics

One-Two-ONE

Where to Be Married

An outdoor wedding can be very lovely on a sunny day, with all the elements close by. It can also be vastly more difficult if the weather challenges the setting, or as unexpected noises interrupt you. Or a dog runs through, distracting everyone's attention. Or there's a light breeze or traffic in the distance and no one can hear what's going on with the wedding couple. We have experienced all of these.

You need to create a container that can give you enough safety and stillness that soul talk can take place and be heard. Outdoor weddings that work often take place within a container of chairs and hedges and portable screens. If you don't have those, you can use the community of witnesses as the container, arranging them around you so that they become the walls of a sacred building, substituting people for the walls shown in the diagram at the end of chapter 11.

If you have an electrical amplification system, then also have a plan for what to do if something goes wrong with it. We have seen the sound system fail on a few occasions. At the last minute, what was working before goes flat, off, gone. Or the microphone is set too far away from the marrying couple—probably because the system was not tested with the bride and groom during the rehearsal—so no one can hear them speak. Many people don't realize that most microphones should actually rest on your chin to function properly. Ought a celebrant give instructions to a bride and groom during the ceremony?

In these situations, the celebrant has to think fast. In the case of standing too far back, if an instruction from the celebrant to stand closer to the microphone will frazzle either bride or groom, the celebrant can hold the microphone up to each as they speak. We have done this a few times.

In the case of a failed sound system, you don't want someone fiddling with the controls and the power cords, fretting up front in the sight of everyone, taking all that attention. Anxieties rise; the buildup of energy wafts away and is challenging to retrieve. This is what Lila did as a celebrant with a sound system that worked in rehearsal but failed at the wedding ceremony: she called everyone to rise from their seats and crowd in close to the couple to hear better. As you're in a theater production, you need to do what theater people do: insist on a long and detailed tech rehearsal. This ought not to involve you, but it ought to involve your director. Even with tech rehearsals, you need a celebrant who is quick-thinking and can adapt to all sorts of interruptions. Or limit your use of technology.

Indoor weddings allow for more obvious containment, and can be easier in some respects. Picture the building in which you have chosen to hold this wedding. Its job is to contain and embrace you and your wedding. You will spend some time designing and enhancing this container with flowers, fabrics, fragrance, friends, and so forth. Your witnesses will be lured into your ceremony by the sights and smells of what you've put there. You invite your friends and family through one circle after another, so that they can assist you in the Sacred Moment.

The StarHouse is an unadorned space with twelve sides, so it lends itself to many different arrangements. Everyone can sit around in a circle. Or everyone can sit facing a single direction that becomes the "front." Or people can sit on three sides of a circle, still with a "front." People have chosen different directions for "front."

A regular church (or synagogue or other traditional structure) makes decisions for you ahead of time. The seats are bolted down; there is a clear front and rear of the space. These structures have determined who's in front and who's facing whom. They can uphold you with the power of the accumulated tradition implicit and explicit in the architecture and statuary and objects within. They can also drag you in a direction that you may not wish to go. Make sure that both of you feel very comfortable about the space in which the ceremony takes place. Too many times we have heard a last-minute confession of discomfort from one partner about the other's choice of the venue.

exercise

The Venue

Ask what you each envision for the container of your ceremony. Is there a strong preference for indoors or outdoors? Why? You can find out why by doing a "Yes, and . . ." exercise, or simply a Heart Talk. Do either of you have places already in mind and heart? If so, put all the possibilities on the table and be sure you speak about them all. Reach a decision that honors the vision of your intention.

The Invitations

The invitation is one of the first communications about your intention to marry that many people will receive. It is a matter of personal taste how involved and detailed the invitation becomes.

We have seen the most beautifully handcrafted invitations, and the most simple and straightforward. Decide that whichever way you choose, you will enjoy the process! If you don't love to make paper art, then don't spend your time doing it. The advent of digital art has made it possible to create customized and lovely invitations. You can also find bulk templates for invitations in stationery stores that can easily be printed with all the details.

Be sure to include all the necessaries: who, what, where, and when. Too often one of these is forgotten. (The last of the Five Ws—why—is the thrust of this book and may need brief mention in an invitation.) If your planning process is running a bit late, you can always send out a "save the date" notification by e-mail or standard mail. We often encourage couples to include a line of verse that gives a hint of their intention in being married, as the invitation sets the tone of the ceremony to come.

The Request for Gifts

Relatives and friends give gifts to you to support your marriage. Most couples set up a registry system to guide the gift choices. Help your friends and family choose gifts that support the mission of your wedding: to grow each other, to establish a household where Love has a prime place, and whatever other goals you have identified through the exercises in chapter 9. A hint for how to deal with these gifts: number them or label each one with an indelible marker so that you know who gave you what. The gift was intended as a specific support from the giver; when years later you can recall who gave that gift, it will energetically reinforce the intention of support from that giver. Even gifts that you consider ugly, odd, or silly have their place. Keep them for a while, and let your appreciation of them grow. If they don't befriend you, then pass them on to someone who will appreciate them.

The Rings

In Greek myth, the demigod Prometheus brought fire from heaven to humanity—the fire of intelligence and insight as well as the physical fire that humans use for cooking and making things. Zeus thought it too early to give these capacities to human beings, and had Prometheus chained to a rock in punishment, with O-shaped circlets around his ankles and wrists. Prometheus relented and vowed to ask permission in the future. To signify this agreement, he wore a ring made of a piece of the chain, set with a piece of the rock cliff to which it had been connected. Rings echo this connection between heaven and earth, and a pledge to heed the guidance of divine principles. Gold replaces the iron shackle and diamond replaces the piece of cliff. They are a refinement of the mineral realm, and they also demonstrate a choice—for a ring can be removed. It echoes a shackle, but is worn willingly.

The wedding ring is something that many people never remove. They can, and they sometimes have to, as when entering an MRI scanner—which is instructive, as the ring can heat up and burn the finger. You are about to wear something that receives electromagnetic waves and heat!

Anything circular can remind you of Concentric Circles, of the progression from outer realms of the ceremony to inner realms in the approach to the core of the wedding, of the grand circle of the O in ONE . . .

The intricacies of the ring's design, its cost, and the size of the jewel on it (if there is one) are less important than the *fact* of the ring. It is a reminder over and over again of the bond that you've created, and the very specific vows and agreements that you have made with each other. The choice of rings can be a ritual in itself. Whether you go shopping for them together or have them designed and crafted, they are a symbol of your choice of union. For years to come, you will look at them on your two hands and remember your wedding. People will ask you to tell the story of your rings as a way to hear about your wedding. It's a form of the origin myth that we spoke about in chapter 2. Some people use a portion of the gold from their ring from a previous marriage, or from their parents' rings, to honor those marriages as valuable training grounds for the present.

We speak in this book about portals and doorways. The wedding ceremony is the doorway through which you travel from relationship to marriage. The core of the ceremony is the portal to the Sacred Moment. In this metaphor, the ring is a doorway too, something you pass through—but wait! You don't pass through. You stay there, connected to both sides. The ring is a doorway in process. Your blood goes through it, back and forth. The ring summons a feeling of flowing through the doorway, every moment.

Let's contrast the engagement ring to the wedding ring. The latter is often simpler. It is the fact of the ring. The former announces to the world that you two are contemplating something special. It can be quite ornate. Traditionally people wear both their rings after their marriage. Why? Isn't the engagement complete after the wedding? Wearing an engagement ring after the marriage can become a reminder of the special focus of this time in which you are planning your wedding, and reading this book—and going through the growth processes seen and recommended here. This is an immensely transformative time, and you have a ring to show that you are in it.

Who forged your rings? Can you feel the memory of heat in them? Who found the ore from which they were made? Who cleaned them and laid them out in the sun? Who holds them before you need them in the ceremony? The ring is your most potent connection with the riches of the earth element.

The Dress and Its Archetypes

Many weddings seem to revolve around the visit of the bride and her mother, sisters, and friends, or any combination of these, to the dress shop, to find the "right" dress. Most men can't understand what all the fuss is about, and they certainly don't understand the price tag. What *is* it all about?

The process goes beyond the actual dress, and, for many, becomes a ticket to the mythic realm (as in the Concentric Circles model in chapter 5). Tradition gives the bride this opportunity to explore the vision of who she wants to be, what she would like to flow through her, and how she can employ the mythic or symbolic realm to make her wedding and marriage truly great. For example, the shape of the gown can indicate the quality of energy as it relates to sacred union. Often the skirt or train of the gown balloons out to connect strongly to the foundations of the earth—to Mother Earth. The veil indicates a mystery with an airy filamentous boundary, or a watery mist between realities. The bulk of the dress hints at the fire within. The dress can accentuate all of the elements.

Mythic/archetypal opportunities are expansive and varied. They can include: Fairytale Princess; Elizabethan Queen; Atlantean Queen; Hollywood Sex Goddess; Celtic Nature Priestess; Indigenous Shaman; Wild Woman; Greek Goddess; Snow White; Titania; Hippolyta . . . This choice is sometimes conscious and sometimes not. It can be a delightful exploration to determine what archetype the bride is drawn to, and also to explore how the groom responds and cocreates with the bride's choice.

In many ways, the bride becomes a flower. Fingernails, hair, eyelashes, makeup, shoes—all of these recall the color and grace of flowers from close up. What declares "flower" from both close up and distance is the dress. We support the bride becoming a flower for the day (and the groom, and bridesmaids, and others in the wedding party). Flowers are an expression of a plant's entire energy, lifting up to the sun. That they fade and crumple is not a tragedy; rather it is a prelude to the next creation, an affirmation that life has cycles. Find the way that a dress can bring out the flower in you. It need not be expensive. If you are having fittings, remember that the dress needs to fit you as flower; it is not you that must fit the dress. Too many women moan at this process because they do not look how they think they should look. Here's a stern reminder: your soul is flowerlike at all times, no matter how your body might compare to that of the latest movie star. The dress simply helps portray that inner fact. Your helpers—friends, mother, aunts—can help by being butterflies flitting around the flowers with you. You may need to remind them that the purpose is for enjoyment of you as flower in all your inner and outer beauty.

Share this process with your partner. Communicating with each other creates another opportunity to share something meaningful. The way a woman chooses her dress is often a reflection of a girlhood belief or longstanding dream: "My wedding is my day to be a queen," or perhaps "Weddings are an overblown and meaningless waste of money, so I'll dress any way I wish." Seldom does a bride say, "I want to become a beautiful flower," though she acts that way. What other mythic associations arise? What are the needs that underlie the dress? You ought to ask partly because the cost of the dress can match all the other wedding costs combined! Be aware what archetype you may be choosing to honor as you design this day, and realize there are alternatives for where to shop and ways to create a glorious magic without spending a fortune.

The job of the dress is to help the bride—and her mother and any of the others that often accompany her on the dress shopping adventures—to leave the mundane and enter into the mythic realm. That boost does not need to take too much time or money. Once the wedding is over, the myth feels more powerful if you let go of the dress. Perhaps you wear it for a reception line. If you have an active party afterward, a different story and a different myth may be acted out, and you can have a different costume more appropriate to that realm of the myth of your wedding.

A coordination of the color and style of clothing for both partners—and for the men and women who surround and support the central couple—indicates that you communicate and cooperate, that you form an artistic community that features a harmony of color and texture. It indicates that you are in ceremonial time, out of worldly time. You are in a small version of heaven, wearing something that is expensive, soft, pure, rare, and often unusable in daily life! All that is fine on a special day.

At the *Midsummer Night's Dream* wedding, the wedding party had clothes made for the event. The men wore leather vests embroidered with bright colors, each vest designed differently. The women wore the kind of thing you would expect to see on a nymph running between tall trees on a full-moon night in the height of summer. The bride's dress lay broadly with many pleats, all white, festooned with feathers.

Our only advice: Don't let the dress become the core of the wedding. It is meant to support and not upstage the real purpose of your ceremony.

The Flowers

We have attended a wedding where there was one perfect flower in a vase at the center of the room, around which the wedding couple and the celebrant gathered. There was a single candle on either side of the blossom. The lights in the hall were turned down, and it was night outside. This spoke as strongly as festoons of flowers everywhere.

We attended one ceremony for which, all night beforehand, a dozen people had strung different-colored chrysanthemum blossoms on long strings to adorn the room. These strings of thousands of flower blossoms softened the walls in every direction, inviting everyone to swoon into the fragrance and the blazing colors.

As the bride is the central flower, all other flowers should support her.

Let flowers serve your wedding, and ideally, have someone else in charge of arranging them.

Flowers

Don't wait for your wedding to become aware of flowers. Why are flowers so wonderful to people? One technique for training consciousness suggests that you stare into the center of a single blossom until the flower disappears, and you are transported through the flower gate into a realm of communion with all of nature. This is best done with a living flower in your garden or in a meadow, but you can also enjoy the flower's offering of beauty if it's sitting in a vase in front of you. Learn to admire different kinds of flowers, not with a sweeping glance but with this same focus on details, on the center. Once you learn the different gifts of different kinds of flowers, and appreciate the different perfumes of each, you will welcome flowers as supports for the core of your wedding. Then you will choose the flowers to accompany your wedding carefully, as you will understand that quality is more important than quantity.

The Altar

We recommend two tables as altars (the general concept is discussed in chapter 7). A medium-sized table can be placed behind where the celebrant will stand, in the ceremonial area so that people can view it beforehand. It can contain photos of family unable to attend, as well as grandparents or great-grandparents—whomever you would like to invite. You can arrange the two families on either side, with a photo of your couple in the middle, that which is linking these two families. At one wedding, the bride included a family tree naming the ancestors going back ten generations.

A small table can be placed between the celebrant and the couple, to hold items that will be used in the wedding. We recommend—though this is completely up to you—a unity candle, a card with the powers/principles that you would like to invite ("In Whose Name"), a vase with a very small bouquet of flowers or a single flower, and bowls with the four elements: earth, water, air, and fire. For anything having fire—for example, lighting a candle—have two methods for lighting. We learned this the hard way . . .

though it became a kind of Sacred Moment when no one could find a lighter that worked!

Time Apart Before the Ceremony

Since ancient times, the technique of separation before union has been used. The marrying couple go separate ways, living apart for three days, not seeing each other and not speaking with each other. This means that you have a director in place dealing with last-minute details of the wedding ceremony itself. It also means that you have your rehearsal three days before the wedding. If you forget details of the ceremony, you know that you can depend on the celebrant to show you what's needed when the time comes.

Before our wedding, David stayed in a small bed-and-breakfast in the mountains by himself, spending most of his time outdoors, hiking high mountain trails. Nature was his guide, companion, and teacher. He met with his close men friends, getting advice from them and speaking about the powers and pitfalls of relationship.

Lila also spent most of her time outdoors. She met with women around a campfire. They told stories, gazing into the wild element of fire in its glory. The time apart allowed both of us the opportunity to reflect on our separate lives before we joined those lives together. The wedding day was clearly a threshold crossing, and in preparation for it, we found we wanted time for deep reflection, meditation, and solitude.

We understand that these days of preparation represent a high ideal, and are not easy to arrange when many relatives and old friends come to town. It's possible that the director could handle these relations for a short time. Three days apart was a luxury, but you may not be able to manage that. Even three hours is valuable.

Time apart does not mean time with other sexual adventures or titillations, "last chances," any of that. The time for sexual adventures is long gone. It also doesn't mean an excuse to distract yourself with a whole new set of stimuli and wild notions. It means time to yourself. It means truly preparing space in yourself so that there can be space in the Sacred Moment and in your marriage—a space your soul can visit, and someday fill to overflowing. (See more in the next section.)

exercise

Time Apart and Back Together

Time apart may occur because of the different demands of your career paths. However, it's good to have a time apart that is based on intention rather than the constraints of job schedules. And it's good to start with much less than three days. Practice now.

Set an intention for the next hour, then spend that hour apart—not on the computer, but rather in a kind of sacred space that honors the other while being apart. Ponder who you are alone, and who you are in relationship. At the end of the hour, return to share what you have realized during your time apart. A healthy relationship is made of two healthy individuals who take time for themselves.

Bachelor and Bachelorette Parties

The stag party (or bucks night) and its counterpart—stagette, bacherlorette, hen or hens night—have in some places become traditions. Your friends aim to create something memorable, perhaps so memorable that you may have a hard time talking about it with your partner. The event can involve extremes of every sort. If a sex game isn't involved, then there are jokes about it. The theme of this-is-my-last-chance-to-go-wild abounds. Everyone goes wild.

What are the roots of these adventures? In many hunter-gatherer societies, young men and women go through a sequence of initiation rites, where they are tested in physical endurance, emotional shocks, and ingenuity of mind. Initiation rites offer an important opportunity for the elders to teach the younger ones about the foundations of the culture, to teach physical skills useful for the survival of oneself in order to support the community, and to teach warriors to be tough. The younger ones learn hunting, plant lore, the sources of medicines, cosmology, methods for fighting, interpersonal relations, many of the skills that we have given in chapter 7, and more. The tests of survival are strenuous and can appear cruel; some of the young ones don't live through it.

In our modern world, the skills necessary for survival have changed, the demands of the educational system are primarily mental, and competitive sports have taken the place of cooperative physical activities. The urge to initiate others has become distorted into hazing, fight clubs, sex clubs, and drinking contests.

The urge to test yourself and your friends has deep roots in traditional societies. We like best the name for these events in France: "Enterrement de vie de garcon/jeune-fille," which translates as, "The burial of the life as a boy/girl." This echoes those primitive initiation rites from earlier societies. Your life shifts; the old is buried. If you wish to be really creative in this regard, read Frazer's *The Golden Bough,* the unabridged version.

When you know the ancient traditions behind these gatherings, you can understand the attraction to adventures and danger. Initiation has become passing out from too much alcohol, or the temptations of hired sex partners.

We ask: Where are the elders in your party, the ones who are using this initiation rite to pass on information, inspiration, and useful techniques? If this is your "last night of freedom," do you really define freedom as relationless sex and alcohol? Doesn't freedom come from being free of those old standbys?

We suggest a contrasting picture: you are athletes preparing for an athletic event. To be successful in that event, you have to be in top form in your body, in your heart, and in your mind. The powers of sexuality, of intimacy, of sensuality, of Love, of the immensity of the ONE surge upward around a wedding. Everyone can feel them, and few know what to do with those rising impulses. You have to ask: does a wild time serve your preparation for a Sacred Moment?

Perhaps you do need a release that blows off some steam, before shifting your network of relationships through marriage. We have already spoken about releasing in several places. You could try some of those techniques. If you have friends that insist that you be blindfolded and led through some kind of experience, do that well before your wedding, a week, a month . . . long enough away that you have time to recover.

The Night Before the Ceremony

The celebrations before or after the ceremony can be as joyful and satisfying as the actual event. Depending on whether this is the first marriage, the second, third, or more, or a rededication ceremony, give some thought to the prominence of these other events. Be sure they don't eclipse the main focus of your wedding.

Consider the place of alcohol. The misuse of alcohol is a major issue in our culture; it is the most widely consumed and generally accepted drug. Most people consent to drinking, and appear not to notice when it gets out of hand. Many assume that alcohol is an inseparable part of a wedding, certainly during the reception afterward, and many assume beforehand too, for the rehearsal dinner, or the bachelor's night out with the men, or whenever. We have observed that this means lots and lots of alcohol, even consumed by people who rarely drink. Alcohol is a powerful entity. Ask yourself if and when you would like to invite this additional guest, Mr. Alcohol.

Alcohol traditionally runs freely at bachelor and bachelorette parties, the last-chance-before-I'm-hitched parties. We have heard about several bucks and hens nights (the terms used in England, Canada, and Australia), where the men adventure forth to be bucks and the women go off to be hens. In every story, both men and women partied hard and late. The wedding ceremony was overcast with the hangovers of several of the key people. This is another opportunity to be aware and awake as you plan your ceremony, and to simply ask what will serve your highest intention. Do you choose to be crippled or ready at your ceremony?

One caution: if you feel that you've succeeded in realizing a Sacred Moment in your ceremony, don't rejoice too quickly afterward with a large "celebration" drink, no matter what your friends urge upon you. The being of alcohol tends to overwhelm the subtle and delicate sweetness of what you've created. Drink several glasses of water as you bask in the glow of the Sacred Moment, and then decide what's appropriate.

After the Ceremony

It helps to have an idea of what's happening after the ceremony before going into the ceremony. Knowing that you will have time to integrate the experience is very helpful.

We recommend that the couple leave the ceremony for some time alone, perhaps only ten minutes, but alone. The celebrant speaks to the witnesses about their responsibility in relation to the new marriage, about the couple as buzzing with the powers of their union, and about the possibility of receiving some of that blessing from them in a reception line. Meanwhile, the couple are calmly breathing by themselves in a secluded place not too far away.

This includes postponing photographs. Professional photographers have gotten into the habit of demanding that everyone gather immediately after the wedding for a series of poses, with different groupings of people, all smiling, all demonstrating, "We were all together and we were all happy!" Don't do it. A photo shoot is a trial at the best of times. "Put your right shoulder out. Lift those flowers. That's it. Smile! Hold it! Hold it! (Click, click, click.) Now kiss the bride. Come on! Don't be shy! (Click, click.)" For a couple trying to nurture a very delicate energetic feeling generated in a ceremony with one or more Sacred Moments, a photo shoot can be overwhelming. Often, the couple had no idea that it would go on so long. Let photos happen after a break of a half hour, at the soonest. If the photographer communicates that he or she is in a hurry because they have another wedding to go to—we've seen this inappropriate communication a few times—then send them on, or have your director or celebrant send them on. Your energetic memories are more important than any photos.

Instead, continue to create the ceremonial structures that nurture the soul of the event. The witnesses form two parallel lines. The couple comes from their secluded place and walks slowly between these two lines. The sense of life force emanating has occurred every time we have seen this, a life force that energizes and rejuvenates the witnesses. In this way you care for your witnesses, who will in turn care for you in the coming years. Once through this form of reception line, the couple can be better integrated into the group.

Many people expect to party immediately after the wedding. Build to that slowly. Imagine that you are carrying something subtle, refined, powerful yet elusive—the life force of that in whose name you have been married. Your access to these powers is at a height at this moment. Don't overwhelm that subtlety with alcohol or whooping it up.

The Post-Wedding Reception

If everyone has been attentive and given freely of his or her energy to the center, they will require some nourishment afterward. You thank them with a full dinner, or with light snacks and drinks.

Don't be persuaded to create an expensive gala if it doesn't serve the tone of your wedding. A great deal of money can be spent on a reception that might serve a couple in better ways! Consider asking good friends to bring a dish instead of buying you a wedding present; or keep the menu simple.

The reception too serves the container of the Sacred Moment. Ideally the reception becomes a time when people integrate what they experienced in the wedding itself. You may need to read that sentence again. The meal afterward is not the centerpiece of the memorabilia of this day. A reception serves to bring together the couple, who sparkle with Love—earthly love, heavenly love, Love through and through—and their community. We instruct our witnesses that, especially at the beginning of the reception, the newlyweds are full of this Love energy, and every touch of their hands and gaze of their eyes is a blessing to everyone else. We encourage a reception line toward the beginning of the reception, and ask that the witnesses pass by with only brief exchanges, receiving the couple's blessing. The witnesses can have longer conversations later.

The Point of the Parties

Around a wedding there are many gatherings and parties. A bridal shower, a sewing bee for tablecloths and even the dress, a women's spa day for close friends of the bride, a "blessing way," luncheon with the in-laws, various bachelor and bachelorette nights, the rehearsal dinner, the reception.

Hold a tight rein—with your director and celebrant and your closest helpers—on what occurs in these settings. Ask yourself repeatedly, "What's the point? Where is this headed?" People will tend to gather in the ways that they're used to. If that includes loud music, alcohol, and other substances, then they will do that. If you would like something more focused—toward the building up and then the integration of a blessing of divine energy, toward the unification of two families and friends through you and your partner—then you have to direct the activities and conversations at your gatherings. Stay on course, and ask ahead of time for support in this from the ones closest to your ceremony. Your focus needs to be on the wedding itself, and on its core. Don't be lured into extra activities that might shift that focus.

In a few weddings that we have supervised, there has been a "Jane, my best friend from college," or "my cousin Andrew, a crazy fun guy," or someone else that comes into the first gathering with what seem to be great ideas. Jane wanted to take everyone night after night from bar to bar, until early the next morning. Andrew wanted to take everyone bungee-jumping, including uncles and aunts that had no business jumping off a height. The bride and groom tried to tone down Jane's and Andrew's invitations, and in the end had to make it clear that this might be fine at another time, but not now. Not only do you have to protect yourself from the wahoo impulses that surge around a wedding; you may also have to protect your witnesses so that they become a good audience for the ceremony.

Your friends and family who have not seen one another for a while will normally tend to renew old relationships. If you would like to integrate the two families with your various groups of friends into a new network of relationships, you might consider directing your helpers in how to accomplish this. One idea that has worked well: set out a bowl into which everyone who comes to a gathering puts his or her name. At one point have a helper take the bowl around, asking everyone to choose a name. Each guest must then locate the chosen person and find out about his or her life. That tends to stir groups together.

One of the purposes of these gatherings is to acknowledge those who have worked hard to make your ceremony a success—your director and helpers—and those who have made your life a success—your parents. You can acknowledge these people over and over again by making toasts, by sharing stories from the past, and by directing friends to speak with the ones whom you wish to thank. When your local friend approaches a relative from your hometown, saying, "Sally has told me about you," a larger community is knit together more firmly.

Let the parties serve the wedding, not blow out its carefully crafted energy.

Photographs and Video

Wedding photography is both an art and a business. As a photographer, Lila is deeply appreciative of what is involved in creating truly great photographs. As a ceremonialist, she understands that there are appropriate times for photographs, and times when they can divert attention from the ceremony itself. You can meet your need to capture the event without detracting from the actual experience.

The clicking and whirring sounds of cameras can be distracting, and you may notice that the mood of a room changes when many (or even a few) people view it through their cameras. You may wish to create some guidelines for the official photographers, as well as for all the people who will show up with their own cameras. A photographer who gets up close to snap pictures during a sensitive part of the ceremony may provide a good closeup photo for the album, but the container of the wedding itself has been strained. We have observed photographers in the center of the room during the core of the ceremony getting "a great shot." By distracting your audience with activity, photographers diminish the energy available to support you in the Sacred Moment. You might ask your celebrant to make specific requests about this before the wedding begins. Determine exactly why you want photos, and have a clear plan and intention for them (for example, a wedding book or distribution to family). You may wish to ask your family and those who have come to bear witness to stay present with the ceremony and allow the paid photographer to be responsible for the photographs.

When it comes to the more delicate parts of the ceremony, at the wedding's core, we suggest that you honor the mystery of the Sacred Moment. Make it special. At some weddings the director has asked the photographer to stop shooting during the exchange of vows, in order to keep the moment quiet and protected. After the announcement from the celebrant, "I now pronounce you husband and wife," or from your community, "We welcome you to your community, as husband and wife," then let the people cheer and the cameras come out to capture images for the future. Leave the mystery of the core for your heart's memory, as no photographs can substitute for what you will retain in your heart. We would even include a video camera on a tripod quietly whirring away: what it gives you will not "capture" the feeling tone of the core.

If you agree with this restriction, the celebrant or the director can announce this early on, as they invite the witnesses to participate in the creation of the beauty of the Sacred Moment. The celebrant can even say, when you are moving into the more delicate parts of the ceremony, "Now is the time to put away cameras and give all your attention to Joseph and Anna."

Honeymoon

As for the next days, research has shown that it's wise to have some kind of honeymoon. When controlled for other factors, such as income level, one study of 3,000 couples found that divorce was 41 percent less likely for those who took a honeymoon. From our point of view, this means that there was some time to integrate what had happened. If the wedding is a success, then the buzz continues in the marriage for some time. Its slow diminishment is not cause for alarm, as this means at least in part that it's been integrated. It helps to have the time to review the ceremony: "What happened?!" Go over the wedding moment by moment, point by point, to the best of your recollection. Don't wait for the photos or the video, as your memory will bring out aspects that the electronics have missed. A honeymoon is the time to recall those memories.

The Event Becomes History

You may begin to collect photographs from friends, relatives, and your official photographer. You may have a video record (though you will find that your photographs are much more accessible). You may have a guest book that people sign with comments. You may have other bits and pieces for a scrapbook. You may put the top of your wedding cake in your freezer. These combine to build a new origin myth, a story about what happened on that day when an old chapter was ended and a new one begun. The most important memories that you hold are the living presences of the Sacred Moments that you created and continue to create. You can find these anytime you choose, through your Shared Affirmation, Heart Talk, and any of the other tools that you have put into place.

Sensitive Relationships

chapter 15

There are those close to you, in your present and in your past, who are part of your wedding, part of your marriage. You need to know a bit more about who they are in your life, as well as who they are in your psyche.

Parents

What is the role of parents? What is in it for them? At a poetry reading Robert Bly presented the picture that there are two marriage ceremonies. One occurs between a man and a woman (or any couple, including same-sex marriages) "upstairs," while "downstairs" there are other, more secret marriages happening, especially the secret marriage between the two sets of parents. We began to look for these parallel marriages in the shadows, and have found them in every case. Either living or dead, these four people—and/or stepparents, important uncles, aunts, and grandparents—join in another kind of marriage, under the floor, out of sight, in the dark. As celebrants, we have little opportunity to interview the parents or significant others. We meet them mostly through the marrying couple.

Sometimes you may get cranky with your spouse and vent a complaint, and find to your surprise that the words and the delivery that come out of you are exactly those of one of your parents. Who let them into your heart, to take over your behavior? This happens. One partner accidentally calls the other "Mom" or "Dad" . . . Such a slip should not require embarrassment, apologies, or the end of the relationship, but rather an awareness that such dynamics move deep down in the psyche for everyone.

It would be very wise to engage in a truth-telling process (as in a Heart Talk—see chapter 7, and the specific questions in chapter 9) on the subject of parents: what you think of them, what kind of relationship you would like to have with them, and what limits you may have to set on their behavior. Getting this clearer in the beginning will help later on. You can honor them as ancestors, and also clarify where their agendas stop and yours take over.

Often, a bride will find her mother hinting that her daughter's wedding ceremony is a chance for her to "do it again" or "do it right this time." That's where the emphasis on the right dress, and the right flowers, and so forth, often comes from. To be conscious in your wedding may require that you give your mother a very important, but not unlimited, part to play. She is not at the core of your wedding. You are.

Psychology, and especially psychoanalysis, understands the very deep impression that parents have made upon you. You aren't going to figure out your "father wound" or "mother wound" or "father complex" or "mother complex" in the runup to your wedding. You can make a start, but don't ever expect to solve the parent issue. Begin with this exercise.

exercise

Parents

Thank your parents. Without them you would not be here. They brought you into the world and cared for you. Thank them, first to yourself. Say aloud to yourself, "Thank you, parents!" Gratitude is the foundation upon which your relationship to them must rest. Later you can thank them personally and find out what they would like to see in your ceremony. For some, you may need to set limits on their involvement; for some, you may need to find jobs for them to do. It's helpful to have them involved but not too involved. The point here is that the relationship with parents should be based on gratitude. "Thank you, parents!" Start there.

Discuss with your partner any area of sensitivity that may exist about either one of your parents. You can communicate requests or concerns to your celebrant and director.

At weddings, the absence of a parent is noted. If the parent has passed on, then sometimes a seat is left for that person, acknowledging that he or she is still present and affecting you from an unseen place.

One wedding that we attended was held up by the absence of a father who had said he was coming. Everyone waited and waited, fifteen minutes, a half hour, forty-five minutes . . . People whispered, "Where is he? Is he all right?" The bride and groom, in different rooms, not yet ready to formally see each other, passed notes back and forth through their friends, wondering what to do. They finally heard that he had been delayed, was all right, and would come when he could. The couple decided to go ahead. Unfortunately, the celebrant did not speak about the gaping absence that had taken over everyone's attention. We would have recommended speaking openly about it to the audience, assuring them that the father was all right, and asking everyone to hold this person as if present.

Some brides have told us that they don't wish to be brought down the aisle by a parent. "I don't want to be 'given away'! How archaic! I'm my own person; I've grown up: I don't belong to them that I should be given away!" Yes, you are your own person—your own One—who can choose to enter into relation with another to make a Two, foundation for experience of the ONE. But here's another perspective: as celebrants, we would like you to be escorted to the front of the wedding by someone, because then you can relax and not have to think about where you need to be, and when. This gives you the opportunity to be more open and vulnerable to the exchange that will occur in the core of the wedding, including the Sacred Moment. It will help the ceremony if you are escorted by someone. This pertains to both bride and groom.

Secondly, the fact that you are accompanied by one or both parents shows your acknowledgment that they have been essential to your existence. They may not have been all you wanted or needed in your childhood, but you have to admit that their union years ago made it possible for you to be here. It's healthy to acknowledge that fact. You might choose a biological parent or parents or, for those with stepparents or parent substitutes, the people who brought you up. The point is that you acknowledge the early part of your life and the central role of your parents (of whatever kind) in it.

Thirdly, the "giving away" is a public acknowledgment that your parents are stepping back, that you are indeed an independent person. This helps bride, groom, audience, and parents to affirm that you are now on your own.

With the celebrant's help, you can do this in a manner that asserts these relationships. The series of handshakes that we described in the previous chapter has been powerful each and every time that we've supervised it.

Relatives

What about the aunts and uncles and cousins and all their children? Most will understand your intention to create a conscious wedding. Some will not. Some will even come with a whole list of needs they expect you to satisfy: a certain kind of pillow on their bed or temperature of toast for breakfast, and a certain quality and quantity of time spent with you. Why are they coming? Why do they burden you with their needs and their embarrassing stories? Because they need you—your vitality and vivacity. They can sense your life force from afar, and are coming to nourish themselves with it. They may not know exactly why they are coming, but replenishment is an important reason. Their not knowing means that they may demand your time and attention at the wrong time, that is, just before the wedding while you as athletes are preparing body, mind, heart, and soul for the big event.

Relatives also bring a kind of power as a gift to you—the power of the stream of ancestors coming through them to you, a stream that goes all the way back to the beginning of time. They may or may not be aware of the gift that they bring you. You—or your celebrant—can help them in this gifting.

Some or many of your relatives are not part of your regular community of friends and colleagues. We have found that they can misunderstand the cues that are given them and easily feel disrespected by some detail or string of details. We highly recommend that you assign one of your friends as a companion to each visiting relative. The companion will greet that relative and make any bridges necessary to other aspects of your community and the ceremony. For example, we've seen many times a wedding couple request that "Reserved" signs be set out in the front rows of the ceremonial space, explaining that these seats are there "for family." That's not enough. When actual names were not added to the "Reserved" signs, we have observed family members enter the space and sit in the back rows, assuming the reserved sections were intended for someone else. In one case, those family members came in, looked around, sat in the back row, and then left just after the wedding, feeling that they had been snubbed. They hadn't been snubbed; it was simply that no one knew who they were. They hadn't announced themselves; they came in too late for the celebrants to greet them; and no one else asked who they were. A companion would cut right through that confusion.

Who would have thought that a relative would take the trouble to feel snubbed, after being invited to your wedding? What people are thinking and feeling cannot be predicted. Of course, were you the director of your own wedding, you could avoid these misunderstandings: you would greet the visitors personally, acknowledge how far they have traveled, thank them profusely for the effort that they've made in coming so far, ask how things are going at home, take them to their seats, inquire, "Is there anything else you need? Some water perhaps?" or care for their every need . . . Do you see that you can't do that? They may want it, but you can't provide that. We need you in a different mood aiming toward the core of the ceremony. You can arrange for a director or a system of companions, and that's the best you can do.

If you are concerned about "fundamentalists" of any sort attending your wedding, and you don't want to offend them, it is important to realize that this sacred space is yours, and we encourage you to be true to it, without creating offence!

We know of a wedding where Uncle Robert couldn't stand hearing the name "God," and threatened to walk out of the room if it was uttered. Uncle Robert's views were so strong that they ruled what was said and not said. The couple backed down and did not include a reference to the name of a power that they felt unified them. "In Whose Name" became the second and third choices, powerful yet missing something that was important. The couple succumbed to the emotional blackmail, as they wished to offend no one. One must ask: Whose wedding is this? Can a couple find a way to invite people to support them in shaping the sacred space that *they* choose, and ask the guests to leave their judgments at the door? Did this solve the problem of Uncle Robert's intolerance? Or will it continue to direct their lives?

In a wedding that we facilitated, the father of the groom insisted that the wedding could not be truly legitimate unless the name of Jesus Christ was prominent. Even though the wedding couple did not have a relationship with Jesus Christ, we were able to craft a section where we made a bridge between the names in which they were marrying—"Sacred Union" and "Love"—and Jesus Christ, thus recognizing the importance of the father's beliefs as part of his uprightness and integrity as an ancestor.

On that occasion, we acknowledged that "Sacred Union" and "Love" were true foundations for believers of every tradition. That includes atheism, agnosticism, and every other -ism that you can imagine.

Your celebrant will be helpful in advising how to meet a relative with a distinct point of view about life, such as the atheism and fundamentalism in the examples above. Bridges can be built, especially if these potentially difficult relatives can be identified ahead of time.

Here's one way to work with different belief systems. Ask your celebrant to say something like: "We are all gathered here today to support the union of these two people. We have come to witness what is sacred to them, and to what they are holding as values in their life together. We ask that you all support the choices of these two, and not be offended by the ceremony that they have created. We are all here to bear witness to their union, based on values that they care about and have reflected on for some time."

Serve your relatives as they serve you by attending your wedding. Don't let them undercut the wedding, or your private time before the wedding, for this impairs your ability to give them what they really wish for—a blessing from the sacred and divine. Then give that blessing fully, knowing that the energy flows through you to them without prejudice.

Make no mistake: you are going through a threshold crossing from together to married. In a successful wedding, you will take your families and communities with you, more than they may have expected. In this wedding, you get their commitment to be there for you in the future. There may come a time when you call in that commitment, so make it clear in the ceremony.

Friends

Family brings the connection with ancestors, the strength of a strong foundation. Friends bring the heart. Choosing the appropriate support for your wedding or ceremony can lead to sensitive moments among friends. Some may feel excluded; others may be unable to attend. We suggest you find ways to ask help from friends who might not have a part in the actual ceremony. We suggest that you send reports to those who can't attend. Delegate as much responsibility as you can to those who support you, and make each job special.

In the previous chapter we spoke about bachelor and bachelorette parties, their counterparts in other countries, and their origins. Previously we spoke about gathering groups of friends together. In David and Lila's wedding, prior to the ceremony, a group of men and a group of women gathered, first to interview and support the same-sex brother and sister, and then to interview and support the partner. Some weddings have picnics or hikes for friends in the days prior to the wedding. These can be valuable so long as you remember that you are preparing for a ceremony. You may have to help your helpers help you by giving clear directions. Your college roommate may wish to go off with you "just like the old days" to have a walk or a drink—or, more than "wish," they may assume that you will do what you used to do together. You may have to set limits on what you can and can't do.

A Circle of Protection

Your wedding may have a group of men and women that you've chosen to be closer to your wedding ceremony. These are the bridesmaids and the groomsmen.

What was the original purpose of the men who accompany the groom: the groomsmen and the best man? This takes us back to times when these men were armed with weapons and ready at a moment's notice to defend the ceremony and everyone in it. We have found in our ceremonial practice that this readiness on the part of the men—and these days the women too—to form a protection around the outside of the ceremony creates a sense of safety that is primal and important. There have been occasions when weddings have been interrupted and upset. A good set of attentive helpers at the front door, and a sense of awareness on the part of a certain chosen few—whether groomsmen, bridesmaids, brothers, sisters, friends given this job—will dispel a deep concern that lives in all of us that something could violate this vulnerable moment. In our sense of Concentric Circles—inverted in the actual ceremony so that the mythic realm lies in the middle and the stories of the world lie outside—the sense of protection forms the outermost circle of the ceremony against the intrusions of the world. At the graduation of the third-year women from the Path of the Ceremonial Arts training at the StarHouse, the women begin in the evening. The men come at a specified time about an hour later, circling the StarHouse on the outside, facing outward. They are not there to peek in at the graduation ceremony, but to provide an energetic protection and container for the ceremony taking place inside. Everyone can feel the power of the encirclement of positive intention. As this takes place on the first weekend in December, these evenings can get cold for the men. Often the women invite them inside at the end of their ceremony, to thank them for that service.

It detracts when the groomsmen don't know this tradition, which is commonly the case. We have seen them many times wandering in behind the groom, looking blank or uncomfortable in their unusual clothes, sometimes giggling, poking one another, winking and waving at friends in the audience. Knowing this bit of history can change all of that. You might place them at strategic points around the room, in full attentiveness to everything going on. They can be placed at the four directions or elsewhere. Reviving some of their traditional role as protectors will enliven the whole ceremony.

Whenever we have instructed the men in their traditional role—that in prior centuries they would have been armed and ready to act at any moment—it has enlivened the men attending. Men these days need to be given something to do. Attentiveness is one such task. The protective weapons of today are not swords but rather attention, which energetically is quite powerful. In every case, this enlivened attention from the groomsmen has enhanced the energy in the whole room. The sense of protection has permitted the groom and bride at the center to be more vulnerable and available emotionally, improving their ability to demonstrate to the audience that they are well matched.

Bridesmaids long ago had a complementary function, to protect the queen for a day, the bride, and more importantly to enhance her powers. They dress in support of the bride, and become the many flowers supporting the central flower.

On occasion, the bride has asked that they join the circle of protection, and we have set it up with the men, alternating female with male around the whole room. What happens when people "hold space"—that is, become aware and awake to the moments of the wedding, especially in the core of ceremony—is palpable. It supports the One becoming Two and inviting the ONE into the ceremony.

Difficult Emotions from Others

Friends and relatives have a job at your wedding: to support you, to help knit together the feelings that flow freely in and around the ceremony. A difficult emotion may sneak in: envy. Someone succumbs to the feeling, "I want that!" Or, jealousy: "I want your partner!" It happens. These emotions arise often unexpectedly.

It may help to understand what that friend is really feeling: "I can feel that the bride and groom love each other deeply. They are strong as One and One, committed as a Two, and have attained the ONE! I feel it so strongly! I don't have that! I want it! I want the ONE all to myself!" The envy or jealousy implies that your friend senses the One, Two, and ONE, and its relative absence in his or her life. The good news is that the friend has grown already from this perception. The bad news is that the reactive emotion can be disruptive to what you're trying to build in the ceremony.

You can design a wedding that directs the potentially destructive energy of envy to the benefit of your Sacred Moment. The celebrant can say to the audience before the couple's entry: "This couple marries in the name of Love [or whatever is the being or principle that the couple has chosen "In Whose Name"]. Love is here and in the ceremony will make its presence felt to the benefit of all here." When held in this manner, the powers of the ONE enter the ceremony and are dispensed to all present, and beyond.

In describing the parallel lines after the ceremony, the celebrant can emphasize that the couple dispenses blessing to everyone. Theirs is an overflowing cup, and there is plenty of positive blessing energy to nurture everyone.

After the couple enters, the celebrant can reaffirm this: "We have Love here. We have Beauty." And any of the names that the couple has chosen to invoke to oversee and interpenetrate the ceremony.

The celebrant thus communicates to the witnesses and to the couple that there is abundant energy arising from the focus of this ceremony. "This blessing is here, among us, available to us. It is happening, and can be more powerful if you strive to be conscious of it. There is enough for everyone."

Story Time

Uncle Robert would really like to tell everyone about the groom's early life. "I remember Bret when he was only so high, and would go crawling around in the ditches looking for frogs. He would come home filthy, with frogs in his pockets. One day he . . ." Sometimes these stories end in a lovely way, and everyone smiles. Sometimes they reveal something that no one, including the bride-to-be, ever knew about Bret. Sometimes these stories are embarrassing for one person, sometimes for everyone. Story time is a way that the traditions of the family are shared. Skeletons are released from closets. Wondrous tales are told. Appreciations are lavished. Old grudges come to the surface. All of them intertwined in a confusion of complex relationships!

There has to be a place where these stories can be told. Family celebrations can often feel like a pressure cooker, where the story has to come out! Relatives of the couples for whom we have been celebrants have taken us aside to tell us stories that they could not keep in. We realized that they needed a forum where they could tell the whole family. Two families are linking through the marriage, and these stories link the two families together. One family might roll its eyes at Uncle Robert's story about Bret and his frogs, as they've heard it before. For the other family, this is part of their new mythology, and they are very interested.

Where can you make space for this interweaving of family mythologies? During the wedding is not a good time, especially if the story is about crawling in ditches and getting filthy. It can take away from the buildup to the Sacred Moment. The night before the wedding is the time usually chosen, though a bomb of a story can make the task of the ceremony more difficult. The reception after the wedding is another time. If you have the opportunity of getting the two families together a few days ahead of time, that would be best.

Children

In Part One we spoke about integrating children into your relationship. We have hinted at ways to include them in a ceremony. We will say a little more here.

That we're talking about children means either that you're remarrying, as in a rededication (which we'll come to in Part Three), or that you're blending your families. When one or both of the partners have parented children for whom they have responsibility, the children are part of the arrangement . . . but how?

Begin by drawing a diagram of stick figures. Start with you and your partner. Connect yourselves together with three lines showing three major modes of communication between you: head (thinking), heart (feeling), and hand (willing or doing). Draw a circle around you. Then another circle. Now you have a rough picture of your individual Ones, the Two of you (first circle), and the larger ONE that expands beyond both of your experiences (second larger circle).

Add a child for whom you are father and mother, who interacts with each of your Ones, becomes integrated into your Two, and on occasion comes to enjoy your sense of ONE. In the standard model of marriage, this is the ideal. The problem is that the standard model is now the minority position.

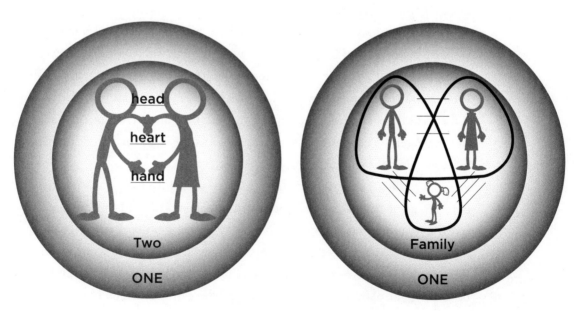

One to One: circles of Two and ONE

How about partners that come with children? Let's say two children from a previous marriage. Along with the children come an allegiance of some kind to the parent's previous partner. It may be distant, if the ex-partner has disappeared and the children are with you all of the time. It may be challenged by an arrangement where the children are with you every other weekend. Or, extremely difficult, you have the children half of the time. Though this may seem logical and fair—"Let's go halves!"—it can be especially trying for the children, whose tensions then become a major part of your marriage story.

Some single parents act as more than Parent–Child with their child. The relationship may have strayed to Adult–Adult or Child–Parent (the child acting as decision-maker, helping the adult who has temporarily fallen apart). You need to be ready to unravel those relationships. Little Tommy may have become used to getting his way with everything: what to eat, if and when to do his homework, taking electronics to bed with him. Little Tommy will expect to interact with the new partner in the same way. Little Tommy may not like to be told that he is a child, and not an equal adult, and not in charge. That last situation is common. When the single parent has been worn down by parenting, a child may have come to act as a Parent, shoes too big for a young person to fill. A child acting like a Parent can become a tyrant.

These dynamics will have to be worked out before a wedding ceremony. We have observed wedding ceremonies where a child sulks or rolls the eyes or makes demands. At home, in private, the kid could not get away with it. The Parent mode of the parent would kick in and order the situation swiftly. Even if this behavior occurred in a shopping center, the Parent could act decisively. But the Parent is now incapacitated, so to speak, because the Parent is seeking a Sacred Moment with the new partner.

What to do with a problem child? Indeed, with any child—as we have observed some model children, unsettled by the enormity of the energy moving in a wedding, become problems. What do you do? A two-year-old needs a child wrangler—that term most often used for cowboys and steers. You need a friend or relative whose main job it is to arrange that the child be in the right place at the right time, and who can take the child out of the sacred space if necessary.

In the ideal wedding, as you move toward the core, just at the edge of entering the most intimate part of the ceremony, you say farewell to all of your loved ones except your partner. The adults will understand, and you will have to explain to the children that you will see them on the other side—in fifteen minutes clock time, which may feel like hours—and you will then be the same and different.

The wrangler can conduct the child (or wranglers, plural, for children, plural) through all of this, firmly, warmly. The children will benefit in the end by what a powerful ceremony will bring into the family's life. They may not understand this, and a logical explanation will likely be insufficient. The warmth of the wrangler will work much better than your explanations.

You may also wish to empower your celebrant to deal lovingly and firmly with a situation of this kind, should it arise. In that case, if something occurs, don't try to hush it up off to the side, because everyone notices. The witnesses begin to squirm, and you've divided their attention. Transparency works best here, so that you engage the witnesses in the difficult decision. The celebrant can announce to everyone, "Amelia seems to be wishing she had some of this attention but the event has upset her. So we'll ask that Amelia go out for the next fifteen minutes, and be reunited with us after the core of the ceremony." Once the delicate parts of the ceremony are over, the celebrant can arrange that Amelia be brought back in and given some of that center-stage attention.

The kind of relationship you have with children is determined by their age. Young children are happy to have a job to do, such as setting place names at a table or lighting candles. Grown children can be included in a constellation that accompanies their parent almost to the ceremonial altar. Even grandchildren can and ought to be included in that accompaniment.

Early and mid-teenagers can pose a significantly different challenge. You may wish to include them in the ceremony, and know that it must be done. Some will add a wonderful presence, and, if asked for their contribution, come forward with the most engaging articulation of the situation. And some may not want to join you, period. Perhaps they think they are indestructible, autonomous, clever, have something to say, or have absolutely nothing to say. Many of these challenging behaviors are natural expressions of their life stage. They may be exaggerated when normal routines are changed because of a new relationship and a wedding. Don't take their intransigence or outbursts personally. A teenager may need a companion, someone other than you who can respond to his or her needs.

We've been preparing you for the difficulties that we have seen happen. You need to prepare for resistance from a child in your ceremony. And you need to prepare for a child entering into your Love-field as into a world of wonder. Their fresh experience of awe at the energy generated can add enormously to the feeling of the wedding. We (Lila and David) have learned much from our children. We gave them a special place of honor at our wedding—not in the core, but with special roles to play. We were blessed by their presence.

If you wish to give your children a place in your wedding, you may need assistance in those delicate negotiations. A celebrant can help, or a mentor, or a friend, or the wrangler. It will help to have a third party speak with your children, as often they feel excluded by the radiance of the Love-field that the Two is creating. Even if they don't stand with you for a part of the wedding, you can seat them in a prominent place that shows you care. They may completely surprise you with their contribution to the ceremony. The fact that you asked will be forever precious to them.

We'd like to cite a few examples about integrating children into a wedding. There are many ways to do this, depending on their age and whether they will be full-time family members or more distant ones.

If it's a more distant, older child, you might give him or her a part to speak, or a poem to read in the Reception/Amplification stage of the ceremony. If the child is going to be a strongly integrated part of the family's daily life, creating a key place for the child, beginning in the early stages of the ceremony and leading up to the Sacred Moment, can be very meaningful, as well as mythic in nature.

In one wedding, the bride was honoring a six-year-old girl. (The bride's previous husband was the father, she the stepmother.) The child would be spending part of the year with the bride and new husband. She gave the child a beautiful pearl on a necklace, saying she would be adding one pearl every year to the string, in honor of the growing they would all do together. At the age of six, the child was deeply affected by this display, and everyone picked up on it. It was a demonstration of both loyalty and development.

Another couple was weaving an extended family together, a child from each of them. They chose to bring both boys into the inner circle of the ceremony. Each presented the other's child with a totem necklace that had been made specifically for the event. They spoke about their vision for creating family together, and the willingness to weave a new kind of fabric from the threads of the four of them. It was quite clear how moving this was to the boys, in ways they could barely comprehend at the time.

Our advice to those bringing children into the marriage is similar to all the other aspects of the wedding: Find a way to ritualize the vision you have for your extended family. Speak to the story where you will live most of your days. Speak as well to the psychological realm, and most importantly to the mythic realm. The ceremony is mythic. Children of all ages live a great deal in the mythic—from fairy tales to video games. Find a way to bridge the mythic with the mythic. A gift given, an opportunity for the child to speak, a way for the "new" parent to honor that child—all this comes out of who the people are, and what the configuration of family will be.

Sometimes you can look to the elements and notice what needs to happen in the relationships that are being created. Does the relationship need to be more grounded? Then suggest that the child find a beautiful stone, crystal, or piece of rock art to offer to the ceremony; or you might gift the child with such a thing, keeping it on the central altar during the ceremony. Perhaps there needs to be some healing energy brought into the ritual, in which case water might be the best choice. Can the blended family seek out that water before the ceremony, together? Can the child be tasked with finding special waters through Internet friends? If a lighthearted quality is needed, the child might want to release a bird, or a helium balloon. We have attended weddings where each of these happened. The bird had been injured, had been cared for, and was now ready for release back into nature. To the balloon was tied a poem of hope written by the child. Together lighting candles of intention for a vision of the future is always a good ritual element. You all hold the match together, and can take the flame from the central Unity Candle and spread it to what the child's hopes and visions are for the future. These are ways to bring into the ceremony what's important to the child, and have that interest and commitment witnessed by everyone.

Cleanup

One of the most difficult parts of organizing any kind of party is cleanup time. People like the buildup, but they don't like the letdown. A healthy ceremony has a steady incline to the peak as well as a steady decline to the mundane world of everyday concerns. Many will assume the ceremony is over at the pronouncement, and out come the electronic devices and the drinks. The celebrant may be needed to help the intensity of the ceremony decline more slowly, so that the delicate feelings experienced in the center can be integrated rather than overwhelmed by new stimulation. One of the best ways to integrate is by helping clean up the ceremonial equipment, the tables and floors, and any of the messes made in preparation for the reception. Even if you are renting a space in which to hold your ceremony, and even if you have only two hours in that space, make some effort to have others tidy it up or clean it, as this activity releases the energy that you built there and helps you integrate it better. Even if you feel you've hired the venue and it's their responsibility to clean it up, understand that the function of cleanup is to slow down the release of the ceremony. Remember: this isn't you, as you are doing something else. This pertains to those to whom you give jobs, which should include as many people as you can.

The Actual Design of the Ceremony

In our work with ceremonies at the StarHouse, and in the teaching of the Path of the Ceremonial Arts, we have developed a simple approach to ritual design. Here are the basic steps, adapted to a wedding ceremony: Preparing Sacred Space, Invocation, Reception (Amplification), Distribution, and Closing. We will briefly introduce these basic steps in sequence, then go into more detail. In summary, it's like climbing a mountain, enjoying the peak, then climbing down again. Each step has its own tasks and flavor.

Take some time together to decide which of these steps you would like to design into your wedding ceremony. There are many options, but this simple arc will help you identify where and how the pieces land.

In designing a yoga class, teachers are advised to cluster the poses in such a way that the class moves smoothly between standing poses, and then down to sitting poses. The teacher also creates a choreography that balances back extension and forward bending, so the individual expands and contracts in a natural rhythm. Choreographing a wedding is similar. There is a sense of flow that will help all participate and relax into it.

Preparing Sacred Space

Design. Your attendants, family, and friends can be on hand to create the altars and set the space to evoke the mood of the ceremony. What does the altar look like, where are the rings placed, what elements of ceremony do you bring to the process, and how do they look, feel, and sound? You are building the container that holds the core of the ceremony.

Purification. To make a public or rented space your own for the day, or even for a few hours, you need to purify it. You may choose to do this with the smoke of a plant, as incense or smudge, to cleanse the air with the product of fire. You may use plenty of water for washing. You may bring fresh earth and clean crystals into the room. You may use the musical tones of instruments and of your own song. Purification works on the space and on those purifying it. It declares, "We cleanse the old and enter the circle of Sacred Time, and so will all who bear witness to our ceremony." It may be that you cannot get into the space until just before the ceremony. Here's a question: will it be you doing the purifying?

Your task is to feel what others have done on your behalf when you enter.

Invocation

This will normally be given by the celebrant. It can happen more than once. Before the bride and groom enter, the celebrant may wish to bring the witnesses into alignment with the inspiration the couple has chosen to guide the ceremony. An invocation, which includes "In Whose Name" this ceremony is called, creates a resonance for the group experience.

An example of an invocation before the couple enters: "Susan and Simon have consulted with me about the nature of their union. It is their wish to be united in the name of Love and Compassion for All Life, so please join me in filling this room with a feeling of Love and Compassion for All Life, so that as they enter, they feel its presence." The celebrant can invoke, or supervise the invocation of, the four directions, as they often are by the very architecture of the churches in which these ceremonies take place. The celebrant can invoke the elements, various deities, and angelic presences.

After the bride and groom have entered and the container has been sealed, a new invocation is appropriate, in the hearing of the couple.

All the preliminaries to the Sacred Moment, including the entry of the groom and bride, the giving away, the readings and music, are part of the invocation of a wedding, leading up to the Sacred Moment. Through these activities you invoke or call upon heavenly beings or great principles to become active in your presence. The stage of invocation has a feeling of lifting, of vertical movement.

Reception/Amplification

After you receive the virtues, energies, and divinities that you have invoked, you amplify what you have received. Your family, friends, and other participants may be involved through readings and other special assignments. After the vertical lifting of the different forms of invocation, the container expands horizontally to include more and more of the witnesses, and the good intentions of all are amplified. The ceremonial activity is moving toward the Sacred Moment.

Coming Into Union: The Sacred Moment

This is the heartbeat of the ceremony. We behold the One—the two individuals entering from different directions and at different times—becoming Two—the partnership affirmed in vows and rings—and then becoming ONE—the communion that they experience in the Sacred Moment, shared with all. This core section of the wedding ends with the pronouncement.

Distribution

The peak has been reached, and the pronouncement spoken. Now everyone must come back to the regular world. But you don't return by jumping off the mountain that you've climbed. You savor and integrate and move back slowly, swifter than the buildup but not, as in many weddings, dropping off, done, party time. Here the couple can turn back to their guests, having experienced their coming into union, and share their Love and radiance. This might involve a group song or chant, a short celebratory piece of music, or simply the joyful exit from the ceremonial space. The celebrant thanks and releases the presences contained by the ceremony, and offers them to the greater good of all. The newlyweds continue to distribute their blessings to others in a reception line. A vibrant ceremony distributes to a wider community.

Closing

The stages of Distribution and Closing intermingle. As they have different purposes, it's helpful to think of them differently, so we separate them here. At the other side of the peak of the ceremony, you intersperse these functions.

Depending on how you created your sacred space, you may now need the celebrant or your friends and family to release the energies that were called in. Perhaps this would include the naming and release of the four directions, as well as the elements, deities, and other "unseen guests" that you invoked. Thanks for coming goes to *all* of your guests, human and otherwise. It's very important that there be a breathing here, a calmness before another lifting up with the events of a reception. The breathing gives an opportunity for reviewing and integrating the many experiences that have just occurred. Cultivate that relaxation into calm, as it assists integration of what just happened.

After the Ceremony

Knowing what will happen after the ceremony helps you design the transition from ritual to play, and can open possibilities for sacred play.

That was the overview. Now for more detail:

Preparing Sacred Space Before the Ceremony

This is an art in itself, and will vary according to needs, visions, and budgets! There is something special about creating sacred space, no matter where the wedding takes place. Some suggestions:

- You set a clear intention that this space becomes a temple for your union, a temporary temple but a temple nonetheless.

- You create a sense of order. Consider the color and placement of flowers and how they contribute to the whole design. Arrange special items carefully on an altar.

- You do not take charge of arrangements on the actual wedding day! As much as you want everything to be just right, it's not where you need to be putting your attention. Allow trusted friends to handle this under the supervision of a director or wedding planner.

- Helpers burn incense or ethyl alcohol, or smudge with sage or cedar, to clear the space of its previous uses.

- Helpers wash the space with water, then spritz the space with diluted flower essence (such as rose oil) before (and perhaps during) the guests' entrance.

- Helpers have music playing as people enter. Decide on the kind of music you both love. Live music is good here also. In addition to music for witnesses entering, you may opt for a focused song or piece after the welcome.

- We strongly recommend against serving alcohol before or during the wedding. You may have to bring it in afterward, bowing to pressures from your witnesses. Beforehand, it tends to weaken the powers of consciousness of your witnesses.

- Helpers seat the witnesses, according, if you wish, to the tradition of bride's people on the left (from the vantage of someone entering from the rear) and groom's on the right, or in some traditions the reverse. You can also choose open seating. Helpers and companions seat family members in the reserved seats toward the front.

Purification. At some weddings we've supervised, methods of purification are offered to the witnesses: the opportunity to wash their hands, in a few cases a ritual washing of the witnesses' feet, or someone with a smudge stick washing the body of each witness with ceremonial smoke, or spraying it with a fine mist of rosewater. In every case, the entry to the ceremony is set so that the witnesses arrive through a hallway and a doorway, or between greeters, that is cheerful and beautiful.

You create a container away from the larger world, away from noise and traffic. You do everything in your power to distance yourself from the larger world of busy people going hither and thither. One of the most important ways that the world continues to intrude is via electronic devices. Having read the latest research on this, we recommend that the phones are turned off—not simply to buzz mode or airplane mode, but off—or put into envelopes at the front door. This goes for your witnesses and any staff that you have at your occasion, including photographers and planners. It would be grand, too, to have any wifi at the venue turned off.

Welcome and greeting from the celebrant. This is also part of the preparation of the sacred space and can include the preliminary invocation mentioned above, as well as the sharing of any specific details of the ceremony that may need to be explained. Note: The wedding couple is not in the room, unless the groom prefers to be present by the time of the welcome.

- The celebrant or a special friend welcomes those who are attending, making them feel at home and important as witnesses to this marriage. The celebrant gives all the stage directions for the play that is about to happen, sets up everyone's parts, and makes sure that everyone is warm and comfortable. The celebrant explains the theme. The celebrant asks that all electronic devices are turned all the way off. The celebrant asks that cameras not be used during the core of the ceremony, and promises a reminder on this point. The celebrant names the beings or principles "In Whose Name" the couple has convened this gathering and ceremony. This already is an invocation; through repetition it will build up power as the ceremony proceeds.

- A helper plays a special song or music (live or recorded) to welcome people and warm them to the ceremony.

- The celebrant guides the group how to pronounce you "husband and wife" on cue toward the end. If you use this device, the witnesses need to practice at the beginning, before the couple enters, under the direction of the celebrant, so that they do not fumble at the end. We prefer it when all the witnesses, on cue, and after practice, can announce: "We now pronounce you husband and wife, partners in life!"

- The celebrant shares any instructions for the very end: the importance of the parallel lines to greet the bride and groom, and how to receive that blessing. The celebrant gives guidelines for throwing rice, birdseed, or flower petals. Rice has recently been frowned upon as destructive to bird life. You need to let people know how they can appropriately express their joy at the end.

- The celebrant invites the witnesses to participate actively before the bride and groom enter. When we serve as celebrants, we ask the witnesses to feel their blessings flowing from their eyes, from their smiles, from their hearts. The celebrant asks them to help create a sacred container where, in the vicinity of the vows, the Sacred Moment can occur, and they will actively feel blessed by this union. The more the witnesses are invited, the more they engage and the more energy there is to work with.

Invocation

This is where the true beginning or "calling in" of the ceremonial time begins. It starts after the welcome by the celebrant, and moves through various stages. You may decide to do things differently from what we describe below. Truthfully, every prop that you have—every flower, corsage, crystal, everything—invokes the Love that permits communion. Every aspect of invocation lifts the whole room higher and higher into more refined realms.

- The groom enters with his men. This can be a solemn time, or it can be light. Either way, it ought to feel strong and intended. The men can stay close to the groom or they can arrange themselves around the space, attentive and protective.

- At a cue from the celebrant, music is played to indicate the entry procession of the bride. The bride enters, and typically, everyone stands to honor her. This is her day. She is queen of this day. We have also noticed that most brides embody a specific aspect of the Divine Feminine. If you are familiar with archetypes, you may find it interesting to determine this. Is it Aphrodite? Artemis? A wild forest sylph, or a Native American princess? The bride can be one or all of these. The same relation to archetypes applies to the groom also—he is a god and a man, at one and the same time.

- The celebrant invokes again, in the hearing of bride and groom, the beings or principles "In Whose Name" they have entered this wedding and marriage.

- The bride's father takes his daughter's hand and places it in the hand of the groom. Or he shakes the right hand of the groom, holding on until he places his daughter's left hand in the groom's right hand. Either will be a potent gesture felt by the whole room. We have met some brides who balk at the idea of being "given away," and that's understandable. It's not for everyone! But it can also be reframed to be an honorable exchange of the "primary man in your life" moving from father to husband. It can also allow for a mythic moment to happen between the men themselves. The father does need to acknowledge that his daughter is starting a new chapter . . . without Dad! At the end, however you get there, the bride and groom hold both of each other's hands.

- The celebrant deliberately names, and thus creates, the concentric circles of a sacred space, where at the center the couple will have their Sacred Moment. A more formal invocation, now that the bride and groom are present, might include the following:
  - Four people call in the four directions (East, South, West, North), and perhaps three more call in Above, Below, and Within. This continues the creation of a strong container.

- Friends or relatives whom you may have asked to call in the directions may bring in a color, a flag, or the element of that direction. We usually associate the elements and directions as follows: East–air, South–fire, West–water, North–earth. In the Southern Hemisphere, we would use South–earth and North–fire, as there the sun rises and sets in the northern part of the sky.
- The celebrant delivers a simple prayer, blessing, or invocation, and perhaps asks the witnesses to close their eyes and envision this Sacred Union.
- Perhaps a special (and brief) song is used to warm your witnesses' hearts. Live singing is best. A few chords on a guitar and a phrase from a song can hold more power than a whole song.

Reception/Amplification

The preparations become increasingly intimate and powerful. The focus becomes more intense and concentrated, so it can open a channel to divine energy to arrive to bless the union.

- Family or friends now offer their voices with poems, readings, or dedications you would like to have heard. We suggest that people be prepared with what they say, reading if necessary, but ideally speaking from memory or spontaneously from the heart. You may have special poems or quotations about the nature of marriage or Love that you would like to have represented. Keep these readings short. We facilitated a wedding where a ninety-second belly dance occurred here, which worked perfectly to set a tone of artful honoring of the human body. Attention can be dispersed if readings or performances are too long and difficult to follow. Here's why we included this part in "reception": Though you might think that quoting Thoreau or Hildegard or St. Paul could be part of the invocation—the influences that are called in to empower the proceedings—by this point, everyone who speaks has already been empowered. The short speeches or songs become vehicles for the powers of the ONE to come into the wedding, bolstering the build-up to the core. They need to be short and interesting. It's the feeling that counts, not the number of words.

- At the celebrant's cue, the couple acknowledges the special people who are present. You may have parents whom you would like to honor. They may have something special that they'd like to present to you. Perhaps you would like to light a candle in gratitude for your ancestors. Perhaps the parents have a blessing for you. We suggest that most of this should be rehearsed in the day or days before; some of it can be spontaneous. Some parents are very clear that they want to bring a nonmaterial gift or offering to the ceremony. It can be lovely to be surprised! Be very clear beforehand about the time limit, however, as it is your day, not theirs. And accept whatever happens in the moment. At this stage in the ceremony, it's the celebrant's job to set limits, not yours.

- Especially if you are creating a larger extended family with children from previous partners, the celebrant now includes these. There are simple ways you can create an artistic ritual here, by having children carry a rose or a flower that has been color-coded to create a lovely bouquet of the "new family." You can honor smaller children by giving them a simple piece of jewelry. You can create a ceremony of all coming together, each holding a piece of string, then weaving together the strands to create a new fabric. Weaving together extended families in ritual makes a powerful beginning for creating a new shape in the family.

- The celebrant manages the unexpected. Let's say Uncle Robert gets up and begins, "I remember Bret when he was only so high," which all of Bret's family will recognize as the Bret and frogs story. Your job as the bride or groom is to breathe and maintain your composure. The celebrant's job may be to interrupt and say, "Thank you, Uncle Robert, we are now moving into the core of our ceremony. We would like to hear the whole story at the reception." There is a better time for stories from relatives who have known you since birth. The end of this section needs to feel warm, inclusive, inspired by the music and poetry, and expectant. You will have briefed your celebrant on which person could speak or which passage be read that will bring the mood to that point. If Uncle Robert is not on that list, the celebrant has to be very careful about what Uncle Robert might say.

Coming Into Union: The Sacred Moment

This is the core of the ceremony, as you take the energy that has been prepared for, invoked, and amplified. Now you're ready to make your vows.

- The Speaking of the Vows and the Affirmations
  - The celebrant announces, for example, "We are entering the core of this ceremony, supported by the beauty around us and by everything that has been offered as word and song." If it is your choice, the celebrant can say, "Remember this is the time to put away your cameras, and to make yourselves available through your presence."
  - The celebrant calls for vows. Speak your vows in the form you've chosen. Do your best to allow for spontaneity!
  - The final vows: In the case of a man and woman, whom we could name Dennis and Denise, the celebrant speaks: "Dennis, please take Denise's hand; feel her, see her. (Pause.) Do you, Dennis, take Denise, whom you now hold by the hand to be your wife and consort?"
    Dennis: "I do."
    Celebrant: "Denise, do you take Dennis whom you now hold by the hand to be your husband and consort?"
    Denise: "I do."

Celebrant: "Do you mutually promise you will love, cherish, and respect one another throughout the years?"

Dennis and Denise: "We do."

- The Exchanging of the Rings
    - Often a couple has identified a ring-bearer, maybe a friend's young daughter dressed up as the ring fairy (who, if very young, comes with a wrangler to guide her down the aisle) or the best man. We recommend that you do not assign this job to children from a previous marriage, as you need to make it clear that, while important, they aren't gatekeepers to your marriage.
    - The celebrant introduces the rings: "Wedding rings are a symbol of an unbroken circle of Love. May they be a daily reminder of your vows to each other and your resolve to live together in unity, Love, and happiness."
    - The celebrant then asks you to repeat words that you've written or approved, words that you don't have to remember but that you do have to choose consciously. It might go something like: "Dennis, please repeat after me: This ring represents the great Oneness/from whence we come/and is a symbol of my eternal dance with you./With this ring, I thee wed/ and pledge my love and commitment." Then the same with Denise, after which, the celebrant summarizes: "Gaze at the ring on your hand and on your partner's hand. Remember to see these rings as an active symbol of Love, and magic—each ring represents the names you called in today [repeat those names]. At any moment of life's challenges, you can gaze at these rings and remember!"
    - Alternatively, make up your own words ahead of time, and remember them as best you can. (The celebrant can prompt you if you stumble.) You might say something like, "This ring represents an endless circle of Love. It has no beginning and no end." Or, "This ring is a symbol of my Love for you. It is forged of gold, representing the light and beauty of our Love."

- The Sacred Moment
  - The core and central mystery, the reason for the rest of the theatrical structure of this day. The mystery visits you in several ways. First, you can't know when soul will speak to soul, or how. Second, you can't script when a Sacred Moment can occur. You have to leave that to a team made of soul, the celebrant, and the ever-changing opportunities that present themselves unexpectedly.
  - Perhaps the celebrant asks the bride and groom to close their eyes. The celebrant can ask, "Is there anything else that you would like to say to each other?" Then see what happens!
  - This request can come at other times in the ceremony, perhaps as a surprise question, posed at a time determined by the celebrant, to evoke an unexpected moment of candor.
  - The Sacred Moment may have occurred spontaneously at any time inside this container, that is, during the vows and exchange of rings. It doesn't always come exactly when called. You have to be ready and willing throughout. Whenever it does occur, the celebrant recognizes and nurtures that moment, then moves on.

- Pronouncement by the celebrant or acknowledgment in some formal way that the marriage has occurred. Suggestions for pronouncements:
  - The traditional. The celebrant simply says, "I now pronounce you husband and wife!"
  - We prefer to engage all the witnesses in this pronouncement. It creates the feeling that the whole extended community is affected by the marriage and is interested in being supportive of it. Thus the celebrant would cue the witnesses, who have at the beginning been trained, "Now we can pronounce together . . ." Everyone joins to say, "We now pronounce you husband and wife, partners in life!"

- Consider also "In Whose Name" you are being married, and include that naming here: "In the name of Compassion and Love, I now pronounce you husband and wife!"

Distribution

This part of the ceremony is the release, the celebration. Hurrah! At this stage you are fired with the passion of the energy that has moved through you and continues to move through you. As divinely inspired beings, you can distribute blessings, as the fountain of this blessing is infinite. Your witnesses receive; the whole world receives. The witnesses can participate. They can sing to you, clap for you, shower you with flowers. They do these things for you, and for what is greater than you, what resides in you at this point as archetypal and holy.

- Celebration and well-wishing
  - Time for the Kiss! Right after the pronouncement, a gesture of intimacy and conclusion. The celebrant invites, "Seal it with a kiss!" A general cheer, upbeat music, a chant that the group has learned at the beginning (we like "Jubilate Deo," easily taught), the throwing of rose petals or birdseed.
  - In a joyous moment the community receives this newly wedded union.
  - The journey out of the inner circles is assisted by an energetic song, an energetic reading, a brief energetic performance. Don't come down from the climax of the pronouncement too quickly.
  - The wedding couple leaves. Traditionally, the newlyweds now have the opportunity to distribute their blessing to those who have attended. A reception line can be set up, but not too soon. The bride and groom could well use some moments alone to seal their communion. There is a lovely wedding tradition in which the bride and groom now go off by themselves before speaking to anyone. They connect in the sacredness of this time together. For ten or fifteen minutes, they deepen in the communion of the experience

before sharing it with the community. A trusted friend, either man or woman, stands guard, back turned to the wedding couple. When the "guard" is in place, the couple can relax more fully into this time of breathing, calming, and grounding the continued buzz in their bodies—before coming out into the social realm again.

- In many traditions, the bride and groom are considered sacred after the ceremony, filled with extraordinary energy, which we find to be accurate in every case of a conscious wedding. As is often true with energy of this kind, there will be a part of your mind that ignores your actual experience, and wonders what next to worry about. Learning to notice these other realms takes either practice or openness of mind or both. If you have done your job, you are filled with the vibration of the sacred and can share the overflow of this energy with everyone at the wedding. This is not just another party. Sacred energy is flooding into you as wedding couple, and through you to others.

Closing

• The bride and groom make formal exits, followed by everyone else in the order of the procession. The couple has left with whatever attendants are necessary. The celebrant now closes the formal aspect of the ceremony. It may be appropriate to ask that he or she announce the opportunity to send a prayer or blessing after the newly married couple. There may be logistics to review as to what happens next. People often need reminders: "There will be water and drinks available outside." Or, "In ten minutes, we will call you together to create two lines for the bride and groom to walk through and dispense their blessings."

• There is also an opportunity here to release any spiritual quality or being called in for the purposes of the ceremony. If the directions or elements have been called in, the celebrant can release them or ask that those who called them in release them. It is an important part of ceremony to thank the unseen beings that have shown up, and to formally let them go.

After the Ceremony

- Decide if you'd like alone time as a couple. If so, choose a secluded, accessible location.

- How will you reenter the social group who have witnessed your ceremony? In place of a reception line where bride, groom, and parents stand in line to greet the witnesses, or at least preceding it, we recommend that the couple walk through two parallel lines of the witnesses, so that the newlyweds can radiate the overflow of energy that continues to move through them. Connect and keep moving. This is more mythic and less chatty than the interaction between people in a reception line. This form helps to distribute the blessing. It relieves you of jumping too quickly into a more talkative social reception.

- Now you can consider posed photographs of the wedding party in various combinations; not sooner.

- What do you serve at your reception? We've been to alcohol-free weddings (ours was also), and it was quite a wonderful experience to realize that alcohol-free drinks and elixirs made from herbs and fruits can be an art unto themselves, and very creative as an alternative. What statement do you want your reception to be of your newly formed sacred union?

- There are plenty of reference materials on who "should" speak at your reception. Remember that the main purpose of the reception is to continue the feeling of marinating in the mythic. Invite those whom you really *desire* to have speak! And, remember, if you're still in the mythic, who's in charge of this? Your director and others, not you. Cultivate the expansiveness for a bit longer by not going too swiftly to the details of the story-and-drama realm of life.

• The same thing goes for the dancing! If it's a high value for you, take dancing lessons in the weeks preceding and wow everyone with some cool moves together. This is really the coming-out party for the two of you to share your Two, your relationship! Enjoy it. Surprise your guests with a song you sing together (if dancing isn't your thing). Or a poem you share, which can be funny or endearing. Encourage someone to bring a variety of music, not only a grinding beat. We'll share a secret that you can now use: we come to every reception with a recording (it used to be a CD, and now it's a little computer drive) of the overture to the opera *William Tell* by Rossini. At some point, we recommend to the master of music that this be put on, and we begin moving to the music, engaging others as a group of horses galloping through the room. It works for all ages, and unites the group in energetic play.

exercise

Listing the Elements of a Wedding

Identify the elements you choose to have as part of your ceremony. Start by having your intention for the ceremony at the top. Then go to the beginning of this chapter, start a page in your journal with number one, and jot down what you now know about the time, place, etc. Continue all the way through these topics, simply writing down the elements that you wish to include.

This will help the celebrant (and wedding planner, or director) understand what is important to you. You may well have more material than you can include in one ceremony. That's why you need to determine the length of your ceremony ahead of time.

Discuss this list with your partner. Don't accept a proposal from your partner until you understand it. Ask out loud, "Why do you want to have that feature in our wedding?"

Don't accept a response from your partner that sounds like this: "Yeah, sure, whatever you want." That means he or she is not involved. You may have to explain a feature or every feature, and in great detail. Each explanation is an opportunity and not a chore. You may have to find out if you've overwhelmed your partner with a six-hour list of must-have features, in which case you need your partner's help to prune it down to the essentials.

Practicing Heart Talk will be your best preparation for finding the truth of what you really wish to have in your wedding.

The Rest of Your Life

You slowly disentangle from the ceremony. You say goodbye to the relatives and friends. The flowers wilt and go to the compost pile, with thanks from you for their service. You put the dress away. You pay the bills for the various businesses that have helped you in this ceremony. You thank the celebrant, director, helpers, companions, and other friends. At every step of this disentanglement, breathe in what came to you during the Sacred Moment. You gave a great party, and one that has consequences—not to be forgotten by everyone in a month's time, but to be remembered. These consequences continue to have impact for a long time.

You disentangle, and yet you have new entanglements. You ponder the new ring on your finger. You reread the vows that you've written together. You tell the story of what happened at the ceremony to those who were unable to attend.

Back and forth you go, from One to Two to ONE to Two to One.

A chapter of your relationship ends with a wedding. Enjoy the happiness of this time, yet don't mourn its fading. You have leaped up a few steps in the school that is relationship, and you continue to mature. All the tools that you learned in this book become even more important, as well as others that you will certainly learn to use along the way.

We have an understanding between us that our wedding, our marriage, is a verb. It didn't happen once and then end—we continue to feel we are actively in the process of marrying.

A Wedding to Remember

Which of all the many ideas that you have read in the foregoing pages excites you? What stays with you? What would you like to have in your wedding? What would you like to have after your wedding?

Perhaps you are part of a religion that has very set forms for a wedding. Watch carefully—you will quite often be able to move flexibly around the edges, and then check that "Meaning" box to which we referred at the very beginning of this book. There are always edges to work with. Even if the entire text of the ceremony is already set, you can still find the Sacred Moment within that framework. You can find a celebrant within every religious tradition who understands that the part that wasn't part of the script, that "accident," was not incidental, but was rather the fleeting core of the whole wedding.

Make yours a wedding to remember. Choose and prepare carefully, then delegate the outward details to your director. Your job is simply and thoroughly to show up, every aspect of you, fully, consciously.

PART THREE

Endings and New Beginnings

"Divortex"

chapter 17

Some books, magazines, and movies suggest that the marriage ceremony is the end of the story. "Happily ever after" is as far as they go. However, statistics show a different story.

A large percentage of marriages "fail." We put that in quotes, because failure is such a subjective label. Divorce might be the mark of success of the marriage: you've grown better human beings in each other, and now it's time to move on, just as you would move from third grade to fourth grade. Or divorce might be a measure of catastrophe, fiasco, and disappointment. When we look back on our previous two marriages each, we don't think they failed. They taught us both a great deal, and brought us to the new life where we could meet each other.

The reasons people separate are legion, and while many divorces might have been avoided, sometimes divorce is the appropriate next step. It may be that the couple lacked tools of communication, or didn't know how to have a Heart Talk. Or perhaps it was appropriate and healthy to change the form of the relationship. Both partners learned and both moved on.

Each of the two can look forward to the next chapter where they change the foundations of the relationship, where they remarry. At present, in 40 percent of marriages in the United States, one or both partners were previously married. They learned from their prior experiences, and are trying it again. Or each can look forward to taking a separate path in life. Either way, everyone ought to understand divorce.

The relationships we create in life are central to the unfolding of a mature individual. It is valuable to find a healthier way to release the forms that no longer serve, rather than ending up in litigious battles that spread toxic energy, damaging the couple and everyone around them, as well as killing trust in the idea of partnership and in Love itself.

A wedding marks a turn into a new chapter, but it's not the end. Preparation for the wedding begins to change you. The ceremony itself works its magic. You

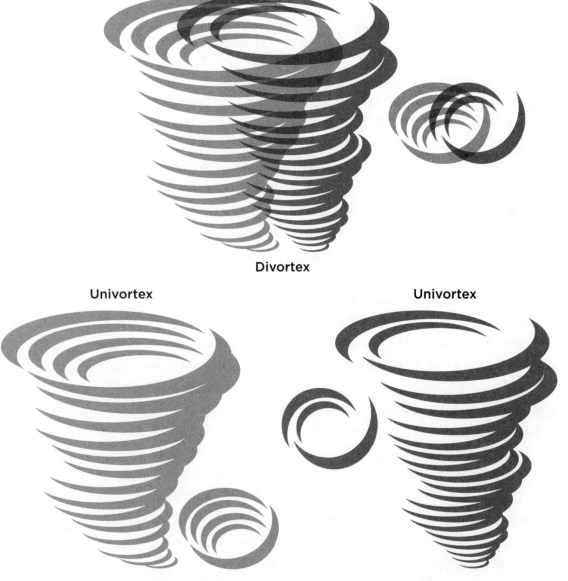

Divortex

Univortex　　　　　　　　　**Univortex**

Divortex becomes two univortices: from the side and from above continue to transform after the wedding, as you experience the energetic ripples of what you accomplished there. Down the road a few years, new issues begin to arise. The landscape has changed. The two individuals look at each other in wonder: "How different we have become!" One or both ask inwardly, "Where is the partner I married?" After that, either they agree to ride life's waves together in a new way, or something sends them in separate directions.

Note that the root of the word "divorce" is *di-vortex*: two vortices or whirlwinds. These two whirling energies are, during marriage, a univortex, a single vortex made of two, intermixed, merged into ONE. However, you don't have a univortex all the time. You have it part of the time. Since ancient days, the balance between two individuals or two realms has been symbolized by the figure on the previous page, which can be seen as a cross-section of two vortices.

One side is me; the other side is you: One to One. When things are going well, we meet in the overlapped area: Two. We only overlap completely in certain moments of Communion, the ONE. Sometimes we separate into two individuals, the One stage; One relating to One is our experience of Two. Separating completely into two Ones occasionally is very healthy.

The most natural relationship moves rhythmically from One to Two to ONE, from individuals to partnership to communion and then back again to individuals, from divortex to univortex to divortex. At certain times the rhythm slows or comes to a stop. Is it a problem or an opportunity?

Perhaps you're stuck in stale places. You ask yourself, "How did I not notice these problems years ago, when I first married this person?" They seemed so small then, or even nonexistent, because you were not grown in that area. Now you've grown up, and the constraints are clear. You would not dress a child in the same pants and shirt year after year. So it is with relationships: if they remain the same shape and size, after a time, they just don't fit.

You might lament, "Oh, if he would only stay the same." Some people try to hold the other down:

> Peter Peter pumpkin eater
> Had a wife but couldn't keep her.
> He put her in a pumpkin shell
> And there he kept her very well.

Have you ever felt the desire to put your partner in a straitjacket, to try to keep him or her the same? That feeling may be genuine, but you have to ask whose problem this is—your partner's or yours? Why is your tolerance for change so low? What wants everything to stay the same?

Excitement or Flatline

Here's another way to look at this. Every person can be understood as a wave pattern, simplified as a wavy line. When you come into relationship with each other, you can either synchronize your energies or they can cancel each other out.

This drawing of synchrony shows two wave patterns pulsing at the same rate; they superimpose to create something much more powerful than either person alone. As we said earlier: where two (or more) are gathered in the name of a quality, that quality will be with them. If that quality is Love, then the combination of the two life energies increases the power for both.

The other diagram, asynchrony, shows the two wave patterns out of phase. When two disharmonious vibrations combine, nothing results. In a relationship, this happens when your rhythms are not combining, when the combination of the two of you has gone flat.

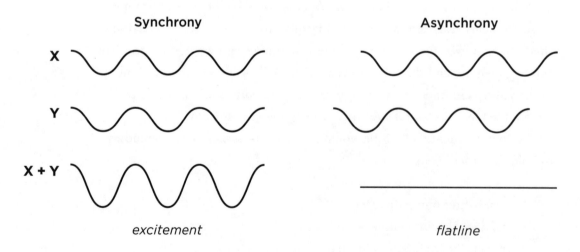

How you combine energy creates excitement or flatline

The One Certainty Is Change

What do you do? Three choices present themselves. You leave, you suffer, or you change. Suffering can be wholly internal, such that no one knows about it, including sometimes yourself. Eventually it will burst out—perhaps first as little innuendos, then as spiky jabs, and finally as a whole avalanche of recriminations. Often the partner is completely surprised: "Where did that come from?" Then you get to be amazed at how you've suffered for years and your partner didn't even notice. That leads to anger at how he or she didn't perceive your suffering. "Wasn't it completely obvious?" you wonder. Well, maybe not. The chains that fetter your personal growth may be quite different from the chains that bind your partner. It's possible that he or she is quite comfortable living a limited life or a life based on the fantasy that "everything is all right."

You have then become the canary in the coal mine. Miners going underground used to carry a caged canary to be a measure of safe oxygen levels. Canaries have a greater sensitivity to lack of oxygen than humans, so when the caged bird stopped singing and hopping, the miners would still have their wits about them for long enough to exit the mine before they too began to suffer from hypoxia. Hard on the canaries, who sometimes fell over dead, but helpful to the miners who could get out to breathe.

If you know you are suffering, you are the canary! You have the responsibility to let the miner know what is happening. Otherwise, you will, in some way, die. Of course, it may take years of oxygen deprivation for you to notice. If you are the canary, who is the miner? Your partner? Maybe. The first miner you must inform is yourself. Some part of you has got the idea that you're going to tough it out, no matter what, and the canary in you has to wake you up to the fact that something isn't working and you need to do something about it.

Don't despair. It's part of the natural process of growing within a relationship. You've just gotten stuck. In Australia they use the appropriate-sounding word "bogged," as when a vehicle gets stuck in mud. Your relationship is bogged and you are the first to notice it.

Speak up. Find a third party to speak to as a couple. This was included in the set of clarifying questions in chapter 9—finding someone that both of you admire as a mentor. That mentor may be able to help you dissolve some weighty chains. Or he or she may advise that you seek someone trained in marriage counseling. Do not consider yourself wrong or bad for seeking counseling. If you are bogged deep, you may need a stronger vehicle to pull you out. There is no shame in that. There is still plenty to do after you've been pulled out. Remember, the most important purpose of a marriage is not being happy—which can often devolve to "looking happy." The most important purpose is growing as human beings. When things get rough, this can be part of that growing process. Make the most of it.

If you get through the canary part, then the basis of your relationship has changed—and the terms of your agreements have changed. You have gone through one of those life-transforming experiences.

What do you feel is different in you from a decade ago (or two decades or three decades)? Have you noticed that other things are important in life? What are they? What is the "name" with which you align your life now? What is the "name" with which you align your relationship? Is that name the same for your partner? How might you find out if that's true?

If you find you are slowed in your growing, and you have tried everything, and you begin to see your spouse differently, then consider a rededication ceremony, covered in the next chapter. If you find that the incompatibilities are too strong, then you can consider a ceremony of release. Your grudges and resentments do not serve you or anyone else.

Complete release requires two steps: first, the release of your previous vows; next, the release of your marriage. Release of your vows is essential as a foundation for a rededication or for a healthy divorce. We give you more about rededication in the next chapter. First you have to let go of the old.

Release of Vows

Some things may have occurred in your marriage that you would like to undo or "do differently." You may have experienced difficulties in the early years of your marriage, and you would like to release all of that. You may have married young and made vows in your youthful wedding ceremony that you feel now were inappropriate, foolish, or inadequate. Times have changed, and now you would make some vows stronger, and others less strong. First you must release those old vows.

How do you undo something that you did? How do you undo a promise that you made "forever"? Here's a verse from Rumi:

> Come, come, whoever you are, this caravan knows no despair.
> Come, come, whoever you are, this caravan knows no despair.
> Even though you have broken your vows,
> Perhaps ten thousand times,
> Come, come again.

Thus speaks the voice of forgiveness. That's the key. You have to forgive yourself for your indiscretions, your mistakes, your errors, all of it. Your partner has to forgive you, and you have to forgive yourself.

You forgive and you release.

How? There are many release techniques. Here are a few we suggest, building on the exercises we gave you in chapter 5:

exercise

Releasing Vows

- Write your vows, or what you recall of them, or whatever agreements you feel that you've made, on a piece of paper, and tie it to a small piece of wood. Build a sacred fire, separately or together. Put the paper and wood into the fire. Ask that the pattern be transformed, let go, digested.

- Draw your relationship in the same way as the vortices at the beginning of this chapter: some parts that are comfortable as One, and some parts that are entangled as Two and don't come apart so easily. What are the areas of entanglement? Label them on your drawing. Put your drawing into the fire, asking for release of these places.

- Bathe in water: your hands, your feet, your whole body. Magnesium salts and sea salt in the bath have the reputation of taking in patterns.

Then they drain away from you, taking those patterns with them,
to be transformed deep below the surface of the earth.

• In the element of air, say what your vows were, and then let them go.
You ask out loud for these words to be let go.

These are preliminaries. Because of the depth of your interpenetration with
each other, it takes time to go through this process. The memories may be hard
to shake. They function in the same way as we see in trauma survivors. Even
the littlest thing, the memory of the exact way that your partner poured hot
water for tea, may obliterate the sense experiences of this moment.

Practice with some of the exercises that we've given you, especially
"Equanimity" (p. 99), which is powerful in neutralizing grudges and
hyper-strong memories. A spiritual teacher once gave us a powerful tool:
"Attachment leads to detachment." You concentrate on where you're going,
on that to which you choose to attach; the old stuff then detaches, falls away,
dissolves. We find that you can do both, actively attach and actively detach.

You might say to yourself: "I choose my sovereignty. I forgive myself for
whatever mistakes I may have made in discernment. I forgive myself for
negative emotions expressed. I ask for healing for the wounds I have suffered,
emotional and physical. I release the vows that I made, and the vows that were
made to me. I release with thanks all the people and spirits who were called
into the wedding. I release the older version of me. I actively and wholeheartedly welcome the new."

You might say to your ex-partner: "I forgive you for whatever behavior may
have caused me pain. I ask forgiveness for anything I did or did not do. I ask
for healing of all wounds, emotional and physical. I release the vows that I
made, and the vows that were made to me. I release with thanks all the people
and spirits who were called into the wedding. I release the outdated version of
you, and welcome the new."

Notice that you do not use "we" in these statements, as the "we" has
changed. Going into the future means affirming the "I-ness" of each

partner—from univortex to divortex, from ONE to Two back to the original One.

Of course, you must design the wording to suit your individual situation. This ceremony is very helpful to the whole of you, especially the subconscious parts that are not touched by reasoning, but rather by ceremony.

This clears out the past (or makes a good start) and readies you either for a rededication, as if marrying anew, or for the further step of release of the marriage.

Ideally, you and your ex-partner can meet and release your ties amicably. However, sometimes things fall apart in such a way that your ex-partner cannot attend a little ceremony such as we describe above. Or perhaps you have come across this idea of severing the old ties years after the ex-partner has gone in a new direction, and perhaps you have no idea how to reach him or her. You can still go through these steps, on your own, in an undisturbed environment. They create an opportunity for you to get straight who is who, to remove the parts of your ex-partner's vortex that are still entwined with your vortex. When you have made Love with another and taken his or her body into yours, or when you have opened your heart to another, an energy imprint comes deep into you. Releasing and letting go is not superficial. Intention to let go marks the first step; letting go the memories, the next. See the ex-partner grow distant emotionally and physically from you. People who maintain good relationships with ex-partners have always redefined the relationships energetically.

If you have a new partner, you can go through this process, of letting go the old flames, together. Acknowledge and let go. Even when the previous partners are not present, the relaxation of your energy around what happened can free you both to move in new directions.

When you release and let go, the old relation-ship-wrecks finally sink and dissolve. Attachment leads to detachment.

Release of the Marriage

From the soul's point of view, the relationship that is ending has been an opportunity to grow. The stories may include terrible things that were done to you, and terrible things you did in revenge. The soul cares little for the scorecard implicit in the stories; the soul cares for how you kept your integrity through it all, for what you learned, and for how you deepened in Love and the capacity to forgive.

To your ex-partner: "I release our marriage. I release our wedding vows. I thank you for what I have learned in Love and in many other ways from our walking of the path of life together. I hope that your journey will help you continue to grow." Remember, that was the commitment you made to each other no matter what else might happen. You undo many vows, and you repeat the basic vow to appreciate the other at the soul level.

We have found that, no matter how much your ex-partner seems to have become an ogre, and no matter how much you feel hurt by him or her, there is a spark of thanks deep in your soul for what you learned from this temporary companion in life. There is a spark of compassion as you understand the source of difficult behavior in the other. Deep down there is a spark of Love. Let that spark grow as you part ways. No matter what stresses arise from legalities, accusations, and other challenges, repeat your forgiveness and your thanks. Over and over until the two vortices have fully separated and you each go on your way.

Renewal and Rededication

A marriage that has aged a decade has aspects of inevitable growth. Everything changes through the passage of time. Though change threatens the part of us that would like everything in its place, think about it: you wouldn't want to squelch and imprison the natural unfolding of life forces moving through you.

After five years, ten years, twenty years, it's natural that you have grown new interests and alliances. Your partner looks different, acts different, feels different. You awaken to the queries: "Is this marriage the best vessel to carry me into my next chapter? Where did the person I married go? Have I changed that much too?" The differences seem too great. You wonder about separation. There is another alternative. We strongly advocate renewal and rededication! It's possible that our culture leans more toward separating than it does toward deepening, reviving, and transforming.

You have built far more positive foundations than you know. If you leave your partner, you will find, as many others have, that there were aspects of your relationship that you took for granted that were very supportive and very high-quality.

It's healthy to feel the urge to move on, to change the rules of engagement, to honor in some way the new themes and issues that are arising in your life. You contemplate moving out and away because the container of your marriage no longer fits. We recommend a rededication ceremony first. That is, choose to move on within a transformation of the container of your present marriage. Consider that it's time to renegotiate some things, and take a good hard look at how you might make important revivifying changes. Choose to marry again.

You can, in fact, "do it better this time." You can learn from your mistakes and create a ceremony for a new marriage that honors, sings, and celebrates the human beings you have become. You've succeeded at assisting each other to grow into different human beings. Celebrate that accomplishment and renew the intention in a new container.

When to Consider a Rededication

We thought it might be helpful to make a list to indicate when a rededication might be considered. This might seem presumptuous because many people have an inner knowing of when it's time for a change. But sometimes we're so inside our creations that we don't consider the obvious. And rededications are not all that obvious or common! So, here are some serious and not-so-serious situations wherein one of you might recommend the idea.

The fire has gone out, and you are having a difficult time reigniting.

Maybe something has gone flat and cool in your jobs, relationships with children and family, your relation to health and fitness. All too often we project outside ourselves, when the fault lies with our own disenchantment or boredom. Routines can be boring! A rededication could bring you both back into focusing on finding new goals, new projects, new perspectives for setting out a fresh course for your relationship. If the fire that's extinguished is directly related to sexuality, then deal with it head on! There are all kinds of courses, books, and experts who can open new doorways to sexual expression.

In one marriage we know, the man received a book from his partner, titled *Sexual Secrets.*

"Thank you, dear. Uh, did you give this book to me for a reason?"

"No, not really. I just thought you would be interested."

Don't believe the disclaimer. It's time for a Heart Talk.

We have found that at any age, there is a fire of passion available. If you're feeling cooled off and uninterested, ask yourself, "Do I wish to feel this way in five years?" If not, then begin to seek out the resources that can guide you into passion in a new way. And plan a rededication.

The very thing you used to find endearing about your partner is now making you crazy.

You know that one! "Her sweet little baby voice, that used to make me feel so special, now drives me up the friggin' wall!" Or, "The Sundays we spent watching sports together used to be special time; now he just drinks beer and eats popcorn without caring if I'm there or not."

Personality habits can run into a rut. We can all make room for improving our communication skills when it comes to the annoying things that make us feel like the other person is driving us nuts. This can be an opportunity for graciousness. David could easily point the finger at Lila's sensitivity to loud nut-crunching as something that is simply her problem. But he chooses not to "fight that battle" because it's so easy to just walk into another room and not create a nerve-grating situation for Lila. We had to come to that understanding through some fairly entertaining conversations about why nut-crunching was an annoying sound. (Of course, we used the Concentric Circles approach, as well as Heart Talk, and even Repeated Questions.) But we got through it, and the resolution works most of the time. Most important for this discussion is to note these indicators of restlessness in you.

You find you'd rather be almost anywhere else than at home with your partner when you have a day or a night off.

There are stages in life, each with its own interests and focus. Being together now is different from what it was a decade ago. Anyone's habits and patterns can become boring, and couples will often enter a collusion together in a way that can reinforce habits that are not particularly revivifying.

Maybe it's time to take up a new sport together, or find a common interest that sparks a new round of engagement. When we travel, we make a point of going to see live theater, because we love the art form and it always gives us something to talk about.

A couple for whom we were celebrants went through an intensely trying time recovering from the Colorado floods in 2013. As life returned to normal, they decided to take up kayaking together. Now they have a focus for their weekends and holidays. It was a new pursuit for them both, and it has given them an entirely new appreciation for spending time together.

You notice that one or both of you is drinking more, or developing other addictions that weren't present when you married.

Good! You've noticed a behavior that has consequences that you have subtly agreed to ignore. How have you agreed to this collusion—the use of the Two to ignore behavior that each knows deep down is destructive? What are other collusions that you may have built? We have our own story about deciding to stop drinking for a year, and that decision flowed effortlessly into eight years. Then we took up the occasional glass of organic wine. When we noticed that it was turning into more than the occasional glass, we decided to create new agreements in support of weeks without drinking, or ways to be mindful of enjoying a drink without letting alcohol get the upper hand.

Collusions occur when the habit begins to direct the program of your lives, rather than consciousness. A couple can develop patterns of hiding out, and they will subtly support that game-playing rather than going head on into the conversation about "what's really going on here, and what do we want to do with our lives?"

One of you has felt an attraction to another person, and has either acted on it or has fantasized about it.

It's the stuff of movies, this one! It is essential to have an agreement in place about what to do *when* this happens, not *if!* Our agreement is that we talk about it. Straight up, without any avoidance. Sometimes it is uncomfortable, but truthfully, when there's spaciousness to simply listen and appreciate your partner's vulnerability and honesty, it is much more effective than feeling jealous or reactive. Creating spaciousness like this in the relationship is the very thing that allows the partner to feel seen and understood, and therefore much less likely to need to act out on the attraction.

Holding onto a fantasy or a secret requires increasingly large parts of your inner world. When you share with your partner what's been going on, the part of you required for that passion or fantasy suddenly becomes much smaller. You could let your relation-ship-wrecks include the one-night stands or secret trysts, and concentrate on revivifying your marriage.

We find little use for the notion of "cheating," though we find a great deal of use for the notion of "learning." The Ashley Madison website is an online dating service for people in relationship who are seeking some spice elsewhere. It had 22 million subscribers in 2013. Its mission statement is "Life is short; have an affair." Is this letting go of the conscious part of marriage? Perhaps you need a break of some kind—from what? Discussing this with your partner can be the best break that you could possibly imagine.

Should an infidelity occur, then deal with it as an opportunity to grow. Don't jump to judgment, separation, and high drama right off the bat. These challenges can be the very thing to open the question of how and where the relationship needs to grow in order to be strong enough to enter the next decade.

The vows you made at your original wedding ceremony have not been noticed, honored, or embodied in some time. What were once shared affirmations haven't been spoken for a while. One, or both, of you has forgotten what is sacred in your marriage.

Noticing this situation is key to finding the core of a rededication ceremony. You may not even remember the vows you took, and they may have been created by the religion or by the minister who married you. Either way, in our understanding of Concentric Circles, this would be a great time to create from your mythic circle! Find that third organizing principle or assemblage point of the relationship, and attune to it from a fresh perspective.

When we establish that new vow in the outer ring of the Concentric Circles model, it will shift the energy as it moves back through the psychological ring and into the inner circle that represents your story. When that note is agreed to and placed in a ritual context, it starts to bear an influence on the new story that you choose to create together. This phase in relationship is so vital, and can help heal even the most difficult of perceived transgressions. Often we find ourselves in difficulty in relationship because we "need the gift" of the problem, as Richard Bach says. If my partner has been unfaithful, what might I need to learn about myself from that situation? How can we grow together and engage a different set of values to address what is not right between us? It is often the depth we have to go to through difficult passages like this that increases the bond of Love.

The Decision to Rededicate

Just as in a wedding you choose to cross a threshold together, so too with a rededication. You choose to cocreate a ritual together, in public or private, to call in your friends, your family, and your spiritual allies to consciously choose a new episode.

A rededication can offer a most meaningful experience and modeling for children and grandchildren as well. When children witness the seriousness of recommitment, it creates a lasting impression. How directly a marriage models relationship potential for children cannot be underestimated.

You know how sometimes people talk about an important experience that they have gone through and say, "It was a life-transforming experience—I will never be the same." Well, when you have gone through a marriage of over seven years in duration, it's likely that either you are miserable from the constraints of it, or you have negotiated—piece by piece, little change by little change—a life-transforming experience.

Or: the canary in the coal mine has felt the lack of nurturing oxygen (a metaphor we introduced in the previous chapter). The canary has spoken, and you have engaged in some kind of work with each other that has renewed your relationship. You have weathered an initiation rite, not in one event, but in thousands of little events accumulated over time. To recognize this transformation is as important as the recognition of your great Love that first brought you together. You are a new couple, agreeing to go onward into new phases of your lives. You know what? Maybe you ought to get married!

When you have more life experience, you have the capacity to choose better what to keep and what to leave behind—in a relationship and in a ceremony to acknowledge that relationship. From a celebrant's point of view, people with more life experience are wonderful to work with, because they really know what they desire in a relationship and in a ceremony. They have a sense of what they wish to avoid, that happened before. They have ideas about what they would like to have in a relationship and its beginning ceremony that they missed the first time. (The percentage of marriages in which one or both partners was previously married has risen dramatically in recent years, standing now at 40 percent of all marriages; these are people who tried something, moved on, and then came back to do it better, having learned from their mistakes.)

To recommit to the relationship that now exists, rather than to the memory of what was, you must let go of previous vows. This will free up an astonishing amount of energy with which you can forge new vows. Ritual has a powerful way of engaging the whole self. Designing a rededication ritual informs your whole self and your partner that you're sincere in creating a working relationship based on present realities, not on outdated memories.

The rededication ritual itself can look very much like a marriage ceremony. It may be lacking in some of the details and numbers of attendees, but it is no less meaningful! We bring ritual into many aspects of our relationship, and we rededicate ourselves to it several times a week. On occasion, we have found ourselves moved by the environment we were in and worked with that as an inspiration. Other times, we have taken advantage of an anniversary to rework visions and intentions. It creates a more memorable anniversary event to have a rededication ritual as part of the passage. A rededication of an existing marriage always involves two steps: release of the old and embrace of the new.

If you are considering rededication, start by asking yourselves what is your intention. Ritual is a powerful tool that refocuses energy toward a desired outcome. When the circumstances around relationships change, create a ritual to honor that. When you reaffirm and rededicate, it is both as if you are affirming and dedicating for the first time, and as if it is something that you know about. You've become an expert.

Releasing the Old

The first step of release is letting go of your previous vows, covered in the previous chapter. You forgive yourself, and you forgive the other. You may have to sit with each other in release of the past more than once. The historical part of the personality wants to cling to old views. It's very healthy to brush all of that out, in order to open up to new potentials more fully. You have to work diligently to see clearly the new person that you have become and the new person that your partner has become, and then to make that clarity evident to a group of witnesses.

Building Anew

You craft what vows might be said at this point in your life. You build anew, as you are taking your relationship in a completely new direction. You can start right at the beginning of this book, using the exercises to build a relationship with this new person in your life. When you rediscover the power of your Two to enter the wonder of the ONE—when you are ready to go down on your knees in awe of this wonder, both of you on your knees!—then you're ready for a rededication.

A rededication ceremony can act as a booster rocket in your relationship work with each other. Everything that we've said about the value of the Sacred Moment can become active here. You prepare by nurturing beauty. You prepare by going through all the questions in chapter 9, here and now, as if at the beginning of your relationship, taking the opportunity of greater maturity to create something exquisite, completely fresh and new.

Many couples rely on their anniversaries for this kind of renewal of interest. However, if you are emphasizing that you are now going off in a new direction, hold your event on another day altogether. Let your earlier wedding and its day of recollection be released, and dedicate yourself to a new level of learning with each other.

If you create a wedding ceremony for rededication, you can have all of the features of a first-time wedding, everything that seems appropriate from Part Two of this book. You may be amazed at the impact it will have. You may be completely surprised by the Sacred Moment: where it arises, and what it brings. You may be amazed at how your more mature attitude ripples out through your witnesses to people who didn't even attend. The story goes out and strengthens the power of Love in the world.

Even though you may be grown up and much more capable than before, engage a celebrant to guide you through this process, so that you may be led in the details, giving your full attention to your openness to the beauties that will flow through your new wedding.

story

Rededication 1

We decided to have a rededication ceremony along with two other couples with whom we were close. The six of us met several times. We relished the idea of reviewing and reviving our marriages. We found certain issues that were common to all, and certain issues that were unique to each couple. Each couple found that "In Whose Name" had changed from their previous marriage.

We decided to hold our rededication as a group, a ceremony that acknowledged the commonalities of recommitment and that also acknowledged the unique character of each individual and each couple.

We shared the desire to be freed from the vows of the previous wedding ceremony, which had occurred decades previously. Times had changed and we now experienced life differently. The circumstances of the relationship, the life stage, the sense of what was important and what was not, had also changed. These preliminary discussions proved very worthwhile.

We all agreed that experiencing a short span of time of being single again was symbolically important. We decided to begin in the center of the ceremonial space as couples, standing together, holding hands, facing out. Then we took off our wedding rings and plopped them into little containers of scented salt water for a good cleanse. We walked out of the center of the circle in six directions as individuals. We intended to enjoy the feeling of being single before rediscovering our mates and partners. The celebrant called each one by name, asking if he or she was ready to commit to something new and dynamic. One at a time, each person in a couple affirmed "Yes!" and returned to the center of the circle, where they redefined and recommitted to a marriage. Then the next couple was reunited, and the third couple reunited. It had the sense of returning to a known partner and the sense of creating something completely new. We danced a simple form choreographed by one of the six that showed each individuality, the partnership, and—indicating the ONE—all six dancing in clearly defined geometrical forms. We asked the witnesses to join us, beholding us with fresh eyes. 🏵

story

Rededication 2

This is from another rededication ceremony, led by the celebrant Circe Moss. She wrote the following about the ceremony:

I love the transformation of their vows; from the broad 'Have and to hold from this day forward . . .' traditional vows from ten years ago to their concise seven vows that are intention statements, based on experience and covering all the bases of life, home, family, and community.

The husband said to the celebrant: "Our culture doesn't see this as worthwhile; what's the big deal about ten years of marriage? We never get celebrated as a couple, as parents. It elevates our relationship."

How do you find something new in a relationship that is ten years old? You design gentle surprises. In this ceremony, the men and boys arrived earlier than expected, and assembled in the backyard. They called out to the groom, who was in the house; he came out to join them. The women and girls assembled in the front yard and called up to the bride, who joined them. The groups had practiced the song of the first dance from the first wedding, words and music that had particular meaning to the remarrying couple. The women sang one stanza to the men: "I love you for sentimental reasons; I hope you do believe me; I'll give you my heart." The men sang one stanza to the women: "I love you and you alone were meant for me; please give your loving heart to me; and say we'll never part." The groom and bride were held by their gender groups, sung to, and then united for the ceremony proper.

The groom told the celebrant: "This is worth celebrating: our marriage, our parenting, our family. The ceremony and the party make it public. Our parents were very pleased (especially the mothers). Our kids liked it too; it's good for them to see their parents in love."

Some of the important inquiries that you can make for a rededication include:

"What defines this relationship now, as the years have passed?"

"What do we hold as sacred in our lives currently?"

"Is there some way that we have fallen asleep in our loving, or in the expression of that Love? How do we awaken and what do we see?"

"If we could have anything in the next chapter of our lives together, what would that be?"

We strongly encourage partners to consider the rededication of vows at least every ten years. Whether it is in a private and personal ceremony, or in a public or family context, it serves the family and community to bear witness to a maturing relationship.

Rededication is new territory, and very important. Please write your stories to us, so that we can have an ongoing account of what rituals and ceremonies you have created for this life transition.

Ancient Souls

In an important way, all weddings have a quality of renewal and rededication. Whether the bodies are young or old, the souls have been through this before. When you witness a wedding, you often feel that these two people are not only enacting a sacred rite; they are *re*-enacting that rite. You have the feeling, "They must have done this before—not only in previous marriages with others, but with each other. These two are soul mates, finding each other again." Souls seek to engage with each other because that engagement is where the greatest soul growth takes place. At the end of your life, you don't take any possessions with you, but you do take what loves you have developed. That is a learning that stays with you. Your greatest love may be your partner. At least, the potential is there, and the purpose of a conscious partnership is to lift that potential to its fullest.

Release and Renew

If you are considering rededication of your relationship, decide first what you are releasing from the old form. It may be what naturally happens with the passing of time: the children are grown up, the business is changing, you have to move from where you live, there were some things you said or did that you'd like to let go, or any number of life stories. What do you intend to release? Then, what would you like to claim or to renew? Write these down separately, and share them. Include the qualities of life as well as the actual physical circumstances. What emotions are involved? What is it you want to create more of? Begin to understand the transformation that you are interested in creating and work toward a Shared Affirmation that honors it. Go on to create vows at all levels (see chapter 13). Once you know those, you can proceed to design a ceremony that will honor that intention. Using the stages of ceremonial design in chapter 16, you can begin to create the most appropriate way to honor this passage.

To design a rededication ceremony, you go through the possibilities presented in this book, and decide which ones you would like to use. To create something wholly new, you start from the beginning.

Every Day a Wedding Day

When you've had the ceremony and a Sacred Moment has visited you in public, preceded by many Sacred Moments in your preparation time with each other, you feel a new kind of awakening. It's like waking into a new day.

After the ceremony is over and all the guests have departed, there you will be: just two people. Perhaps with children from previous partnerships, and perhaps with pets, and possessions, and demanding relatives, all of that! But basically, before the wedding, two people; after the ceremony, two people. Has anything changed? If you've shown up for each other in the Sacred Moments, it certainly has! This is one situation where the events of one day can change your life forever. You have reached from your singular One through the Two of partnership into a communion of ONE so strong that everyone feels it. Then you practice how you can achieve the communion of ONE over and over again.

Every day can be a wedding day.

story

LILA and DAVID   Every Day a Wedding Day

Setting: on a beach, in a car, in a grocery store, anyplace.

Lila: "Will you marry me?"

David: "Yes! Now! This minute, fully!"

Every day, you can share your affirmation. Every day can have attention to beauty. Every day can have respect for others, wishing them well and helping where needed. Every day can be imbued with Love from beginning to end. There is a hint in the word "relationship": that "re-," or return, that you see also in "rededication" and "renewal." It must be made real every day, over and over again, repeated. You journey in your Relation-Ship in new ways to ancient lands.

Every day can have a Sacred Moment—perhaps at the core of the day. Perhaps the Sacred Moment can happen every moment, as you cocreate this beautiful world, in joy.

exercise

This Sacred Moment

At any moment in your day, you can awaken and look around you, and look within you. Notice your garments—they are your costume. Notice the buildings—they are your sacred place. Notice the people around you—they are creating with you the ceremony of life. Notice your Beloved—she or he winks and nods and interacts heart to heart in this Sacred Moment, a continuous Sacred Moment of Life. And this moment too. And this one. And this ONE. Every thing, every thought, every feeling participates. Awake, aware, conscious.

Sample Weddings

appendix

Following the organizational outline that we recommend for a wedding ceremony in chapter 16, we have included two sample wedding outlines here. This gives the skeletal structure, to be filled out by the suggestions that we gave in Part Two.

1. Maura and Andrew's Wedding, Boulder, Colorado

Length of ceremony, from entry of witnesses to closing:
nearly two hours
Theme: Shakespeare's *A Midsummer Night's Dream*

The theme showed up on the wedding invitation, including encouragement for attendees to dress like a character in the play. David and Lila included some quotes from the play in their comments during the ceremony, which we gave in chapter 14, as well as comments in support of a foray into the mysterious deep forest that we were all joining in the ceremony.

Pre-Wedding

The design phase included four meetings with the couple and the celebrants.

This wedding had a full two days of preparation and events, which is an increasingly popular approach so that visitors from out of town can enjoy a weekend away and the two families and sets of friends can meet each other. The couple started Friday with a sweat lodge from the Lakota Native American tradition, wherein prayers are shared in steamy darkness. This was followed by the wedding rehearsal at the StarHouse, and a bridal party picnic on the grounds after that. After the dinner, another event in the StarHouse included theater games, intermixing the witnesses in various combinations. This activity also prepared the space (purification) for the wedding on Sunday.

Saturday included a hike into Rocky Mountain National Park that provided an opportunity to get some exercise in nature. On Saturday afternoon, the women spent time at a local spa (the word is taken from the initial letters of *salus per aquam*, "health through water," thus relating to purification and to the elements, which were prominent in this wedding). The rehearsal dinner was that evening, organized by the groom's parents, including various speeches and an honoring of the bride and groom in ways that had been prepared in the previous weeks.

Wedding Day

PREPARING SACRED SPACE

The temple was set with a beautiful arrangement of glass spheres with flowers inside that were hung from the ceiling. They defined the central space (the core of the wedding) from above, a delightful feature. A small central altar held a Unity Candle and flowers.

The guests were asked to remove their shoes, and their feet were washed by friends of the bride and groom. People were smudged with sage smoke before entering. This was purification of the space and people to a degree unusual for weddings, and helped tremendously to set ceremonial time apart from normal time.

Live music was playing as people entered.

INVOCATION

The two celebrants welcomed the guests and invited them to bring what was sacred to each of them, so that they could focus on blessing the couple. As celebrants, we also gave them a quick overview on creating a container in order that the Sacred Moment could be felt in the core of the ceremony. We read a quote here from *A Midsummer Night's Dream* to enhance the theme. The couple chose "Divine Unity" and "Wild Love" as their response to "In Whose Name" these qualities were invoked. Then the whole group practiced the pronouncement which would be made all together at the end:

"We now pronounce you Husband and Wife, consorts for life."

The bridal party then entered, first the groom and his men. All stood for the bride, who looked like the Fairy Queen from *A Midsummer Night's Dream,* to be sure! The father handed the bride over to the groom with touching intention (and the hand choreography detailed in chapter 14). Following that, the four directions were called in by the bridal party members, and once again the invocation was made to Divine Unity and Wild Love.

RECEPTION/AMPLIFICATION

During this part of the ceremony, the bride and groom sat, as people of their choice presented songs, readings, a poem, and a speech. During this time, their rings were circulating on a pillow through the room, so that people could honor and bless the rings.

The parents of both were invited to stand, light a candle, and speak a blessing. This was followed by sacred music (a *kirtan* in the Hindu tradition). The words were taught by the musician, very simple repetitions of Sanskrit words that joined everyone in the room in live music in which they could participate by listening, singing, or both. After this, there was a period of silence for two to three minutes, which made the bridge from amplification into the core of the ceremony.

COMING INTO UNION/SACRED MOMENT

The celebrants started this phase with another invocation that called in the land upon which we all stood and the ancestors, especially of the marrying couple. We invited each person present to find his or her own spiritual connection as the couple stepped in more closely to make their vows.

The musician provided one minute of fast drumming modeled on shamanic practices, which engaged everyone in the same rhythm. This served as a border between past and present. The couple faced each other and were led by the celebrants through the process of speaking their vows. They had written them out, and insisted on reading them. As the reading voice is often faster and more monotonous than spontaneous speaking, the celebrants had trained them how to read more slowly, with pauses, in order to catch the meaning of each densely packed vow. As each partner spoke, the celebrants asked the other to close their eyes while the partner gazed on the Beloved. The one with eyes closed took a breath or two and was asked to deepen into any other words they might wish to say. Each responded with an exchange of sweet words, accompanied by tears and warmth. Genuineness permitted a sense of the Sacred Moment to arise, soul speaking to soul, one of many moments during this wedding.

The celebrant then spoke these words: "Andrew, do you take Maura, whom you now hold by the hand, to be your wife and consort for all of time?"

He answered, "I do!"

The role switched so that Maura could answer the same question. "I do!"

Celebrant: "Do you mutually promise that you will love, cherish, and respect one another throughout the years?"

Couple: "We do."

Celebrant: "Wedding rings are a symbol of the unbroken circle of Love. May they be a daily reminder of your vows to each other and your resolve to live together in unity, Love, and happiness."

Celebrant (first to groom, then to bride, spoken in short phrases so the words could be repeated as the ring was held and then placed on the Beloved's finger): "Please repeat after me: This ring represents the great Oneness from whence we come, and is a symbol of my eternal dance with you. With this ring, I thee wed—and pledge my Love and commitment."

Bride and Groom then lit a Unity Candle on the central altar.

The participants were then cued to make the pronouncement: "We now pronounce you husband and wife, consorts for life!"

DISTRIBUTION

They kissed, and, to the sounds of live and lively music, exited with the bridal party following. The couple went to a seating area in the woods to breathe and calm. The celebrants asked the participants to join in the releasing of butterflies, and throwing birdseed. The witnesses formed two lines so the couple could walk between them; the butterflies were released at the beginning of that reception line, then birdseed thrown as the couple passed through. They were especially radiant. A wedding this detailed and active with relatives and friends feels like a marathon of meaning. If the couple's energy can hold up, then everyone is swept into the mythic realm for a long period.

CLOSING

After the couple had exited the ceremonial space, the celebrants spoke the truth of the moment in the words of the theme of the wedding:

> You have but slumbered here
> While these visions did appear.

The midsummer dream had come to an end. People slowly awoke to the present. The directions were released. People were encouraged to begin their movement to the door to put on their shoes, then to gather outside for the reception lines. Some of the wedding party were engaged in folding chairs and cleaning up the items of the ceremony. Others joined in. It's very healthy to have jobs for people at the end of the ceremony. It helps people come down slowly with simple tasks.

After the parallel lines in which the witnesses received the blessing of the bride and groom, tasty elixirs were served, combinations of fruit juices, herbal extracts, and flower essences. This helped slow the process of return to the mundane, while, practically speaking, rehydrating everyone after a long ceremony.

2. Billy and Belina's Wedding, Charleston, South Carolina

Length of ceremony: about 30 minutes, not including the delay
Theme: "Vintage Beach"

Billy and Belina chose what they called a "vintage beach" theme—white linen on large tables and as costume and trim, in this stylish Southern seaport. They also brought in features of furniture and ornamentation that their wedding planner termed "a flare of *Alice in Wonderland.*"

Pre-Wedding

The design phase involved several long conversations with the celebrant (David). This included homework in between conversations, over a six-month period. Several of the exercises in this book were used to help define the purpose of the ceremony. The process of choosing "In Whose Name" took a long time, which provided for very fruitful discussions about where meaning resides in the universe.

The wedding was preceded by casual family time in different locations and houses. The guests were given a list of suggestions for what they could do in Charleston, and outings happened in an informal manner, mixing the witnesses together in different groupings.

A rehearsal occurred in a location different from the venue. (This is not unusual. The venue may not always be available for rehearsals. But you can approximate the distances and do a walk-through with members of the wedding party anywhere.)

The rehearsal dinner was a catered event, held at a private residence with close family and friends, as well as out-of-town guests.

Wedding Day

PREPARING SACRED SPACE

This was an outdoor wedding by the harbor in Charleston.

The venue had been beautifully established with couches on the lawn, and an altar area set with the four elements (for the rings to be blessed). The central altar was set with a backdrop to define the space, and surrounded by tiki torches and flowers. The participants walked through a door that did not have walls on either side, just a door in a frame reserved for them—it was enchanting. There were little bars serving water and flavored juices that could be had before the ceremony, as it was a warm day.

When people dress up, as for a Charleston wedding, it is a kind of purification that can be stunning to behold. Preparations are mutually supportive.

Being outdoors poses special challenges. There was a microphone set up and the technical person assured the celebrant, "This will do the job." The celebrant insisted on testing it ahead of time, and figured out quickly that the amplification would not be adequate if the microphone was left in its stand. This knowledge gave the celebrant time to plan how to set up the scene: he would have to hold the microphone for himself and close to the mouths of the bride and groom, making only one hand useable.

INVOCATION

The celebrant offered welcoming comments and preparation for the ceremony. The couple had chosen to have a group pronouncement at the end: "We now pronounce you husband and wife, partners in life!" All the guests practiced saying it together. The guests were told that the couple had chosen to be married in the name of "God" and "Love."

A challenge came at this point. Between the site of the ceremony on the lawn near the ocean and the rooms where the members of the wedding party were preparing was a distance of sixty yards. Signals for entry were missed; the wedding planner was not to be found, as she had been called away to deal with an emergency with the food for after the wedding; the witnesses were left sitting in the hot sun. After the initial instructions from the celebrant, they waited. After fifteen minutes, the celebrant sent a messenger across the lawn to encourage the wedding party to come forward. This delay stretched the witnesses' energy.

While waiting for the messenger to rouse the wedding party, the celebrant spoke about the elements on the altar, how they concentrated the earth, water, air, and fire of the surroundings. The celebrant pointed out details of the surroundings in terms of the four elements—the land where they were gathered, the water of the ocean close by, the air full of the scent of flowers, the warmth of the sun—all connected by the warmth of Love, which was one of the names this couple had called in as their foundation. A celebrant needs to be able to fill in like this, not with small talk, but with large talk. However, there are limits to infilling, and the hot sun was beginning to affect the witnesses.

The processional followed. The bride was accompanied by her brother, as her father had passed. When asked, "Who gives this woman in marriage?" the brother responded, "I do, in my father's name."

RECEPTION/AMPLIFICATION

Both bride and groom had lost their fathers, so the next part of the ceremony was an honoring of the fathers who had passed. The tiki torches were lit by family members, and each father was named.

The celebrant spoke for about five minutes regarding Sacred Union, with instructions to the couple and witnesses about how to support this marriage. The couple had chosen not to have readings or songs.

COMING INTO UNION/SACRED MOMENT

Personal vows here were spoken by bride and groom. The celebrant held the microphone as each spoke, and stepped forward so that the couple could half face the audience and half face each other. They had brought little cards to remind them of the words they had prepared. They spoke their vows in their own time, not reading from the cards but using them as prompts.

When the celebrant asked the groom, a man who had the reputation of privacy with his feelings to the point of aloofness, if there was anything else he wanted to say, the groom burst out, "I just want to finish this—and MARRY this woman!" It was a delightful eruption of genuine feeling, in which he turned toward his bride and lifted his arm to embrace her. That revealing of what lay in his heart and the clear signal from his whole body provided the point of release of the strictness of the form. A tear came down the bride's face. Everyone breathed deeply, and laughed with relief. The groom loosened up, and a wide smile came over his face, and the face of his bride. The witnesses were now fully attentive, and joining the process. Perhaps it was the Guiding Hand at work; perhaps it was soul rising to meet soul. It was certainly a Sacred Moment.

The groom's niece presented the rings. The bride, then the groom, passed the rings through the four elements, "upon which we all depend: earth, air, fire, and water." The couple chose the more traditional ring vow, phrases spoken by the celebrant and repeated by bride and groom: "With this ring, I thee wed, in the spirit of God, Love, Divine Union—and blessed by Jesus Christ. In the presence of these witnesses, I, Belina, take you, Billy, to be my husband. To have and to hold, for richer and poorer, in sickness and in health; to love and to cherish from this day forward, as long as we both shall live."

The community made the pronouncement. The two kissed, and music followed.

DISTRIBUTION

The couple left for a private ten minutes of calming and breathing. The celebrant asked the witnesses to breathe, and bask in the expression of Love that had just occurred. The celebrant gave the witnesses instructions to drink water or juice, enjoy each other's company for ten minutes, and then gather in a long tunnel so the couple could walk through, dispensing their blessings. This outpouring by the witnesses was met energetically by the couple and had the feeling of a Sacred Moment.

CLOSING

In a ceremony where the directions are not called in, nor divine beings, nor elements formally recognized as special, or where such activity is not understood, the celebrant does not ask the witnesses to let these helpers go. The celebrant does this himself or herself, privately.

Making Choices

Both these ceremonies show a uniqueness of approach that met what each couple envisioned. One was longer and required more orchestration and direction. The other was short and to the point. Both contained Sacred Moments where the gathered community had a sense of connection, blessing, and appreciation for the couple and their coming into Union.

Index to the Exercises

One way to use the exercises is to close your eyes and let your finger drop to the page. Try the indicated exercise. A guiding hand may be at work or at play with you.

Index

Acknowledgments

We thank those pioneers of healthy relationship and marriage with whom we have loved, played, and worked, and wish them a happy voyage in their Ship of Relation. We thank those who trained us, via previous relationships, the hardest and most certain path of learning.

A great thanks to Haven Iverson and Donna Zerner for believing in this book, to Allegra Huston for her many excellent editing suggestions, and to Tami Simon and all those who make Sounds True a boon of plenty for the earth.

About the Authors

LILA SOPHIA TRESEMER is a group facilitator, playwright, photographer, ceremonialist, and minister. She produced the companion DVD to this book, *Couple's Illumination.* Her commitment to the Divine Feminine is evidenced in her Sophia work (SophiaLineage.com). She cofounded the Path of the Ceremonial Arts, an ongoing three-year training for women that is now fifteen years old (at TheStarHouse.org). She continues to cocreate programs for sacred living and remembrance in Boulder (SophiaLineage.com), Australia (MountainSeas.com.au), and elsewhere. Lila is dedicated to building a global community that honors the Divine Feminine, supports Sacred Union, and celebrates the divinity in all beings. Her most recent book, *Don't Go Back to Sleep,* traces a young woman struggling with the legacy of genetic damage through her father's exposure to Agent Orange, who finds resolution in a dramatic ceremony at the StarHouse. Lila is adjunct faculty for the certificate program in anthroposophic psychology at the Anthroposophic Psychology Associates of North America (APANA). Visit apana-services.net.

DAVID TRESEMER, PhD, has a doctorate in psychology, and is core faculty for the certificate program in anthroposophic psychology at the Anthroposophic Psychology Associates of North America (APANA-services. net). His latest book is *The Counselor . . . As If Soul and Spirit Matter* (as editor and contributor), as well as *The Sophia Element Meditations* (serialized through SophiaLineage.com). He has written in many areas, ranging from *The Scythe Book: Mowing Hay, Cutting Weeds, and Harvesting Small Grains with Hand Tools,* to a book about mythic theater, *War in Heaven: Accessing Myth Through Drama,* and a book about astrology-seen-intelligently, *Star Wisdom and Rudolf Steiner: A Life Seen Through the Oracle of the Solar Cross,* as well as *The Venus Eclipse of the Sun.*

TOGETHER

David and Lila have written several plays produced in the United States, including *My Magdalene* (winner of Moondance 2004, Best Script), about which we created a DVD, *Re-Discovering Mary Magdalene.* Another play is *Darwin in the Dreaming,* which we were asked to perform at the 2009 Parliament of World Religions in Melbourne, Australia. (We can say with some authority that writing plays together, where every word must be perfect for the moment, can test a partnership!)

Lila wrote and produced and David narrated a part of a study on one of the anatomical systems of the human body—the nervous system—presented with helpful graphics in the DVD *Brain Illumination.* Our second project was the DVD *Couple's Illumination: Creating a Conscious Partnership,* which complements this book.

Both of us are ministers in a transdenominational church, and one of our greatest joys is helping couples to find a Sacred Union of their own design. This is the third marriage for each of us (we married each other in 1995), so we have had some practice. From each relationship, and from each ceremony, we have learned immensely, and for this learning we are grateful to our former partners.

You can find out more about us at David-Lila.com. We invite your origin stories ("How did you two meet?"), rededication stories, and other comments at that site. And, naturally, we also act as celebrants at conscious weddings!

About Sounds True

Sounds True is a multimedia publisher whose mission is to inspire and support personal transformation and spiritual awakening. Founded in 1985 and located in Boulder, Colorado, we work with many of the leading spiritual teachers, thinkers, healers, and visionary artists of our time. We strive with every title to preserve the essential "living wisdom" of the author or artist. It is our goal to create products that not only provide information to a reader or listener, but that also embody the quality of a wisdom transmission.

For those seeking genuine transformation, Sounds True is your trusted partner. At SoundsTrue.com you will find a wealth of free resources to support your journey, including exclusive weekly audio interviews, free downloads, interactive learning tools, and other special savings on all our titles.

To learn more, please visit SoundsTrue.com/freegifts or call us toll free at 800-333-9185.

SOUNDS TRUE
many voices, one journey